JOHN STUART MILL'S
ON LIBERTY

John Stuart Mill's
On Liberty

JOHN C. REES

Constructed from published and
unpublished sources by
G. L. WILLIAMS

CLARENDON PRESS · OXFORD
1985

Oxford University Press, Walton Street, Oxford OX2 6DP

London New York Toronto
Delhi Bombay Calcutta Madras Karachi
Kuala Lumpur Singapore Hong Kong Tokyo
Nairobi Dar es Salaam Cape Town
Melbourne Auckland

and associated companies in
Beirut Berlin Ibadan Mexico City Nicosia

Oxford is a trade mark of Oxford University Press

Published in the United States
by Oxford University Press, New York

British Library Cataloguing in Publication Data
Rees, John, 1919–1980
John Stuart Mill's On liberty.
1. Mill, John Stuart—Political science
2. Liberty
I. Title II. Williams, G.L.
323.44'092'4 JC223.M66
ISBN 0-19-824766-4

Library of Congress Cataloging in Publication Data
Rees, J. C. (John Collwyn)
John Stuart Mill's On liberty.
Bibliography: p.
Includes index.
1. Mill, John Stuart, 1806–1873. On liberty.
2. Liberty I. Williams, Geraint, 1942–
II. Title.
JC585.M75R44 1985 323.44 85-7267
ISBN 0-19-824766-4 (U.S.)

Set by DMB (Typesetting), Oxford
Printed and bound in Great Britain by
Biddles Ltd, Guildford and King's Lynn

Er cof

PREFACE

THIS volume is not merely a collection of articles by a renowned Mill scholar, nor simply a tribute to his qualities as a thinker; it is a book by John Rees. It lacks his final touch, but its planning and preliminary execution go back a number of years. Thus the articles previously published are included here not simply on the grounds of their merit but because John Rees saw them as drafts for chapters of his planned book. Most of his published work on Mill was in fact a series of stepping stones towards the book. Similarly, the new material was designed for the book, and so my role has been to seek to discover and then follow the author's wishes rather than to select and edit on my own account. I have not attempted to revise and polish where there might be a danger that my own views might intrude. I have worked in the belief that an imperfectly polished work by John Rees is better than one completed by an inferior hand. Thus while there is a sadness that John Rees's own meticulous scholarship has not overseen the book in its final version, the individual chapters are his: they do I believe fit neatly together, according to his own conception of the book. In it we can see the two talents which he brought to bear on the study of Mill, those of a historian of ideas and those of the political philosopher. This volume is a blend of historical and textural research with the philosophical analysis of liberty; indeed he saw those activities as allies in the search for proper understanding rather than as alternative methods. This is the key to his approach and the reason for his vast influence in the area of Mill study.

John Rees was born in Maesteg, South Wales in 1919. He studied law at Cambridge between 1937 and 1940 and politics and economics at the London School of Economics between 1943 and 1947. He lectured at the Universities of Southampton, Birmingham, and Leicester before becoming the first Professor of Political Theory and Government at University College, Swansea in 1955. Having established the foundations of a healthy and growing department he took the unique step of resigning his Chair in 1962 in the belief that the administrative burdens were preventing the fullest pursuit of scholarship. He became a lecturer once more, and later a Reader, enjoying a Visiting Professorship at the University College of Los Angeles in 1963–4 and a Visiting Fellowship at All Souls, Oxford in 1967–8. He died in 1980.

This barest of outlines may seem to miss out almost everything of importance, but it does serve to point to his love of knowledge and to his integrity, two key features of his life and work. Whilst these qualities contributed to his vast reputation amongst Mill scholars they also ironically led to the present situation, the imperfectly revised book we see here. For John Rees's influence, resulting from his authoritative and polished works, was seen as much in the attention he paid to others as the care with which he tackled Mill. A great deal of his time and energy was spent in advising, helping, and evaluating the works of others. He corresponded widely and helped so thoroughly that his own work, though benefiting in the long run, was often delayed. What he wrote in print was only a part of what he wrote; his letters and comments to others were equally important to him as a teacher, scholar, and friend.

And like his published work, his interests were wide-ranging: though Mill and freedom were closest to his heart, he published and corresponded on subjects ranging from the Greeks to Lenin, to the nature of justice, to the idea of equality, to the methodology of the social sciences. As his concerns in political theory were extensive, so were his interests outside this field. He was as incisive and rigorous whether the topic was university life, jazz, rugby, or whisky, and in these areas as in political theory he combined high seriousness with great good humour. His list of the ten top jazz records of all time, or the world's finest rugby fifteen, or the best malt whiskies were as carefully considered and debated—and enjoyed—as his conversation and writings on political theory. Variety was as important to him as to Mill. He did not tread one narrow path through life, but gloried in the pursuit of many goals.

He would I think have agreed with the reply Confucius gave when asked what was the way of the good man—There are no footsteps—but we can rejoice at least that his life and work has left for us some clear footprints of the paths trodden by an excellent teacher, a renowned scholar, and a stimulating friend. This great reputation which John Rees enjoyed was built up over a period of some twenty-five years. His first work, the classic study of *Mill and his Early Critics*, was published in 1956. In it he showed that the general reaction to *On Liberty* was much more hostile than later commentators had supposed. Mill's attempt to defend a principle of liberty on utilitarian grounds was attacked from the beginning. As a historian of political thought this work shows John Rees at his very best, but it also highlights a problem in political philosophy which is more than simply historical. Whilst the book was marvellously illuminating as a survey of a period in nineteenth-century thought (incorporated here as Chapter III), and whilst it showed that Mill had not in fact written a work *On Social Freedom* which espoused a positive conception of freedom (this argument incorporated here as an appendix), it left the major philosophical problem of interpreting Mill's principle unsolved. The task of the historian raised a problem for the philosopher, and John Rees's next major contribution to Mill scholarship turned to this question. Was it possible to distinguish, as Mill had seemed to, between actions concerning only the agent and actions concerning others? Could this distinction provide the key to those areas left free to the individual and those where interference could be justified? In 'A Re-reading of Mill on Liberty' (incorporated here as Chapter V) John Rees attempted to rescue Mill from what most traditional interpreters had seen as a rather crude and fallacious distinction. It is difficult to overestimate the influence on later Mill study of John Rees's distinction between actions which affect *others* and actions which affect others' *interests*. He argued that Mill's principle justifying interference applied to the more limited range suggested by the latter formulation and not to the extensive range indicated by the former. A great deal of later comment on Mill's principle revolves around this interpretation. Much clearly rested on a fuller analysis of the concept of interests, and John Rees became dissatisfied with his earlier view expressed in 1960 and came to believe that *On Liberty* had to be related to Mill's discussion of justice in *Utilitarianism*. From there he, amongst others, developed the notion that Mill's idea of harm was to be understood in terms of those rights and interests which society must

guarantee as necessary, but not sufficient, conditions for individual development. A full examination of this issue was to
be the final chapter of this book. As it was, John Rees gave a
lecture on 'Justice and Liberty' to the Royal Institute of Philosophy in 1980; as with all his work the paper was intended for
polishing and perfecting before publication. Where revisions
were clearly indicated I have made them; after some thought
I have included it as Chapter VI in the belief that John Rees's
final thoughts on the problem of Mill and liberty are of value
and interest even if imperfectly finished.

While pursuing this problem of settling his final interpretation of Mill's principle John Rees was busily engaged in the
more general controversies over Mill, either defending him
against the charge of illiberalism in 'Was Mill for Liberty?' or
against those who advanced various arguments that *On Liberty*
was at odds with other fundamental beliefs expressed elsewhere
in Mill's writings, in 'The Thesis of the Two Mills'. (These are
both incorporated here as Chapter IV). To complete the historical picture and to round off his philosophical argument, one
thing remained—to show how Mill's views on freedom developed from his early background and to show the extent of the
continuity with his utilitarian inheritance. Chapter I explores
the views of Bentham and James Mill in an attempt to show
that whilst Mill did indeed move far beyond the earlier utilitarian tradition the ground for many of his later ideas of liberty
had been well prepared by his two early teachers. Chapter II
continues the study of the early Mill, establishing his views on
freedom before he met Harriet Taylor and then assessing her
influence as well as that of Carlyle, the Saint-Simonians, and
Channing.

Thus the book has a chronological framework, from early
influences to contemporary critics to modern critics, and at the
same time moves forward philosophically towards an interpretation of Mill's much disputed principle. I hope that my recon-
struction does justice to John Rees's talents both as a historian
of ideas and as a philosopher, and that the book reflects his
belief that these qualities are partners in the search for truth
rather than contenders in a demarcation dispute. In trying to
intrude as little as possible in this work I trust that the vigour,
clarity, and depth of John's writings shine as brilliantly as

his memory does to those fortunate enough to have known and honoured him. As someone who was in turn a student, colleague, and friend of John Rees's, preparing this volume has been as much a celebration of his life as a tribute to his scholarship: the book is John's.

Sheffield, 1984   GERAINT L. WILLIAMS

ACKNOWLEDGEMENTS

IN constructing this book from published and unpublished sources I am grateful to the University of Sheffield for granting me study leave and to the British Academy for providing me with financial assistance. I am indebted to Leicester University Press who have kindly given permission for the inclusion of *Mill and his Early Critics*. The book also contains material which originally appeared in *Political Studies*, VI (1958), VIII (1960), XIV (1966), XXV (1977). These are reprinted by permission of Oxford University Press, to whom I am most grateful. The final chapter is based on a lecture given to the Royal Institute of Philosophy, to whom I am similarly grateful. In addition I would like to thank Mrs Betty Rees for her encouragement and help. Lastly, thanks to Sarah Cooke who was most helpful in typing and preparing the manuscript.

CONTENTS

INTRODUCTION

IT is sometimes argued that the historian of political thought is concerned to understand not to criticize; that the way the works of great thinkers are often handled by persons with a philosophic interest is unhistorical and therefore fraught with danger, and further that it violates the philosophical distinction between 'explanation' and 'judgement'.

Indeed it would obviously be absurd to criticize a Greek commander during the Persian Wars in the fifth century BC for not getting a clear picture of the enemy's dispositions before battle, when by 'clear picture' we mean the sort of thing we could now get by aerial reconnaissance. It was simply not open to a Greek general to do that—any more than to Hannibal, Cromwell, or Napoleon. It might be equally absurd to pour ridicule on a tribal group for the practice of consulting oracles and administering 'henge' to live chickens to determine who had been casting spells. We have to try to see things from their point of view. Military historians and anthropologists try to do this.

Now, philosophers who attempt to assess the arguments of Plato or Mill or Marx are often supposed to share the errors of the unsophisticated military historian and the naïve observer of primitive practices; that is, they assume that Plato, say, can be regarded as being joined with us in an assault on a problem that is the same for both of us, whereas in fact the concepts and assumptions of a fifth-century Greek were quite different from ours. Therefore it is claimed to be dangerous to approach Plato and assess the validity of his arguments by means of our standards of validity. Our task is to understand Plato in his own terms.

Now, I do not deny that the prior task is one of understanding—of seeing Plato or Marx or Mill in the context of their own times—of seeing the force of the concepts they use and the assumptions that lie at the back of them. A philosopher must master what, say in the case of Plato, the classical scholar has to offer him. It is certainly important to understand what a writer is doing, the context in which he writes and the intellectual tradition to which he belongs and which gives much of the character and confidence to his views. But I do wish to deny that this is the only appropriate context for their interpretation and thus the sole proper means of appreciating them. I do not see how a historian of political thought could do his job properly unless he were to bring a critical eye to bear on the opinions of the writers he is studying. Let us take some examples: having done the essential preliminary work, we discover that Plato often argues in a manner similar to the way we argue. For example, the argument between Socrates and Polemarchus in the early part of the *Republic*: 'Is it right to return a dagger one has borrowed to someone who has since gone mad?' Now, if the classical scholars have done their job properly in their translations, this is the problem Socrates was discussing and the argument makes sense to us. So when Plato goes on to construct his ideal state and requires of his rulers that they have knowledge of the Good, the question may be fairly asked, how can it be ensured that abstract knowledge of that sort is correctly applied to concrete social problems? For, as Socrates has shown, the principle of 'returning what you have borrowed' has exceptions—circumstances matter. Circumstances must matter too for the decisions of the Philosopher-King to be right. Has Plato shown us any means, independent of the Philosopher-King's own decision, for determining whether he has acted wisely?

Now, philosophic interest in this kind of question arises not from the desire to score points off Plato but rather from a concern to explore the nature and implications of Plato's own arguments. We want to know what knowledge of the Good is, how it is translated into correct political decisions. For the Greeks were certainly aware of the difference between a commitment to moral principles and the difficult job of applying them in actual complex situations.

So I would argue that a philosophic interest is necessary to extract the most in the way of understanding what Plato said, that what appears to us to be a limitation in his argument is a spur to go on and see if he had an answer to the problem. In this way we are led on to a fuller and deeper understanding of his ideas—even if we emerge with a conviction that they were limited—by our standards, wrong—but not only by our standards, for some Greeks in Plato's time held views closer to ours than to Plato's. It is difficult to see how philosophy could have developed in the way it has, and how it could develop further, if a ban had been or were to be successfully imposed on citing critically the views of philosophers from another age. Thus, for example, Plato's *Crito* in which Socrates defends his refusal to escape from prison where he awaits the death penalty, is a wonderfully useful example of the sort of reasoning that often precedes decision—a decision we want to reach by thinking about the issues rather than acting impulsively. It shows how general principles and personal circumstances are intertwined and that they do not yield an automatic and logically compelling conclusion. The principles and the circumstances will be, and have been, different for other people, but the pattern and relationship of the components in Socrates's argument have been many times repeated, and so, at least in this sense, the *Crito* has a significance that transcends the context in which it was born. What is instructive about it is that, despite the enormous cultural gap between the scene of its composition and our own time, it tells us something vitally important about the nature of reasoning up to a moral or political decision. And in this sense it is a vital contribution to a continuing problem about what can be said about political obligation. An obsession with contextualism would make nonsense of philosophy and thus miss a great deal both in the understanding of a past philosopher and in the problems he dealt with.

Let us move from Plato to Mill. Many of the philosophic difficulties we find in the essay *On Liberty* or in the *Utilitarianism* were felt to be so by his contemporaries. This is surely strong prima-facie evidence that when we approach the essays in a philosophic spirit we are not necessarily engaged in a hazardous task in the sense that our understanding is bound to be defective because of some 'intellectual gap'. If we can be wrong in our interpretation of Mill this only makes sense if someone is right. And if it is claimed that any interpretation is likely to be risky because Mill was himself confused, how could one know that, independently of some philosophic conception of what it is to be confused on these matters? It is indeed commonly said that Mill was confused because he drew a distinction between self-regarding and other-regarding actions and that no such distinction is possible. Mill makes a distinction, certainly. We try to understand what sort of distinction it is, and this pre-supposes a certain amount of analytical ability, a typical piece of philosophical equipment. We say it seems to be a distinction between actions that affect, and actions that do not affect, others. But this is not a viable distinction. Mill, moreover, did not want to prevent people from saying or publishing things that caused others pain. So what was he trying to say?

In other words, as a result of a critique of one possible mean-ing of his principle we are led on to try another one. The same could happen to the latter—and so on. A critical philosophic attitude is indispensable for coming to a better understanding of what Mill said, and the interpretation commonly accepted at any one time may be open to objections that stimulate others to improve on it. But at that time it cannot surmount the objec-tions, and seeing what these are is part of the understanding of what Mill wrote.

The philosophical approach, then, is not one at odds with the study of the history of political thought but one essential to its fruitful study. In the case of a book on Mill's essay *On Liberty*, how absurd it would be to refrain from asking critical questions about his 'principle of liberty'—how would one set about offer-ing this as opposed to that interpretation without employing the critical tools of the philosopher? The texts which great political philosophers leave behind do not have meanings which are ob-vious or beyond dispute; hence the need for critical interpre-tation as well as attention to certain biographical details and to the intellectual scene to which the writer belonged. In the case of Mill's thought—its tensions, ambivalences, and vacillations —careful scrutiny of the texts is essential, as is a study of his intellectual history.

My main concern will be with the arguments in Mill's *On Liberty*, with what people have thought about those arguments and how they stand today. My interest in Mill's classic text derived from a preoccupation with liberty as such, what it meant and how important it was in relation to other values. This has of course a tremendous contemporary significance. But thinking about liberty cannot go far without taking account of Mill, and in this way I became interested in his essay for its own sake as well as its place in the history of the western idea of liberty. I wanted to see how he arrived at his own distinctive views and how his ideas on liberty were related to the other parts of his political theory, to his ethics, and to his views on the logic of the social studies. Clearly, over such a wide field as this the treatment cannot be uniformly detailed and so many aspects of Mill's thought have not been done the justice they deserve. I have always sought to keep the question of liberty in the centre of the picture.

In the first chapter I shall discuss the importance to Mill's final views of his intellectual starting point. To a very large extent Mill had been provided at an early age with beliefs in various spheres of human thought—how influential was this inheritance? In the second chapter I shall turn to various new influences which may also have contributed to his mature view of liberty. Next I shall survey the impact of Mill's *On Liberty* on his contemporaries, and in the fourth chapter I shall consider the views of some modern commentators who see the work as in conflict with the rest of his views or as essentially illiberal, as opposed to the view I shall have outlined in my first two chapters, that the way to *On Liberty* is a comprehensible growth and that the work is a part of his whole outlook—not at odds with it. In chapters five and six Mill's principle of liberty will be discussed. Finally, as an appendix I shall consider an essay *On Social Freedom* which was once thought to be Mill's response to the kind of criticisms levelled at him by his contemporaries.

As the book will have Mill's essay *On Liberty* as its focus it might be appropriate before we begin that enterprise to say a few brief words of a more general nature about Mill and his writings.

John Stuart Mill was born in London on 20 May 1806, the eldest son of James Mill, a leading disciple and friend of Bentham. In his *Autobiography* the younger Mill describes the remarkable education he received from his father, beginning Greek at the age of three and Latin at eight. At fifteen, massively instructed in a wide range of subjects, including economics, history, philosophy, and even some branches of the natural sciences, he first read Bentham and emerged with a unifying conception of things and a sense of purpose in life. In

1823 he followed his father into the service of the East India Company until his retirement in 1853. Regular employment did not prevent him from vigorously promoting the Benthamite cause by speech and pen, but during a lengthy period of depression which started in 1826 he became convinced that there were serious weaknesses in his inherited opinions. At the same time he was subject to new influences 'which enlarged my early narrow creed', among them Wordsworth, Coleridge, Carlyle, Goethe, the Saint-Simonians, and Comte. In these crucial years he came to value poetry and art both for themselves and as a means of cultivating the feelings and character; to move to a fuller conception of happiness as involving the development of one's personality in a rich and diverse manner; to appreciate the Saint-Simonian division of history into organic and critical periods; to see that political institutions must be related to the state of society; and to accept the important role an intellectual élite could play in shaping, and making coherent, the attitudes and beliefs of a society in a stage of transition. It was at this time too that his fears about the growth of mass conformity and its stifling effect on individual freedom took firm root. In the decade from 1831 Mill published several articles containing clear signs of his changed outlook; notable among them are the series on the 'Spirit of the Age' (1831), the essay on 'Civilization' (1836), and his studies of Bentham (1836) and Coleridge (1840). His judgement on Bentham is especially significant, manifesting some of the vital differences which were to distinguish Mill from his educators. He praises Bentham's contribution to the philosophy of law and his work for the reform of legal institutions; he greatly admires his methodological principle of breaking up wholes into their parts and abstractions into things; but he is harsh on a conception of man which, he claims, has no room for the pursuit of spiritual perfection as an end in itself. Moreover, Bentham's theory of government, he argues, ignores the dangers from a despotic public opinion and the importance of establishing checks on the will of the majority. And on both of these related matters Mill was strongly confirmed in his new attitude by a careful study of Tocqueville's *Democracy in America*, which he reviewed at length as the two parts appeared in 1835 and 1840. Meanwhile Mill had met Harriet Taylor, the wife of a London businessman, and there soon began what he called 'the most valuable friendship of my life'. They were married in 1851, two years after Mr Taylor's death.

Mill's first major work, the *System of Logic*, was published in 1843 and ran to several editions, as did the *Principles of Political Economy* after it appeared in 1848. With these two works Mill's reputation as an outstanding thinker of his day became firmly established. The successive editions of the *Political Economy* show a greater sympathy towards socialism and for the claims of the working classes than Mill's inherited opinions would have permitted, and it is probably here that Mrs Mill's influence, if it is to be admitted at all, would be most generally allowed. *On Liberty* (1859) came out in the year after Harriet's death and Mill insisted that it was a joint production which they had both gone over several times. Mill now spent much of each year in France where his stepdaughter, Helen Taylor, managed the small house at Avignon near Harriet's grave. His main work on political institutions, *Considerations on Representative Government*, appeared in 1861, and in the same year he wrote a set of essays on moral philosophy for *Fraser's Magazine* which came out as a book, *Utilitarianism*, in 1863. The most notable of his remaining works are *Auguste Comte and Positivism* (1865) and *The Subjection of Women* (1869). From 1865 to 1868 Mill represented Westminster in Parliament. He died at Avignon in 1874. His *Autobiography*, edited by Helen Taylor, was published later in the same year.

I

The Way to *On Liberty*

I

MILL'S writings stretch over a period of almost fifty years. There would be something profoundly unimaginative and unhistorical about any attempt to present this entire output as all of a piece, self-consistent and governed by an unchanging set of basic principles.[1] Mill himself provided more than enough evidence to suggest that the course of his intellectual development was marked by important changes of outlook, a fact which emerges in any case quite clearly from a study of what he wrote at different stages of his life.[2] There is this well-known passage in the *Autobiography*:

> After 1829 I withdrew from attendance on the Debating Society.[3] I had had enough of speech-making, and was glad to carry on my private studies and meditations without any immediate call for outward assertion of their results. I found the fabric of my old and taught opinions giving way in many fresh places, and I never allowed it to fall to pieces, but was incessantly occupied in weaving it anew. I never, in the course of my transition, was content to remain, for ever so short a time, confused and unsettled. When I had taken in any new idea, I could not rest till I had adjusted its relation to my old opinions, and ascertained exactly how far its effect ought to extend in modifying or superseding them.[4]

From about 1840 (probably earlier rather than later) Mill entered what he called the 'third period' of his 'mental progress'. His early Benthamite years had been followed by the absorption of new currents of thought which carried with them a phase of severe criticism of his 'old and taught opinions'. Now he had 'completely turned back from what there had been of excess in my reaction against Benthamism'.[5] *On Liberty* was of course written during this third period, and it has been widely recognized to contain much that fails to harmonize with the ideas he learned from his father and Bentham. An important question is whether it stands in contrast not only to his intellectual inheritance but also to what he wrote after 'the only actual revolution which has ever taken place in my modes of thinking was . . . complete'.[6]

That there is something distinctive, perhaps unique, about *On Liberty* has been sensed or confidently asserted by quite a few writers, though not all for the same reasons. Let me cite some examples.

F. C. Montague, writing in the 1880s, said that Mill's case for freedom was based 'on the ground of expediency', but his argument was also influenced by the doctrine which holds freedom to be 'man's natural and indefeasible right'.[7] Montague is in effect claiming that the foundations of Mill's essay are composed of a mixture of utilitarian and natural right theories, a view echoed over fifty years later by George Sabine:

> Though Bentham and James Mill had assumed that free discussion was necessary to good government, they had never been much inclined to stress liberty as a personal right. Among ideals of character intellectual honesty, candor, and objectivity appealed to Mill supremely, and in consequence freedom of thought and expression became for him ultimate social values. The argument of his essay went far beyond a mere utilitarian defense of liberty.

Sabine goes on to say that the practical limits of liberty set by Mill did not follow 'a single clear principle' because he combined a theory of natural rights with the principle of utility. Hence 'Mill's tendency to mix these two discrepant lines of argument left his conclusions pretty much to be determined by his own inclinations and habits of judgment'.[8]

Leslie Stephen, referring to his brother's *Liberty, Equality, Fraternity* (1873) as 'the most elaborate attack upon the *Liberty*', observed that 'the book is substantially a criticism of Mill from the older Utilitarian point of view. It shows, therefore, how Mill diverged from Bentham'.[9] And Lane Lancaster is very specific about the respects in which Mill did diverge:

> When he speaks of spontaneity as having *intrinsic* worth or as deserving regard on its own account; when he asserts that it is the privilege and proper condition of human beings to use experience in their own way; when he insists that the character of a man is of equal importance with his acts; and when he speaks wistfully of the kinds of men and women that 'nature can and will produce', he is voicing moral aspirations which go far beyond the principle of utility.[10]

But what is said to make for the special quality of *On Liberty* is
not simply that Mill was no longer an orthodox Benthamite
and that he built his case for liberty on a broader base than the
principle of utility; it is said to lie in his affirmation of a romantic conception of individuality. Thus Walter Houghton, writing
of Mill and Arnold as the major Victorian champions of 'the
ideal of self-development', with a common source in Goethe,
finds it necessary to say of Mill's particular version:

Nevertheless, Mill's interpretation of this ideal is neither Greek nor
Goethean—nor Arnoldian: it is Romantic. . . . What Mill wanted was
freedom for the individual to go his own way and live his own life;
freedom, in short, to cultivate and call forth all that was unique in
himself, within the limits imposed by the rights and interests of
others. Development meant the development of his special capacities
for intellectual, moral, and aesthetic life, not their harmonious
flowering in a balanced personality.[11]

Meaning perhaps not precisely the same by 'romantic',
R. P. Anschutz claims that Mill 'often behaved with a reckless
disregard of consequences more suitable to a romantic than to a
utilitarian'. 'He is thoroughly romantic, again,' continues
Anschutz, 'and thoroughly representative of his age, in the
eagerness with which he seeks out and endeavours to assimilate
every last exotic line of thought which shows any signs of
vitality'.[12] More important, however, is Anschutz's contention
that there is a conflict between the two views of human nature
which are expressed in different parts of Mill's philosophy, and
that this conflict is the source of the inconsistencies he finds in
his thought, illustrated for instance in Mill's treatment of the
free-will *versus* determinism problem. According to Anschutz,
Mill's belief in the universal law of causation committed him to
the view that every person's character is shaped by circumstances. Human behaviour is thus determined by the 'causes
called motives according to as strict laws as those which exist
in the world of mere matter'. On this view, claims Anschutz,
a human being cannot possess any more individuality than a
physical object. But Mill also believes that every man has, 'to
a certain extent', a power of altering his own character, and
this commits him to seeing man as something quite different
from a physical object whose behaviour can be explained simply

and entirely by the principle of the composition of physical forces. Mill's exposition of the naturalistic or scientific view of man, so Anschutz maintains, is to be found mainly in the *Logic*; and one of the principal manifestations of the romantic or self-formative view is the *Liberty*.[13]

One of the most recent and sustained arguments for seeing *On Liberty* as occupying a special place in Mill's writings, even among those of the 'third period', is Gertrude Himmelfarb's *On Liberty and Liberalism*,[14] to which we shall have occasion to return in more detail later on. For the moment let us note her contention that Harriet Taylor (or 'Mrs Mill', as she was to become) played a major role in the composition of *On Liberty*. She compares a short essay written by Harriet around 1830 with *On Liberty* and finds the resemblance 'striking'. Himmelfarb goes on:

And not only in its general theme—the value of individuality, the distrust of society, and the contempt for conformity—but also in many of its details: eccentricity raised to the level of principle, the relativity of truth, the connection between good and error, and the idea that force itself is conducive to the good. Above all, it resembles *On Liberty* in its posture—that of the romantic rebel standing alone against the overwhelming pressures of society . . .[15]

And what is distinctive about *On Liberty*, she asserts, is that Mill did not have the same conception of freedom either before or after he wrote the essay; so it was not characteristic of his attitude to liberty even in the period of his maturity. She describes this conception in these terms:

It was the absolute value of liberty, the absolute sovereignty of the individual, that distinguished this work from Mill's other writings and from the liberalism of his contemporaries. And it was this absolutistic doctrine that the influence of his wife and the circumstances of his life help account for.[16]

What on the face of it would seem to be an altogether different reason for singling out *On Liberty* is advanced by Paul Feyerabend. He regards it as a repudiation of those parts of the *Logic* which constitute a philosophy of science, setting out firm principles for the conduct of scientific activity. Since Mill published the *Logic* in 1843 and revised the successive editions right up to the eighth and final edition in 1872, thus apparently standing by one of his principal works (in the *Autobiography* he said: 'The "Liberty" is likely to survive longer than anything else that I have written, with the possible exception of the "Logic" . . . '), Feyerabend's claim is a bold one and it will be discussed in detail in a later chapter. For the present it will be enough to note that Mill's doctrine of individuality is central to Feyerabend's argument, invoked in support of his attack on current orthodoxies in the philosophy of science and set in contrast to the rigid and inhibiting position taken up in the *Logic*. And it is this same doctrine, as we have seen, with its call for self-cultivation and the assertion of one's own unique self, which has been taken to constitute the romantic element in Mill and is said to impart a distinctive flavour to *On Liberty* among his writings. In this respect at least Feyerabend's case shares a common factor with some of the other writers who see *On Liberty* as having a special place in Mill's philosophy.[17]

II

There is little point in multiplying examples; we shall encounter others when we come to consider the critical reaction to *On Liberty*. Our concern at this stage is simply to provide illustrations of two contentions, namely: first, that *On Liberty* constitutes a breach with Mill's intellectual inheritance, a claim which would be widely, though by no means universally, accepted; and secondly, that *On Liberty* is unique even within the range of Mill's mature writings, clashing at important points with doctrines stated in his major works on logic, ethics, political economy, and his other writings on politics. Now, in order to assess these claims we need standards of reference, and in the next chapter I propose to take, in respect of the first claim, Mill's early writings and speeches up to, roughly, 1830. Here I shall be concerned with the views of his father (particularly those expressed in the essays on 'Government' and the 'Liberty of the Press') and Bentham (chiefly the *Principles of Morals and Legislation*), out of which the views expressed in his early writings were largely taken but from which there can also be extracted much that was to enter into *On Liberty*.

Up to the year 1826 Mill considered himself an orthodox Benthamite. He tells us in the *Autobiography* how in the winter of 1821–2 his father 'put into my hands Bentham's principal speculations, as interpreted . . . by Dumont, in the Traité de Législation. The reading of this book was an epoch in my life; one of the turning points in my mental history.'[18] He then goes on to record:

When I laid down the last volume of the Traité, I had become a different being. The 'principle of utility' understood as Bentham understood it, and applied in the manner in which he applied it through these three volumes, fell exactly into its place as the keystone which held together the detached and fragmentary component parts of my knowledge and beliefs. It gave unity to my conceptions of things. I now had opinions; a creed, a doctrine, a philosophy; in one among the best senses of the word, a religion; the inculcation and diffusion of which could be made the principal outward purpose of a life.[19]

Over the next few years Mill was an ardent and active propagator of Benthamite policies, and for him and his circle of young friends it was his father's version of the creed that served as the guiding influence, especially the essay on 'Government'.[20] Apart from the evidence of the *Autobiography*, several speeches given in the 1820s show Mill arguing the radical case by means of concepts and terms to be found in his father's essay. By 1829, however, he began to have doubts about his father's mode of argument, and the appearance of Macaulay's attack on the essay in the *Edinburgh Review* (March 1829) served to increase his dissatisfaction to the point where he felt it necessary to question his father's conception of method in a fundamental way. Eventually, in the sixth book of the *Logic*, Mill worked out his own views on method; and later argued his own case for representative government. Taken together with the essay *On Liberty* they constitute a distinctive approach to social science and political theory.

The essay on 'Government' originated as an article for the supplement to the *Encyclopaedia Britannica* and was first published in 1820. It appeared later in pamphlet form, by itself or along with other essays by James Mill, several times during the 1820s and played a part in the agitation for the extension of the franchise. It is evident that Mill felt constrained to keep his argument within certain limits, for in a letter of September 1819 he reassured the editor of the *Encyclopaedia* that 'You need be under no alarm about my article 'Government'. I shall say nothing capable of alarming even a whig.'[21] Whatever allowances may have to be made in respect of the special circumstances in which it was written, there can be no doubt that the main structure of the argument represented James Mill's considered viewpoint. Certainly it constituted one of the most forceful, succinct, and influential statements of utilitarian political theory; and, as we have seen, was thus regarded by his son.

The same reasons that make government a necessary condition of an ordered society where man can reap the fruits of his own labour point to representative government as the sole effective safeguard against oppressive rulers; for such rulers always tend to be. This is James Mill's central thesis. The reasons are what Mill takes to be the laws of human nature, and it is from these laws as his premises that he proceeds to demonstrate the necessity of representative government. By the latter he means an elected assembly with control over the executive and whose interests are to be identical with those of the entire community. This identification of the interests of rulers and ruled is something that has to be devised, and the chief means of securing it is by extending the franchise to the point where the interests of the voters and the interests of the community as a whole are indistinguishable. In regular elections based on such a franchise lies the principal method for ensuring that the governors have regard for the universal interest and for preventing its being twisted to some partial or sinister interest. Thus whilst Hobbes, arguing deductively from the nature of man, asserted that nothing less than absolute government was adequate to impose a check on the destructive tendencies of human nature, Mill insisted that the evils men would inevitably suffer under absolute government could only be remedied by making government responsible to its subjects, and this it could never be unless it were also representative.

In more detail the argument runs as follows. The task of rulers is to promote the greatest happiness of the greatest number, or 'to increase to the utmost the pleasures, and diminish to the utmost the pains, which men derive from one another'.[22]

Now human conduct is intelligible only in terms of the search for pleasure and the avoidance of pain. Or, to put it more precisely: men's actions are governed by their wills, their wills by their desires, and 'their desires are directed to pleasure and relief from pain as *ends*, and to wealth and power as the principal means'.[23] It must be accepted that the means of subsistence and the main sources of our pleasures are relatively scarce and have to be produced by human effort. Were they naturally plentiful there would be no reason for conflict among men. Since men will take from each other whatever they can without injury to themselves, government is established to prevent mutual depredation—'when a great number of men combine, and delegate to a small number the power necessary for protecting them all'.[24] But with the establishment of government the great problem is how to avert the abuse of power since, being men, rulers are under the same temptation as are all men to deprive others of the means of pleasure, to accumulate wealth and power. Hence the very reasons for having government at all make it necessary to impose checks on the activities of governors. The entire community can, of course, have no sinister interest, and thus it might seem that the only certain guarantee against misrule would be democracy, i.e. a community literally governing itself. This, however, is impractical. Failing democracy, might there not be safety in reducing the number of rulers to as few as possible on the grounds that the things a man can want to possess are not unlimited, and therefore the fewer the governed have over them the less likely they are to be oppressed? But this would be to misread human nature. It is true that on the face of it historical evidence yields no clear answer; hence 'we must penetrate to the springs within'.[25] What the laws of human nature show is that the demand for power ('security for the conformity between the will of one man and the acts of other men')[26] stops only at the point when the actions of every member of the community conforms to the will of the rulers. Mill concludes: 'It is proved, therefore, by the closest deduction from the acknowledged laws of human nature, and by direct and decisive experiments, that the ruling One, or the ruling Few, would, if checks did not operate in the way of prevention, reduce the great mass of the people to their power, at least to the condition of negroes in the

West Indies'.[27] It is therefore on the existence of checks that the avoidance of misrule must depend. The community can impose checks on behalf of itself by choosing representatives to act as a controlling body over the executive. This checking body would need to have sufficient power to curb the executive and at the same time possess an identity of interest with the community, for unless there were such an identity of interests the representatives will use their power for their own advantage. Representatives must therefore serve for a limited period, though eligible for re-election, and should be elected by a body whose interests are the same as those of the entire community. An electorate consisting of all males over forty would, Mill appears to consider, fulfil these requirements. In 'the principles of the representative system', therefore, we find 'all that is necessary to constitute a security for good government'.[28]

Now, implicit in James Mill's argument is the necessity for freedom of expression. How can electors choose wisely unless they have reliable information about the views and conduct of their representatives and of the rulers whom the representatives are to check? Indeed, how could it be said that they exercise any kind of genuine choice unless they can hear all sides of the questions which are at issue? In an article on the 'Liberty of the Press', written shortly after the essay on 'Government' and included in the same supplement to the *Encyclopaedia Britannica*, Mill makes these points explicit. Moreover, they tie up with other aspects of his thought which signify the enormous importance he attached to freedom of expression, a conviction which John Stuart was educated to share from his earliest days. A passage in the *Autobiography* tells of the influence which his father's opinions had in giving a special flavour to the Benthamite propaganda of the young Philosophic Radicals; of the 'almost unbounded confidence' they all had in the great power for good of representative government and complete freedom of discussion. It goes on:

So complete was my father's reliance on the influence of reason over the minds of mankind, whenever it is allowed to reach them, that he felt as if all would be gained if the whole population were taught to read, if all sorts of opinions were allowed to be addressed to them by word and in writing, and if by means of the suffrage they could nominate a legislature to give effect to the opinions they adopted. He thought that when the legislature no longer represented a class interest, it would aim at the general interest, honestly and with adequate wisdom; since the people would be sufficiently under the guidance of educated intelligence, to make in general a good choice of persons to represent them, and having done so, to leave to those whom they had chosen a liberal discretion.[29]

But, John Stuart hastens to add, if a democratic suffrage was 'the principal article of his political creed', it was advocated 'not on the ground of liberty, Rights of Man, or any of the phrases, more or less significant, by which, up to that time, democracy had usually been defended, but as the most essential of "securities for good government"'.[30]

As we have summarized so far, the place of liberty in James Mill's political theory would seem to be purely instrumental. In John Stuart's words, it was an essential security for good government. Good government itself consisted in promoting the universal interest, which in turn is to be elucidated in terms of the greatest happiness of the greatest number, and since the notion of happiness was taken in its Benthamite sense (which is not to say that it gives rise to no problems), liberty is thus regarded as contributing, directly or indirectly, to maximizing pleasure. But liberty in James Mill's scheme of things was also closely connected with the importance he attached to the use of reason, and the latter was itself inseparable from his deep conviction that we are all under a solemn obligation to seek the truth. The moral fervour with which he held this belief stemmed partly from the view that much that was evil in human institutions had its origin in ignorance and the persistent disregard of truth. Truth for him was both a necessary condition, *and a constituent element*, of an improved state of mankind. The impartial consideration of evidence out of regard for truth and fairness he held to be one of the leading virtues, whilst 'the habit of forming opinions, and acting upon them, without evidence is one of the most immoral habits of the mind . . . the foundation of most of what is vicious and degraded in human character'.[31] But for this habit, Mill contends, the improvement of mankind would have been much more rapid. 'How', he asks, 'could institutions, at variance with the interests of the community, which are a mockery of human nature, and act as a pestilential atmosphere upon the race, hold their endless existence, if the human mind was not ruined by the habit of adopting opinions, without evdence?'[32] Adopting opinions without evidence goes with 'feeling little concern about the grounds of one's opinions' and taking up opinions merely because they are currently fashionable.[33] James Mill's contempt for these practices passed on to his son and became an essential part of his case for liberty in every stage of his intellectual development.

Reason and truth were therefore necessary instruments of progress. But, I want to suggest, James Mill's notion of progress cannot be defined independently of them. They enter into his account of progress not only as necessary conditions for its achievement but also as constituent elements of what was to be attained. Thus the departure from a strictly utilitarian treatment of social values, though not openly announced, begins as *part* of John Stuart's 'old and taught opinions'. Moreover, the so-called élitist strand in John Stuart's thought is presaged in the way the eventual triumph of reason and truth is identified by James Mill with the fortunes of a particular social group. 'The opinion of the wise and disinterested', he declared, 'though they are small in number, always, or at least generally, prevails at last, and becomes the opinion of the world'.[34] And this tendency was 'the ground of all our hopes for the amelioration of mankind'. It is solid ground too, for 'when an opinion, founded on truth, and tending to good, is once declared, and when there is the means of making it generally known, and of calling to it continually the attention of mankind, it is sure to make its way, and by degrees to bear down all that opposes it'.[35]

One of the problems facing John Stuart was that whilst he took over these beliefs from his father and endeavoured to work them into his own treatise on liberty, the tendencies of his day seemed to him to stand in the way of their fulfilment. Hence the alternation of optimism and despair, hope and fear, which is such a marked characteristic of his attitude to the future prospects of freedom; an attitude that stands in striking contrast to that of his father. James Mill's optimism stemmed in part from the consequences which he foresaw from the discovery of the printing press and the spread of the printed word. Knowledge could no longer be confined to a small minority, even if its genesis were thus restricted. This would have momentous significance for the conduct of government, effecting 'not a change merely, but a perfect revolution, in the art of governing mankind'.[36] But there was another source for James Mill's belief in progress, namely, that the increasingly literate people would derive its opinion from the 'wise and disinterested' few whose function was to bring enlightenment to the rest of society. The people, freed from its traditional loyalties, would be brought 'under the guidance of educated intelligence'. Now, wisdom and virtue, so he contended, were to be found mostly in the middle classes, and the opinions of the people below the middle rank were largely taken from them. James Mill therefore saw it as one of the most favourable signs of promise for human improvement that the middle classes were growing in number and influence; and with the extension of the franchise they would become the ultimate power.

The notion of an intellectual élite exercising an important social and political role had a very definite attraction for John Stuart, and its origin in his case has commonly been traced to Coleridge, the Saint-Simonians, and Comte. Our account of James Mill's political thought suggests that the source could well have been much nearer home. What seems scarcely to have crossed the mind of the father, namely, that this new power of the middle class would express itself in the shape of a mediocre and oppressive public opinion, was to become a dominant theme in the writings of the son.

III

Up to this point we have dealt briefly with the place of liberty in James Mill's theory of representative government and the part he saw it playing in the progress of mankind. But there is an important aspect of his article on the 'Liberty of the Press' which we have not yet considered, and that is the problem of the *limits* to liberty, a matter John Stuart tried to 'settle' by the famous principle set out in the essay, *On Liberty*. There, early on in the third chapter, he says: 'No one pretends that actions should be as free as opinions . . . [and] even opinions lose their immunity when the circumstances in which they are expressed are such as to constitute their expression a positive instigation to some mischievous act'.[37] I do not wish to anticipate our examination of the problems raised by the attempt to distinguish 'opinions' from 'actions'; rather, I want to indicate the guidelines offered by James Mill for delimiting the spheres in which actions and opinions should be free of social control.

James Mill defines the range of his problem as follows:

We are then to inquire, in the first place, what are the acts of the press with respect to *private reputation*: and next, what are the acts with respect to *government*, which it is desirable that punishment should be employed to restrain.[38]

The second part of the inquiry includes a detailed argument in support of the general point that freedom of the press is an essential security for good government. Going over some of the ground already covered in 'Government', Mill asks: ' . . . what is meant by a vicious government?' One that sacrifices the interests of the many to the few, for 'where there is nothing to check that propensity, all the evils of misgovernment . . . are the inevitable consequence'. And 'there can be no adequate check without the freedom of the press . . . [indeed] it is doubtful whether a power in the people of choosing their own rulers, without the liberty of the press, would be an advantage'.

It is perfectly clear, that all chance of advantage to the people, from having the choice of their rulers, depends upon their making a good choice. . . . [But] the very foundation of a good choice is knowledge. The fuller and more perfect the knowledge, the better the chance . . . of a good choice. How can the people receive the most perfect knowledge relative to the characters of those who present themselves to their choice, but by information conveyed freely, and without reserve, from one to another?[39]

To attempt to restrict what may be said in criticism of governments, e.g. that unjust censure should be forbidden, Mill asks: 'But what censures are just and unjust . . . who is to judge?' He follows this up with a passage which is an admirable illustration of John Stuart's remark about the reliance his father put 'on the influence of reason over the minds of mankind'.

Where there is no motive to attach a man to error, it is natural to him to embrace the truth; especially if pains are taken to adapt the explanation to his capacity. Every man, possessed of reason, is accustomed

to weigh evidence, and to be guided and determined by its pre-
ponderance. When various conclusions are, with their evidence, presented with equal care and with equal skill, there is a moral certainty,
though some few may be misguided, that the greater number will
judge right . . .[40]

This is a proposition, adds Mill, on which his whole case
depends, but 'there is . . . hardly any law of human nature
more generally recognized, wherever there is not a motive to
deny its existence.'[41]

Now it would seem as if Mill is leading up to the conclusion
that there should be no restraints at all on the press. In fact,
however, he is in favour of some limits. One type of restriction
he allows stems from a distinction he draws between what he
describes as 'that species of resistance which is necessary, in the
last resort, to secure the people against the abuse of the powers
of government . . . either to withdraw them from the hands in
which they have hitherto been deposited, or greatly to modify
the terms upon which they are held' and 'resistance to the operations of government in detail'.[42] With regard to the former,
for reasons into which we need not enter, he maintains that
exhortation by the press to this kind of resistance ought not to
be treated as an offence. However, when it comes to obstruct-
ing the processes of a government which 'possesses and deserves
the fullest confidence of the community at large', the encouragement of such acts ought to be treated as offences because
they are clearly 'hurtful acts'. But they are 'hurtful' in an indirect sort of way, since 'satisfaction by the party offending to
the party injured' is often out of the question.[43] The examples
Mill gives are: violent interference with court or legislative pro-
ceedings, and forcible prevention of an administrative official
from carrying out his duties. Thus a hand-bill, 'distributed at
a critical moment', could excite a mob to obstruct a public
officer. The 'hurt' or 'injury' involved in such cases derives
from the threat they constitute to the protection of rights, for
which government is instituted. The notion of a 'hurt' or an
'injury' is therefore closely related to the violation of rights and
the existence of a set of governmental arrangements which
upholds a system of rights. How Mill understood the idea of
'a right' and how the violation of a right is connected with
'pain' are matters we shall take up presently, and it will be

worth looking at them with some care since the construction to be put on the concept of an 'injury' or conduct which is 'injurious' (causes 'harm' or 'damage') is one of the key questions raised by the controversy over how to interpret John Stuart's principle of liberty.

The other restriction on the press allowed by Mill—in relation to government—is simply an extension to the area of public administration of a principle he would include in the civil code, namely, false imputation: 'the imputing to a functionary a criminal act, which there was no ground, nor even any appearance of ground, to impute to him'. So he concludes:

In all other respects, we have seen that the press ought to be free; that if there is any limit to the power of delivering unfavourable opinions, respecting either the functionaries, or the institutions of government, and of recommending those opinions by any media . . . the benefits which may be derived from the freedom of the press are so greatly infringed, that hardly any security for good government can remain.[44]

The other sphere where Mill considers the press to be peculiarly well-placed to inflict injury is that of private rights. He points out that the press *could* be involved in the commission of any offence, or almost any offence (e.g., theft, fraud, or murder), against private persons and as such it would be liable to whatever penalties the law imposes for the offence in question. But it is in respect of 'reputation' that it holds an especially powerful position and it is with this problem that he is largely concerned; and here again he employs concepts which were later to play a major role in John Stuart's essay *On Liberty*.

'No act', says Mill, 'can be regarded as an offence with respect to an individual, which is not a violation of some of his rights'.[45] For an analysis of the notion of 'a right' he refers the reader to the article on 'Jurisprudence' which was also written for the supplement to the *Encyclopaedia Britannica*. There he makes it plain that the terms 'offence', 'a right', 'injury', and 'hurtful' are closely interdependent. In view of the well-known Utilitarian aversion to the idea of 'natural rights' and the claim that John Stuart relies (perhaps unwittingly) on precisely that idea in *On Liberty*, it is important to establish just how James Mill understood the term, 'a right'.

It is not at all clear at first sight whether he wishes to maintain that all rights are legal rights. For instance, he allows sense to the question, 'what rights *ought* to be constituted?', giving the answer that utility determines what *should* be rights. Thus it is certain that he intends to link the idea of rights firmly to the standard of the greatest happiness. 'Men', he says, 'are susceptible of happiness only in proportion as rights are protected'. He goes on:

All rights . . . are rights to objects of human desire . . . All objects which men desire, are desired either as the end or as means. The pleasurable state of mind is the end, consisting of the feelings of the mind. . . . All rights, then, when the term is closely investigated, are found to mean powers: powers with respect to things. What anyone means when he says that a thing is his property, is that he has the power of using it in a certain way.[46]

And, later, he says:

All rights, when the essence of them is spoken of, are powers: powers to an individual, which the governing members of the community guarantee; powers, more or less extensive, of making either a person or a thing subservient to the gratification of his desires.[47]

One feels compelled to ask, given that there can be bad governments and that the powers which *should* be guaranteed may not be constituted as rights, whether the rights actually protected by the law are always consistent with utility. And Mill's answer must be 'no', an answer which would seem to imply a distinction between 'constituted' and 'unconstituted' rights, which in turn suggests that not all rights are legal rights; or, alternatively, that the powers which men *should* possess only become 'rights' when they are guaranteed by law. However we put it, the conclusion seems inescapable that the rights which men enjoy under the law, i.e. 'constituted' rights, may conflict with the demands of utility. Moreover, the problem arises whether an analysis of the concept of 'a right' can be successfully carried out solely in terms of the greatest happiness standard. But this is too large and complex a matter to be explored in passing, so let us return to Mill's discussion of rights, in particular the idea of 'violation' of a right.

By a violation of a right he understands 'all those acts by which the powers conveyed by a right are prevented from operating according to the will of the owner'.[48] An act of this sort involves an 'injury' to the possessor of the right and it is also designated as 'hurtful'. But, Mill says, it is not expedient that penalties should be attached by law to the whole class of injurious or hurtful acts. Here he follows Bentham's system of classification for determining how those acts fit for punishment are to be differentiated from the rest. But, he emphasizes, 'acts are declared to be offences and are made subject to punishment solely for the protection of rights'. They may carry legal penalties for either one of two reasons: first, because there is a *direct* infringement of rights, as when an injury is inflicted on an individual or some individuals; and secondly, because rights have been affected *indirectly* by an interference with the operations of government which exist to protect rights. The latter, he says, 'though mediately and not immediately hurtful, are apt to be more extensively mischievous than the former'.[49]

Further light is shed on Mill's use of these key concepts— 'rights', 'injurious', 'hurtful'—by his treatment of 'the rights which ought to be established with respect to reputation'. He takes as his guiding principle for fixing limits to the freedom of the press on this subject the following proposition: 'that every man should be considered as having a right to the character he deserves; that is, to be spoken of according to his actions'.[50] How might this right be violated? It is 'hurtful' to a man, says Mill, if it is believed that he has committed or has a disposition to commit, certain sorts of actions. An 'injury' is inflicted on him if it is thought that he has committed, or has a disposition to commit, legal offences such as theft, perjury, or murder. But it is also 'hurtful', and constitutes an 'injury', if it is thought that his actions are 'those to which the penalties of public disrepute and dislike are annexed'.[51] When the belief is false the injured party is entitled to compensation; and punishment may also be inflicted to prevent similar offences in the future. Thus far, it will be noticed, Mill has not extended 'the rights of reputation' beyond the limits required for protection against the imputation of falsehood. But at this point he considers whether they ought to be taken further and goes on to make the following observation:

There can be no doubt that the feelings of the individual may be as painful, where the actions of a disreputable nature are, truly, as where they are falsely, imputed to him. It is equally certain, that no painful feelings ought to be wilfully excited in any man, where no good, sufficient to overbalance that evil, is its natural consequence.[52]

He sees no case at all for increasing the range of protection to cover actions which are correctly stated to be breaches of the law, save for one exception—'unless the law is a bad law'. (He does not explain how this qualification would receive legal expression or be administered by the courts.) But where the actions are not illegal and their painful consequences are restricted entirely to the disapproval and dislike of society the matter is harder to decide. On the one hand Mill feels it would be a great benefit to society to have all actions of this sort freely publicized because it would induce men to abstain from them as 'at present . . . any well educated person . . . [abstains] from those acts which constitute the ill manners of the vulgar'. His argument is worth quoting at length:

If the hatred and contempt of the people . . . were always rightly directed, and rightly proportioned; if they never operated against any actions but those which were hurtful, either to the individual himself, or to others, and never, but in the degree in which they were hurtful, the case would be clear; the advantage which would be derived from the true exposure of any man's actions of any sort, would exceed beyond calculation the attendant evil. The great difficulty of insuring the practice of morality, in those numerous and highly important cases, to which the legal sanction, or the *security of pains and penalties*, does not extend, consists in the want of a motive always present, and powerful enough to counteract the instant motive which urges to the instant offence. That motive almost every man would derive from the knowledge that he had the eyes upon him of all those, the good opinion of whom it was his interest to preserve; that no immoral act of his would escape their observation, and a proportionate share of their hatred and contempt.[53]

Among the things which catch our attention in this passage, one which could be instructively compared with John Stuart's attitude to the pressures of public opinion, is the fact that it is only in respect of 'hurtful' actions that social disapproval and dislike are to operate; and that Mill appears to identify a 'hurtful' with an 'immoral' action. However, let us follow the course of the argument, for Mill goes on to explain that he had to use the conditional mood because 'the unfavourable sentiments of our fellow-men . . . do not always fall where they ought . . . [because] it very often happens that men's antipathies are excited to actions from which no evil ensues, either to him who performs them, or to any body else'.[54] It is, he insists, 'to limit *his sphere of innocent enjoyment*'[55] to prevent a man from deriving pleasure from such actions. And among the examples he cites are the eating of animal food in prohibited periods in societies dominated by the Roman Catholic Church; and the drinking of wine, which 'would render a Mahomedan execrable to the whole of his tribe'. These are cases of the infliction of an 'evil' not counterbalanced by 'the smallest portion of good'; they are examples of the 'misdirection of the favourable and unfavourable sentiments of mankind . . . [a] perversion and corruption of their moral sentiments . . . [largely] the work of priests, contriving the means of increasing their influence'. But the 'aristocratical class' too has had a hand in the perversion of the moral sentiments, in order to secure to themselves 'a more easy dominion over the rest of their fellow-creatures'.[56]

Mill concludes, then, that it would be hurtful to a man for the press to give such publicity to his actions, even when truthfully reported, as to expose him to social disapproval if the latter takes the form of groundless antipathies of the sort just exemplified. Yet he hesitates to recommend a definite and unqualified prohibition on hurtful publicity of this nature, partly because there may be difficulties in the way of establishing an accurate and commonly agreed line of distinction between the class of cases when publicity would be beneficial and the set of cases when it would not. Furthermore, the balance of advantage on the side of permitting the truth to be fully disclosed is, he maintains, overwhelming. Not only are the occasions on which the propagation of the truth would be beneficial much more numerous, they are also more important, for they include 'the whole field of morality'.

Every body believes and proclaims, that the universal practice of the moral virtues would ensure the highest measure of human happiness . . . Toward the attainment of this most desirable state of things, nothing in the world is capable of contributing so much as the full exercise of truth upon all immoral actions,—all actions, the practice of which is calculated to lessen the amount of human happiness.[57]

To be set against this, on the debit side, is the evil 'which would be incurred by the antipathies of misguided minds against actions innocent in themselves'. No one, Mill asserts, would claim that they are comparable. Besides, the source of the evil is not beyond remedy, for the antipathies that serve to inflict injury stem from 'a mental disease . . . toward the cure of which truth is likely to operate as the most effectual of all expedients'. And this optimism is reflected in Mill's concluding judgement that though it would be vain to expect agreement on a principle of demarcation in *all* cases, there are some which could be identified 'with sufficient exactness' as to justify reparation when the injury caused is occasioned by actions that are 'innoxious' and 'ought to be of no importance in the estimate of human worth'.[58]

IV

There can be no doubt that John Stuart was thoroughly familiar with the *Encyclopaedia* articles. Apart from the general, and ample, evidence testifying to his knowledge of his father's writings there are the specific references to the essays on 'Government' and 'Liberty of the Press'. In the *Autobiography* we are told that the essay on 'Government' 'was regarded probably by all of us as a masterpiece of political wisdom' (though they disapproved of the exclusion of women from the suffrage).[59] Macaulay's attack on the essay and the ensuing debate was a landmark in Mill's intellectual development, and his ideas on method in the social sciences were shaped by the effort he made to assess the merits and defects of the conflicting opinions in the controversy. As for 'Liberty of the Press', John Stuart declares his indebtedness to this essay in his own article on the subject, published in the *Westminster Review* in 1825. But what is less easy to establish is the extent to which some of the leading ideas in these articles find expression in *On Liberty*. Our plan of advance at this stage will therefore be to ascertain what sort of theory, or principle, of liberty can be extracted from these essays. In the course of our inquiry we shall have to refer back to Bentham and cast forward glances at *On Liberty*.

To prevent misrule, to secure an identity of interest between governors and governed, there must be a system of checks, for the laws of human nature show that unlimited power results in oppression. Hence the need for an extended franchise and regular elections. But, Mill asserts, none of these measures would be effective without a free press. Freedom of discussion was not, however, just an instrument to ensure good government. It was vital for the triumph of reason and truth, and these values, as Mill talks of them, seem both to define and contribute to the greatest happiness. How far should freedom of discussion extend? Apart from the general duty to comply with the law (i.e. to abstain from incitement to murder and other crimes, not to be involved in fraud, and so forth) . . . the only restrictions Mill wants to see imposed are confined to incitement to the obstruction of state machinery, false imputation, and 'certain cases' of misguided disapproval of innocent actions. What really concerns us, though, is the manner in which Mill arrived at his conclusions. We have seen that he invoked the notion of 'a right' and the idea of a 'hurtful' or an 'injurious' action. And his line of demarcation both in respect of 'actions' and 'opinion'—to adopt John Stuart's distinction for the moment—would seem to turn on these notions. Here we come to a problem which has all the appearance of being the same as, or closely similar to, the one that lies at the heart of *On Liberty*. Can the idea of what is 'hurtful' or 'injurious' serve to delineate a range of actions (including the expression of opinions) so as to secure an optimum of, fix proper limits to, liberty? Did James Mill's use of this criterion constitute the model on which John Stuart based his own principle of liberty?

Before we can even begin to answer these questions we must take a closer look at what Mill understood by an 'injurious' or a 'hurtful' action. Incidentally, if he meant to imply a distinction between 'injurious' and 'hurtful' he never indicates what it is. On the contrary, there are places where he treats them as synonymous, and we shall assume that they are so.

Although Mill says that no act is an offence which is not a violation of rights, and that every infringement of a right involves an injury, it is clear that he has an idea of what constitutes an injury independently of its being an offence, i.e. an action prohibited by law. Whether or not an action is injurious is to be decided by appealing to the principle of utility (as indeed is the question of what should be established as rights). An injury is the evil, pain, or mischief (to be treated as synonymous) which results from an action; but not all cases of the infliction of pain are to be regarded as injuries. We have noticed, for instance, Mill's reference to 'unfounded antipathies', perversions of morality: the painful feelings experienced by persons sharing such antipathies are not to be counted as injuries.

It hardly needs to be said that in most of this Mill is following Bentham. In his discussion of injurious acts he mentions Bentham specifically as having laid down the fundamental principles of the subject.[60] Bentham defined an offence as an act which has a natural tendency to produce mischievous consequences and which is prohibited by law. Since the law is often imperfectly framed some acts are wrongly declared to be offences, and some acts which are not offences ought to be made so. According to the principle of utility 'the good of the community' is the standard of what actions ought to be made offences, and this requires that no act should be made an offence 'which is not liable, in some way or other, to be detrimental to the community'.[61] What is mischievous or detrimental is given by the principle of utility, for Bentham stipulates that:

By utility is meant that property in any object, whereby it tends to produce benefit, advantage, pleasure, good, or happiness, (all this in the present case comes to the same thing) or (what comes again to the same thing) to prevent the happening of mischief, pain, evil, or unhappiness to the party whose interest is considered: if that party be the community in general, then the happiness of the community: if a particular individual, then the happiness of that individual. . . . An action then may be said to be conformable to the principle of utility, or, for shortness sake, to utility, (meaning with respect to the community at large) when the tendency it has to augment the happiness of the community is greater than any it has to diminish it.[62]

Later, he adds 'profit', 'convenience', and 'emolument' to his list of 'pleasure terms'; and 'loss', 'inconvenience', and 'disadvantage' to his 'pain terms'.[63] Thus 'injury' and 'hurt' do not figure as such in Bentham's list, but it is obvious from the way Mill uses the terms and from his specific reference to Bentham's analysis of 'injurious acts' that he treats them as having the same force as the other terms on the 'pain' side of Bentham's scheme of classification.

A major component, then, of Mill's conception of the proper limits to liberty derives from the need to prevent, or minimize, injury; and the notion of injury is supplied by the principle of utility. However, as we have seen, not all cases of injury are to be classed as 'offences', i.e. made subject to legal prohibition. Not only are there some sorts of actions which are 'unmeet' for legal punishment, for reasons we shall touch on later, but there are also those actions which fall within the sphere of public disapproval and dislike, i.e. acts which are hurtful and which, 'without being punishable by the law, are attended with disrepute'. These are overlapping categories, and with regard to the latter we should take notice of Mill's opinion that 'the pains which are derived from the unfavourable sentiments of mankind' are a 'powerful agency for the prevention of injurious acts'.[64]

The category of injurious acts rightly subject to legal punishment would seem to be common to both James and John Stuart Mill. Certainly James Mill held that the liberty of the subject, in a country like Britain at any rate, ought to be restricted, at the very least, by those rules of law which rightly prohibit injurious actions. And there are passages in *On Liberty* which give the appearance of accepting this principle:

If any one does an act hurtful to others, there is a *prima facie* case for punishing him, by law, or, where legal penalties are not safely applicable, by general disapprobation.

A person may cause evil to others not only by his actions but by his inaction, and in either case he is justly accountable to them for the injury. The latter case, it is true, requires a much more cautious exercise of compulsion than the former.[65]

Elsewhere, of course, John Stuart speaks of 'harm', sometimes 'damage', though everything points to their having the same force as 'injury' or 'hurtful'. But whereas in the case of James Mill the principle of utility, which tells us what is injurious or hurtful and also determines when injurious actions should be subject to legal punishment, is taken from Bentham, the utility to which John Stuart appeals is 'utility in the largest sense, grounded on the permanent interests of a man as a progressive being'.[66] And there is surely a clue to the meaning of 'utility in the largest sense' in the *Autobiography*, where the leading theme of *On Liberty* is described as:

. . . the importance, to man and society, of a large variety in types of character, and of giving full freedom to human nature to expand itself in innumerable and conflicting directions.[67]

One of the main problems facing us, therefore, is whether father and son employed divergent, possibly incompatible, conceptions of 'utility'. If so, what are the implications of these different versions for the use of key notions like 'harm' and 'injury'? When Bentham or James Mill describe a type of action as mischievous, causing evil, injurious, or hurtful it would seem that any doubt about its tendency being of that sort could be cleared up by an empirical test, i.e. whether it causes pain, or more pain than pleasure on balance. It may well be that doubts over the allegedly 'harmful' nature of a kind of action could not be settled that way when the criterion to which we have to appeal is 'utility in the largest sense'. But might it not be a very large assumption to suppose that the standard to which Bentham and the elder Mill appealed does in fact provide a clear and simple empirical solution? Consider, for instance, the distinction James Mill draws between injurious actions which are rightly met with public disapproval and those 'innoxious actions' subjected to the groundless antipathies of a perverted morality. Can the notion of injury, as used by Mill, sustain a viable distinction of this nature? The question has an added interest in that John Stuart would seem to have made the same distinction in *On Liberty*. He complains there that 'the likings and dislikings of society, or of some powerful portion of it, are thus the main thing which has practically determined the rules laid down for general observance, under the penalties of law or opinion', and refers to these 'likings and dislikings', in language taken over from Bentham and his father, as 'sympathies and antipathies which [have] little or nothing to do with the interests of society'.[68]

V

Several issues arise here in connection with the categories of punishment society is said to have at its disposal for the preven-

tion of injurious actions, but two in particular call for attention:
(i) the appropriate spheres of legal punishment on the one hand
and social disapproval on the other; and (ii) the distinction between an 'antipathy' and genuine moral condemnation. These
problems are closely bound up with such questions as the relationship between 'injury' and 'painful feelings', whether certain kinds of injurious actions are 'meet' or 'unmeet' for legal
punishment, direct and indirect injury, and the business of
'self-regarding offences', some of which will come up for consideration at a later stage. First, then, the respective areas of
law and public opinion as instruments of social control.

One finds it commonly stated that J. S. Mill stood in contrast to other democratic theorists by the emphasis he put on
the 'tyranny of public opinion'. Is this a significant point of
difference between himself and his father? Early on in the
Liberty he declares

> Protection . . . against the tyranny of the magistrate is not enough:
> there needs protection also against the tyranny of the prevailing
> opinion and feeling; against the tendency of society to impose, by
> other means than civil penalties, its own ideas and practices as rules
> of conduct on those who dissent from them; to fetter the develop-
> ment, and, if possible, prevent the formation, of any individuality not
> in harmony with its ways, and compels all characters to fashion them-
> selves upon the model of its own.[69]

It has been frequently assumed that the plea was made with the
doctrines of Bentham and his father largely in mind and there
is much to support the assumption. For example, in his cele-
brated article on Bentham, first published in 1838 and later
reprinted in *Dissertations and Discussions* in the same year as the
appearance of *On Liberty* (1859), he asks of the 'Benthamic
theory of government' whether it is ' . . . at all times and
places, good for mankind to be under the absolute authority of
the majority of themselves. . . . Is it, we say, the proper condition of man, in all ages and nations, to be under the despotism
of Public Opinion?' He goes on:

> . . . Bentham . . . not content with enthroning the majority as sov-
> ereign, by means of universal suffrage without king or house of lords
> . . . exhausted all the resources of ingenuity in devising means for
> riveting the yoke of public opinion closer and closer round the necks

of all public functionaries, and excluding every possibility of the
exercise of the slightest or most temporary influence either by a
minority, or by the functionary's own notions of right. . . . The power
of the majority is salutary in so far as it is used *defensively*, not *offensively*
—as its exertion is tempered by respect for the personality of the
individual, and reverence for the superiority of cultivated intelligence.[70]

Since this passage is by no means an isolated example, and its
message is reiterated in *On Liberty* itself, we are surely entitled
to say that in this respect at least there does seem to be an important break with his inherited beliefs. But where did James
Mill stand in the matter? The possibility that he did not share
what John Stuart represents to be Bentham's position is suggested by some remarks in the *Autobiography* which those subscribing to what might be called the standard account of the
relationship between James Mill and his son have tended to
neglect.[71] One thing, John Stuart tells us, which he felt to be
a 'good augury' was his father's high appreciation of Tocqueville's *Democracy in America*. His father also approved of an article
on 'Civilization' (1836) 'into which I threw many of my new
opinions', including an anticipation of the fears he was to
express about the desolation of public opinion in 'Bentham'.
We need, however, to enter a note of caution at this point
because Mill goes on to say that 'all speculation . . . on the
future developments of my father's opinions . . . was doomed
to be cut short' by his father's death in June 1836; which may
make it reasonable to conclude that James Mill's published
writings up to this time did not harmonize with his reaction to
Tocqueville and his son's new opinions.

Nevertheless, quite apart from what could be read into his
favourable estimate of Tocqueville and his reaction to John
Stuart's article on 'Civilization', James Mill had in fact uttered
a warning note about the misdirection of public opinion. His
concern over unfounded antipathies reflects his belief that
public disapproval should fall on actions which cause real injury, as opposed to 'innoxious' conduct that merely arouses
dislike. But the concern goes along with the conviction that the
'unfavourable sentiments of mankind' are, and can be made
more effectively so, a powerful instrument for securing the
practice of the moral virtues. The pains 'derived from the un-

favourable sentiments of mankind' are, he says, 'capable of rising to a height with which hardly any other pains incident to our nature can be compared'; adding, and 'if sufficiently at command, [they] would almost supersede the use of other means'.[72] This 'powerful agency for the prevention of injurious acts' is thus seen to have both a positive and a negative role, namely, to induce men to take the path of virtue and hence promote the greatest happiness, and also to deter them from inflicting injury on their fellow-men. Unfortunately, however, there is some uncertainty about its scope and mode of operation which the words, 'if sufficiently at command', do not suffice to convey. Bentham was much more definite:

The influences of the *moral* and *religious* sanctions, or, in other words, of the motives of *love of reputation* and *religion*, are other causes, the force of which may, upon particular occasions, come to be greater than that of any punishment which the legislator is able, or at least which he will *think proper*, to apply. . . . But the force of these influences is variable and different in different times and places . . . These, therefore, it can never be proper to look upon as safe grounds for establishing absolute impunity . . . [73]

The greater reliability of legal punishment as compared with other forms of sanction does not, in Mill's view, dispense with the need for the weapon of public disrepute to reinforce the aims of the legislator in the imposition of official prohibitions. The pressure of social disapprobation is therefore brought to bear in two spheres: to support the law, and to act as a deterrent independently of the law. Yet we are still without a principle, or set of guidelines, to mark off the area where the pains of disrepute should operate on their own. The most appropriate place to look for guidance, however, is Bentham's treatment of 'cases unmeet for punishment' and his discussion of the 'limits between private ethics and the art of legislation', the implicit acceptance of which is evident in Mill's article on 'Jurisprudence'.[74] We can, incidentally, do no more than note at this juncture the interesting claim made by David Lyons that in his discussion of the second topic 'Bentham presents a clear case against unlimited paternalistic legislation, one that anticipates the main line of Mill's much later essay *On Liberty*'.[75]

There are some kinds of actions which do not call for punishment, says Bentham. It follows from his conception of the general purpose served by law that punishment should only be inflicted in accordance with the principle of utility. The basis of his approach is sketched thus:

> The general object which all laws have, or ought to have, is to augment the total happiness of the community; and therefore, in the first place, to exclude, as far as may be, every thing that tends to subtract from that happiness: in other words, to exclude mischief.
>
> But all punishment is mischief: all punishment in itself is evil. Upon the principle of utility, if it ought at all to be admitted, it ought only to be admitted in so far as it promises to exclude some greater evil.[76]

From which he proceeds to enumerate four types of case when punishment ought not to be applied: where it is 'groundless', 'inefficacious', 'unprofitable', and 'needless'. We can dispense with detailed explanation of these categories and concentrate on the aspects which relate to the issue at hand. For instance, punishment is stated to be 'groundless' when the 'mischief' produced is outweighed by an 'act which was necessary to the production of a benefit which was of greater value than the mischief',[77] e.g. by way of preventing 'instant calamity'. Punishment is said to be 'inefficacious' when the penalty specified can have no effect, e.g. on insane persons. But it is in regard to cases when punishment would be 'unprofitable' that we have an especially pertinent category, which is defined in these terms:

> Where, on the one hand, the nature of the offence, on the other hand, that of the punishment, are, *in the ordinary state of things*, such, that when compared together, the evil of the latter will turn out to be greater than that of the former.[78]

'These are the cases', asserts Bentham, 'which constitute the great field for the exclusive interference of private ethics'.[79] Let us follow the course of his argument.[80]

'Ethics at large may be defined', he says, as 'the art of directing men's actions to the production of the greatest possible quantity of happiness, on the part of those whose interest is in view'. In so far as it is 'the art of directing a man's own actions'

it is 'private ethics' or the 'art of self-government'. Now, a
man's conduct may be divided into actions 'as none but himself
are interested in' and actions 'as may affect the happiness of
those about him'. To the extent that his happiness depends on
the former it depends on his 'duty to himself' and the quality he
must call on to fulfil this duty is *prudence*. To the extent that his
happiness 'and that of any other person or persons whose interests are considered' depends on such parts of his conduct 'as
may affect the interests of those about him' it depends on his
'duty to others', and the qualities involved in fulfilling this duty
are 'probity' and 'beneficence'. Private ethics, then, aims at
happiness; but so does legislation, which is a branch of the art
of government. To this extent they 'go hand in hand', yet the
actions they are concerned with, 'though in a great measure,
are not *perfectly and throughout* the same'. Bentham explains:

There is no case in which a private man ought not to direct his own
conduct to the production of his own happiness, and that of his fellow-
creatures: but there are cases in which the legislator ought not (in a
direct way at least, and by means of punishment applied immediately
to particular *individual* acts) to attempt to direct the conduct of the
several other members of the community. Every act which promises
to be beneficial upon the whole to the community (himself included)
each individual ought to perform of himself: but it is not every such
act that the legislator ought to compel him to perform. Every act
which promises to be pernicious upon the whole to the community
(himself included) each individual ought to abstain from of himself:
but it is not every such act that the legislator ought to compel him to
abstain from.[81]

How, then, to draw the line and demarcate the area in which
the legislator ought not, directly at any rate, to intervene? The
mode of intervention is punishment and Bentham has already
specified the cases which are 'unmeet for punishment', so we
can deduce from those cases when the legislator must not interfere, and private ethics has, or should have, a role to play—
where to draw the demarcation line. And, to repeat, it is when
punishment would be 'unprofitable' that private ethics has to
perform its main function, when punishment is 'too expensive
. . . because the evil of the punishment exceeds that of the
offence'. It is important to notice that there is an 'evil', thus

Bentham has to show that though the acts be 'really pernicious' they are nevertheless not 'fit objects for the legislator to control'.

Punishment is unprofitable when it is 'too expensive'; but also when it threatens to involve innocent persons. If the danger of detection is, or is considered to be, small then punishment loses its character of 'certainty' and its amount has to be correspondingly raised. In these circumstances we are faced with two conflicting evils, 'the evil of the disease and the evil of the painful and inefficacious remedy'. Bentham surmises that it is partly due to this dilemma that 'fornication, for example, or the illicit commerce between the sexes' is commonly liable to either no penalty at all or to one much less painful than the legislator might be inclined to inflict.

The danger of involving the innocent derives from the difficulty of providing a precise enough definition of the injurious action, either because of 'the nature of the actions themselves' or because of a failure to frame an exact formulation of the offence. Hence the reluctance to impose legislative prohibitions on such actions 'as come under the notion of rudeness, for example, or treachery, or ingratitude'. Bentham then observes —and there are likely to be some who will discern a sinister implication in his remarks:

The attempt to bring acts of so vague and questionable a nature under the control of law, will argue either a very immature age, in which the difficulties which give birth to that danger are not descried; or a very enlightened age, in which they are overcome.[82]

Although he has now indicated where the line between private ethics and legislation should be drawn Bentham attempts to elucidate its nature by invoking the distinction he made among moral duties, namely, prudence, probity, and beneficence. He says that the rules of prudence are 'those which seem to stand least in need of the assistance of legislation'. If a man fails to fulfil his duty to himself it must be due to a lack of understanding of what makes for his own happiness. He rejects the suggestion that the legislator may be in a better position to know and hence able to determine how a man should act in this sphere, remarking:

It is plain, that of individuals the legislator can know nothing: concerning those points of conduct which depend upon the particular circumstances of each individual, it is plain, therefore, that he can determine nothing to advantage. It is only with respect to those broad lines of conduct in which all persons, or very large and permanent descriptions of persons, may be in a way to engage, that he can have any pretence for interfering; and even here the propriety of his interference will, in most instances, lie very open to dispute. . . . All he can hope to do, is to increase the efficacy of private ethics, by giving strength and direction to the influence of the moral sanction.[83]

Why the unprofitability of punishment should have struck him as such a strong reason for legislative non-intervention in the field of private ethics is well illustrated by an example Bentham introduces at this stage. A government that sought to stamp out either drunkenness or fornication by making them legal offences would have no chance of success: 'not all the tortures which ingenuity could invent would compass it'. In the course of attempting the impossible it would produce an amount of evil exceeding 'a thousand-fold' the mischief of the offence. The search for evidence would spread dismay through every family, 'tearing the bonds of sympathy asunder, and rooting out the influence of all the social motives'.

The rules of probity (i.e. those making up the negative side of a man's duty to others), unlike the rules of prudence, do require legislative intervention:

There are few cases in which it *would* be expedient to punish a man for hurting *himself*: but there are few cases, if any, in which it would *not* be expedient to punish a man for injuring his neighbour.[84]

The fulfilment of the rules of beneficence (the positive side of a man's duty to others), on the other hand, ought to be left 'in great measure' to the control of private ethics. The motives which prompt the actions are all-important here: sympathy, love of amity, or love of reputation—not self-regarding motives 'brought into play by the force of political constraint'. And it is their presence that leads us to say of a man's conduct that it is free and voluntary. But there are cases when the law should intervene, especially where persons can be saved from danger:

. . . why should it not be made the duty of every man to save another from mischief, when it can be done without prejudicing himself, as well as to abstain from bringing it on him? . . . A drunken man, falling with his face downwards into a puddle, is in danger of suffocation:

lifting his head a little on one side would save him: another man sees
this and lets him lie . . . Who is there that (in this case) would think
punishment misapplied?[85]

VI

It is possible to give a brief and apparently very simple answer
to the question we have been exploring, i.e. how Bentham and
James Mill distinguished the respective parts to be played by
law and public opinion in preventing injurious actions. It is
this: public opinion ('the unfavourable sentiments of mankind'
or 'the moral sanction') steps in, operates by itself, and imposes
its distinctive sorts of penalty ('pains capable of rising to a
height with which hardly any other pains incident to our nature
can be compared') when it is inexpedient to inflict legal punishment. (Of course, public opinion also works with, and to reinforce, the law, so that he who is punished for doing an injury
experiences the pains of public disapproval as well.)

It would be anticipating matters too much to pursue the
question in detail here, but if someone were to ask whether this
answer was later incorporated into *On Liberty* our reply would
depend to some extent on our being able to clarify a number
of difficulties and obscurities which lurk behind the outward
simplicity of the answer. These arise partly out of Bentham's
account of 'private ethics', which we deal with elsewhere; and
also concern certain issues mentioned earlier, i.e. 'antipathies'
and 'self-regarding offences'. Even so, there does seem to be
this much in common between *On Liberty* and the position of
Bentham and James Mill: in neither case are penalties to be
imposed, whether by legal punishment or the moral sanction,
for actions which cause no injury. But does this amount to a
great deal? For Bentham and James Mill the notion of injury is
either synonymous with, or reducible to, pain ('indirect injury'
is a complication we can ignore for the moment), as indeed are
the notions of what is 'inexpedient' and 'unprofitable'. It may
turn out to be the case, as we have already suggested, that John
Stuart's criterion of 'harm' cannot be similarly translated into,
or reduced to, pain; which could well mean that the common
appeal to 'injury' (or 'harm') as the touchstone is misleading
and conceals an important difference in standards of reference.

It would show itself too over the question whether unprofitability, in the sense that Bentham meant it, is an appropriate
test for deciding on legislative non-intervention; and it may
enter into, or even have been a significant factor in shaping,
John Stuart's opinions about the power of public opinion. For
on the face of it, if 'injury' and 'harm' are virtually equivalent
in meaning, are both reducible to 'pain' or 'painful feelings',
then given the principle to which they all subscribed, i.e. no
legal or social punishment without injury (or harm), it is difficult to account for the striking contrast between the attitude of
John Stuart and that of his teachers toward the pressures of
public opinion. The difficulty is reinforced when we consider
what appears to have been a common outlook on the part of
John Stuart, his father, and Bentham on the subject of 'antipathies'.

The contrasting attitudes toward public opinion are exemplified by the passage from John Stuart's article on Bentham
quoted earlier, and they are also manifest in the marked difference between the alarmist view taken in *On Liberty* about the
increasing power of the mediocre many to impose norms of
conduct based merely on their own prejudices and James Mill's
confidence, expressed in the article on 'Liberty of the Press',
that:

In our own country, for example, the classes of actions which, though
they injure nobody, expose a man to the unfavourable sentiments of
others, are not numerous. The number of persons who would be
exposed to inconvenience on the declaration of truth, in regard to
them, would be small in comparison with those who would benefit by
its declaration in the case of all really hurtful acts.[86]

The 'unfavourable sentiments of others' Mill talks of here are
the 'unfounded antipathies' which he regards as a corruption
of the moral sentiments. They are 'unfounded' because the
actions at which they are directed cause no evil, 'either to him
who performs them, or to anybody else'. (We should notice in
passing the suggestion that one can cause evil to oneself—more
of this later.) A man exposed to such antipathies, to 'the hatred
and contempt of his fellow-creatures', is visited with 'an evil,
uncompensated by the smallest portion of good'. On the other
hand, when hatred and contempt are directed at actions which

are *hurtful*, 'either to the individual himself, or to others', the advantage exceeds 'beyond calculation the attendant evil'.[87] The distinction Mill is drawing between, as it might be put, justified moral condemnation and baseless prejudice depends on the nature of the act, whether or not it is hurtful; and Mill, following Bentham, took it to be established beyond reasonable doubt that 'utility', in contrast to certain alternative moral concepts, offered an *objective* standard for making moral judgements, a conviction shared by John Stuart. Utilitarianism, he says, 'does supply, if not always an easy, at all events a tangible mode' of deciding differences of opinion on moral questions.[88] What impressed him particularly when he first read Bentham, so he tells us in the *Autobiography*:

. . . was the chapter in which Bentham passed judgement on the common modes of reasoning in morals and legislation . . . and characterized them as dogmatism in disguise, imposing its sentiments upon others under cover of sounding expressions which convey no reason for the sentiment, but set up the sentiment as its own reason.[89]

The chapter John Stuart is referring to is Chapter II of Bentham's *An Introduction to the Principles of Morals and Legislation*, entitled 'Of Principles adverse to that of Utility', and it is there that he discusses what he calls 'the principle of sympathy and antipathy'. James Mill's remarks about 'antipathies' in the article on the 'Liberty of the Press' have their source in this chapter; and it is the origin of John Stuart's opposition, stated in *On Liberty* and elsewhere, to making the mere 'likings and dislikings of society' the ground of moral judgement.

'By the principle of sympathy and antipathy', says Bentham:

. . . I mean that principle which approves or disapproves of certain actions, not on account of their tending to augment the happiness, nor yet on account of their tending to diminish the happiness of the party whose interest is in question, but merely because a man finds himself disposed to approve or disapprove of them: holding up that approbation or disapprobation as a sufficient reason for itself, and disclaiming the necessity of looking out for any extrinsic ground.[90]

Bentham does not think it really deserves to be called a 'principle'. It is 'the negation of all principle', for 'what one expects to find in a principle is something that points out some external consideration, as a means of warranting and guiding the internal sentiments of approbation and disapprobation'. He goes on:

In looking over the catalogue of human actions (says a partizan of this principle) in order to determine which of them are to be marked with the seal of disapprobation, you need but to take counsel of your own feelings: whatever you find in yourself a propensity to condemn, is wrong for that very reason. For the same reason it is also meet for punishment . . . In that same *proportion* also is it meet for punishment: if you hate much, punish much: if you hate little, punish little: punish as you hate.[91]

Bentham makes the charge that moral concepts, or 'the various systems that have been formed concerning the standard of right and wrong', which conflict with the principle of utility are no more than devices for dispensing with the need to appeal to an external standard; they all come down to the principle of sympathy and antipathy in the final analysis. Among the 'systems' which he puts into this category are those which appeal to a 'moral sense', to 'an eternal and immutable Rule of Right', to 'the Fitness of Things', and 'Natural Justice' or the 'Law of Nature'. All these 'systems', as he describes them, employ different phrases, but they are just contrivances 'for prevailing upon the reader to accept of the author's sentiment or opinion as a reason for itself'. Moreover, there is a mischief common to them all: they serve as 'a cloke, and pretence, and aliment, to despotism'. Though these principles, 'if such they can be called', are found more often in morals than in politics yet, he exclaims, 'I have more than once known the pretended law of nature set up in legislative debates, in opposition to arguments derived from the principle of utility'. He reasserts the claim of utility to be the proper standard of moral judgement by drawing our attention to what he considers to be a common confusion, namely, the failure to distinguish the motive or cause of an action from its justification, i.e. the difference between that which produces the act and 'the ground or reason which warrants a legislator, or other by-stander, in regarding that act with an eye of approbation'. Antipathy can be the cause of an action which has good effects, but this does not make antipathy a good reason for the action; for antipathies are often the cause of actions with evil effects. So, maintains Bentham, antipathy can never be a good reason for action, any more than 'resentment', which he regards as 'but a modification of antipathy'. He concludes:

The only right ground of action, that can possibly subsist, is, after all, the consideration of utility, which, if it is a right principle of action, and of approbation, in any one case, is so in every other. Other principles in abundance, that is, other motives, may be the reasons why it might or ought to have been done. Antipathy or resentment requires always to be regulated, to prevent its doing mischief: to be regulated by what? always by the principle of utility. The principle of utility neither requires nor admits of any other regulator than itself.[92]

There have been, and still are, many philosophers who would take Bentham to task for attempting to *define* morality in terms of utility and ruling out any judgement which claims to be moral as improperly so unless there is an appeal to an 'external' consideration. But we must resist the temptation, once again, to enter substantively at this point into a problem of continuing controversy. There is, however, another commonly made criticism which has immediate relevance: it is the contention that since actions toward which people feel antipathetic at least cause pain to those who are disgusted or outraged by them, or strongly disapprove of them, they ought to count as injurious for that very reason. Are not the notions of 'injurious' and 'hurtful' supposed to be synonymous with, or analysable into, 'pain'? And is there not a danger that the idea of utility will evaporate if we begin to discriminate among the pains which people experience? To this objection there is a reply implicit in the concept of a 'groundless antipathy' as James Mill held it. Were it not for the antipathy there would be no pain, whereas in the case of, say, arson, assault, fraud, or theft, there is definite damage the nature of which can be objectively determined, as well as the pain to be identified with feelings of moral disapprobation. Whether or not this reply is regarded as cogent, there can be little doubt that John Stuart accepted the distinction drawn by his father and Bentham between mere feelings of disapprobation and genuine moral disapproval and that it forms part of the case he makes in *On Liberty* for the principle of self-protection. We have already noticed his refusal, in the *Liberty*, to base legal and social punishment on the likings and dislikings of society.[93] But perhaps the clearest and most explicit adoption of his teachers' position occurs in the essay on Whewell, written in the same decade as *On Liberty*. Defending Bentham against Whewell's criticism, Mill contends that the feelings of antipathy which people share with others are often, and wrongly, assumed to be universal. Nor can they entertain the possibility that such feelings of right and wrong as they have always experienced could be mistaken. 'This', he claims, 'is the mental infirmity which Bentham's philosophy tends especially to correct, and Dr. Whewell's to perpetuate'. He continues:

Things which were really believed by all mankind, and for which all were convinced that they had the unequivocal evidence of their senses, have been proved to be false: as that the sun rises and sets. Can immunity from similar error be claimed for the moral feelings? when all experience shows that those feelings are eminently artificial, and the product of culture. . . . Bentham, therefore, did not judge too severely a kind of ethics whereby any implanted sentiment which is tolerably general may be erected into a moral law, binding, under penalties, on all mankind. The contest between the morality which appeals to an external standard, and that which grounds itself on internal conviction, is the contest of progressive morality against stationary—of reason and argument against the deification of mere opinion and habit.[94]

In this passage a morality 'which grounds itself on internal conviction' is nevertheless spoken of as a 'morality'. Bentham and James Mill are reluctant to allow that such a thing could be a morality at all. But I doubt that much turns on this, for when it comes to specifying what actions are 'unmeet' for legal punishment, but properly subject to the 'moral sanction', the criterion of 'moral' common to them all is utility; though we always have to bear in mind that John Stuart's conception of utility may be significantly different from Bentham's. They all insist on the necessity of appealing to an 'external' standard, which means that antipathies, of themselves, can never be good reasons for applying restraints on conduct. So we are led to repeat the question: since it is only in respect of hurtful actions that restrictions may justifiably be imposed, and since no action is deemed hurtful if it merely excites feelings of disapproval, how are we to account for John Stuart's distinctive stand against the undue pressure of public opinion? His reading of Tocqueville and others who made him more sharply aware of tendencies inimical to liberty provides no more than a partial explanation. We must identify some element in his doctrine that designates encroachments on individuality, which his father and Bentham either welcomed or regarded with indifference, as an unwarrantable restriction of liberty. According to the doctrine of *On Liberty* these encroachments constitute an improper interference with 'self-regarding' conduct: the individual is being held accountable for actions that cause no harm to others. Is the difference between John Stuart on the one hand, and his father and Bentham on the other, due to the fact that the latter allow 'self-regarding' conduct to be controlled? Or is it that they define the class of 'self-regarding' actions more narrowly? Or is it that John Stuart's notion of 'harm' is less extensive than, and involves different criteria from, theirs?

Let us approach those questions somewhat indirectly. Bentham's definition of an offence, we saw, lays it down that no act should be made an offence unless it has a tendency, 'in some way or other', to be detrimental to the community. He divides offences into five classes, one of which consists of 'self-regarding' offences. These are acts which 'in the first instance are detrimental to the offender himself, and to no one else, unless it be by their being detrimental to himself'.[95] He thinks it will often be doubtful 'whether they are productive of any primary mischief at all' because the person who performs the act, and is most affected by it, 'shows by his conduct that he is not sensible of it'. Such mischief as they produce is 'apt to be unobvious'; even so they tend to be 'more obnoxious to the censure of the world than public offences' because of the influence of two false principles—asceticism and antipathy.[96] The disposition to punish them, he says, owes more to antipathy against the offender than sympathy for the public; which suggests that, in Bentham's view, antipathy rather than utility plays the major role in inducing legislatures to impose penalties on self-regarding misconduct. Taken with his remark that it is *often* doubtful whether what is thought to be self-regarding misconduct does cause mischief to the agent, and his assertion that 'there are few cases in which it *would* be expedient to punish a man for hurting *himself*', we are led to wonder what he did consider to be a self-regarding offence. From the examples he cites it is not at all clear which he is in favour of seeking to deter by the legal or the moral sanction and which he would simply leave alone.[97] The presumption is strong that he thought *some* self-regarding actions do cause injury and are rightly subject to social control. Certainly James Mill took this view, for we noted his remark about antipathies being directed at actions 'from which no evil ensues, either to him who performs them, or to any body else', which occurs shortly after another remark to the same effect (if public disapproval 'never operated against any actions but those which were hurtful, either to the individual himself, or to others . . . ') in the article on 'Liberty of the Press'. In sharp contrast, John Stuart declares, in *On Liberty*, that 'self-regarding faults . . . are not properly immoralities':

. . . to whatever pitch they may be carried [they] do not constitute wickedness. They may be proofs of any amount of folly, or want of personal dignity and self-respect; but they are only a subject of moral reprobation when they involve a breach of duty to others, for whose sake the individual is bound to have care for himself.[98]

And, a little later, he adds that it is only when 'the mischief which a person does to himself' violates 'a distinct and assignable obligation to any other person or persons' does it cease to be self-regarding and becomes 'amenable to moral disapprobation in the proper sense of the term'.[99]

John Stuart's position can be illustrated by the example of drunkenness. This is one of the self-regarding offences listed by Bentham, and it is interesting to compare the ways in which they deal with it. Bentham treats it as a breach of the rules of prudence; and of the rules of moral duty these, he says, require legislative intervention least of all. Legal punishment would be 'unprofitable', and so the best the legislator can do is 'to increase the efficacy of private ethics, by giving strength and direction to the influence of the moral sanction'.[100] John Stuart, on the other hand, treats it as a self-regarding fault and he goes some way further to elucidating the distinction between a self-regarding fault and an injurious action in the following passage:

. . . when a person disables himself, by conduct purely self-regarding, from the performance of some definite duty incumbent on him to the public, he is guilty of a social offence. No person ought to be punished simply for being drunk; but a soldier or a policeman should be punished for being drunk on duty. Whenever, in short, there is a definite damage, or a definite risk of damage, either to an individual or to the public, the case is taken out of the province of liberty, and placed in that of morality or law.[101]

There is an interesting comparison to be drawn too between the ways James Mill and John Stuart deal with certain practices of the 'Mahomedans'. James Mill, it will be recalled, treats the case of the antipathies excited by the drinking of wine in a Mahomedan community as an example of the perversion of the moral sentiments, since no 'evil' ensues from the action, to the drinker or anyone else. Because the antipathies are unfounded the action ought not to be subjected to legal prohibition or moral disapproval. John Stuart also refers to the 'antipathies' aroused by persons refusing to practise religious abstinences which are strictly observed by those whose feelings are outraged, as when 'Mussulmans' are revolted at the sight of someone eating pork. What if, he asks, the majority in a Mahomedan country were to put a ban on the eating of pork? 'Would it be a legitimate exercise of the moral authority of public opinion?' It would not, because 'with the personal tastes and self-regarding concerns of individuals the public has no business to interfere'.[102] The disapproval of the offending action is therefore said in both cases to stem from an antipathy, and since there is no 'external' consideration by reference to which the action can be judged to be injurious or harmful it is, in James Mill's terms, a groundless antipathy. So they both condemn any attempt to impose restrictions on the drinking of wine or the eating of pork. For James Mill, 'it is to limit [the] sphere of innocent enjoyment'. For John Stuart, it is interference with a self-regarding action. Now it *looks* as if James Mill's 'sphere of innocent enjoyment' is equivalent to John Stuart's area of self-regarding actions. After all, they are both committed to there being a self-regarding sphere of some sort, a sphere 'created' and delimited by the principle that harm or injury is a necessary condition for exercising justifiable social control by means of either the moral sanction or legal prohibition. But although John Stuart may have been influenced by his father's idea of a 'sphere of innocent enjoyment' to develop his own conception of an area of self-regarding activity, we have encountered at least one factor, and are leaving it open that there may be two, making for a difference of content in that area. James Mill allows moral disapproval to be directed at *self*-inflicted injuries, whereas John Stuart's criterion is harm to *others*; and James Mill's 'injury' and John Stuart's 'harm' may contain significantly different criteria of judgement.

A preliminary exploration of what sort of difference there might be between James Mill and John Stuart, in respect of their notions of 'injury' and 'harm', could begin by taking up the suggestion that it corresponds to the distinction between 'negative' and 'positive' liberty. For James Mill and Bentham, the argument would run, the 'province of liberty' is what remains when we have subtracted from the total range of human actions those which it is expedient to restrict, by legal prohibition or moral disapproval. For John Stuart, on the other hand, a 'province of liberty' is a necessary condition for the cultivation of individuality, self-development, and hence serves a vital positive function. But quite apart from objections to the use of the positive/negative distinction in this way, the contrast is overdrawn since it neglects the positive value of an area of liberty as a necessary condition for enabling men to attain the objects of their desire, the primary utilitarian good and acknowledged to be so (subject to the proviso that it causes no injury or harm to others) not only by James Mill and Bentham but also by John Stuart. Yet it will not do to portray John Stuart as simply subscribing to the Benthamite version of the greatest happiness principle. His remarks in Utilitarianism about the quality of pleasures have provoked a continuing discussion out of which there has not so far emerged a single and definite interpretation or assessment of their significance. In my view, however, they provide one of several indications that he moved far beyond his Utilitarian inheritance and are closely connected with his conception of individuality and self-development. Moreover, the notion of 'harm', as John Stuart used it, needs to be understood in this light. James Mill and Bentham did not evince any great concern about the cultivation of individuality or about the dangers which John Stuart saw threatening it from the growing power of public opinion. Nevertheless our account of the opinions of James Mill and Bentham points strongly to the conclusion that however much John Stuart may have struck out on his own path the ground had been thoroughly well-prepared by them.

II

Early Views and Influences

I

THE idea of writing *On Liberty* struck John Stuart, so we are told in the *Autobiography*, when he was 'mounting the steps of the Capitol' in Rome in January 1855. We are also told that he had already written 'a short essay' on the subject in 1854 and that the book, which appeared in 1859, was the work of his wife and himself in the two years before he retired from the East India Company in 1858.[1] This account conflicts, in part, with what Mill said in a letter written to his wife after he had arrived in Rome.

On my way here . . . [to Rome] I came back to an idea we have talked about and thought that the best thing to write and publish at present would be a volume on Liberty. . . . I wish I had brought with me here the paper on Liberty that I wrote for our volume of Essays—perhaps my dearest will kindly read it through and tell me whether it will do as the foundation of one part of the volume in question—If she thinks so I will try to write and publish it in 1856 if my health permits as I hope it will.[2]

The extent and nature of Harriet's contribution to *On Liberty* is a matter of dispute, but the wording of Mill's letter suggests that the original paper of 1854 was his own work. How it differed from the essay that has come down to us we do not know. What is certain, however, is that, whether in 1854 or when they embarked on the final version, Mill did not come to the subject with a completely 'open' mind. Some of the ingredients out of which *On Liberty* was fashioned were described in the previous chapter. Here, in this chapter, I want to show how the influence of Bentham and his father was reflected in the speeches he gave, and the articles and letters he wrote, in the years before he met Harriet Taylor in 1830. This would seem an odd date to choose were it not for the fact that I want not only to compare the position Mill took up in his Benthamite period with what he was to say later in *On Liberty*, but also to establish at least one important point in regard to Harriet's role; namely, that the beliefs and opinions he held in this period which can be shown to enter in a significant way into the argument of the *Liberty* can, obviously, not be attributed to her influence.

We have already noticed the claim made by David Lyons that in Chapter XVII of his *Principles of Morals and Legislation* 'Bentham presents a clear case against unlimited paternalistic legislation, one that anticipates the main line of Mill's much later essay *On Liberty*'. In apparently complete opposition to such a claim stands what might be called the 'pro-Harriet school', which credits her with having provided the chief inspiration for what is distinctive about *On Liberty*. There is, it is true, ample room for manœuvre when expressions like 'main line' and 'what is distinctive' are used, and so there could turn out to be some way of accommodating both points of view. But if we are not satisfied that Mill's inherited opinions suffice to cover all the principal features of the *Liberty* then we are left with the question of how to account for the difference. Do we have to accept the contention that if the Benthamite legacy is subtracted from *On Liberty* the remainder is what Mill owed to Harriet? (Let us assume we can get over the problem of how to characterize the 'remainder'.) On the other hand it might well be the case that in the early years of his rejection of orthodox Benthamism (i.e. between 1827 and 1830) Mill absorbed currents of thought the nature of which, combined with what he retained from his intellectual inheritance, is a sufficient explanation of the final mixture we find in *On Liberty*. And, further, the argument would run, Mill's reading of Tocqueville, von Humboldt, and other writers after 1830 served to reinforce the impact of these new ideas. All of which is, of course, quite compatible with Harriet's influence being in the same direction. But now the position would be far more complex than that suggested by the simple monocausal explanation of the pro-Harriet school. Moreover, to sort out the precise, or even approximate, degree of weight to be assigned to each factor is likely to prove beyond the resources of the historian of ideas. However, let us now turn to what Mill wrote in the decade before he met Harriet.

We have seen that a central problem for Bentham and James Mill was how to secure an identity of interest between rulers and ruled. Rulers should be induced to aim at the greatest happiness of their subjects but, since they are impelled by the same motives as all other men, i.e. to seek money and power as the principal avenues to pleasure, special safeguards have to be adopted in order to compel them to promote the general interest. Were there no checks on their conduct, rulers would oppress and sacrifice the interests of those under their control. It is, therefore, of vital importance to institute checks which will make the governors responsive to the interests of the governed. Now, there are involved here a number of concepts and arguments to which the young John Stuart was deeply committed in the 1820s; indeed, to most of which he adhered for the rest of his life. Thus we find him saying, for instance:

The form of government which I seek, and with which I will be satisfied, is that which will secure at the smallest expense an identity of interest between the governed and the governors. This identity does not now exist. The reason is that an immense majority of the House of Commons, who are the real governors, are chosen by a narrow oligarchy.[3]

And again:

The British Constitution is the Constitution of the rich. It has made this country the paradise of the wealthy. It has annexed to wealth a greater share of political power, and a greater command over the minds of men, than were ever possessed by it elsewhere.[4]

Taken together, these two passages illustrate the way Mill united the general and the particular, a characteristic of his writings in this period. There is a constant appeal to the general principles of Benthamite theory, and their application to specific conditions is usually made in the context of British politics. As he put it in another of his early speeches, the particular remedies proposed by Bentham for the cure of misgovernment were related to the actual state of affairs in Britain but were, nevertheless, based on a theoretical foundation.

Universal suffrage and annual parliaments, let me tell the hon. gentleman, are in Mr. Bentham's apprehension nothing more than a particular set of means for giving effect to his system. The one great principle of Mr. Bentham's system is, that the body which, like the House of Commons in this country, holds substantially in its own hands the governing power should be chosen by, and accountable to, some portion or other of the people whose interest is not materially different from that of the whole. Now this, I am ready to maintain in the face of the hon. gentleman, is a universal principle in politics . . .[5]

And, if we may be allowed one more example:

As long as the House of Commons has a sinister interest of its own, or is dependent on persons who have, bad government is certain. Good government can only be secured by making it dependent upon persons who have no sinister interest, and the only persons who have no sinister interest are the people. Dependence upon the people therefore is the only security. Let the House of Commons be dependent upon the people, and I am satisfied.[6]

From the account given thus far of his opinions in the 1820s it will not come as a surprise to learn that Mill was regarded by his contemporaries as a mere mouthpiece for propagating Benthamite political theory; or, as he himself records in the *Autobiography*, 'a "made" or manufactured man, having had a certain impress of opinion stamped on me which I could only reproduce . . .'[7]. When he states the general principles from which his arguments for reform are derived this verdict would seem to be no less justified. Consider this extract from a speech on the influence of the aristocracy:

The materials of which a government is composed are not gods, nor angels, but men. Now rather an extensive observation of the conduct of men in all ages has shown that, extraordinary instances of heroism excepted which of course are not to be reckoned upon, their actions are pretty constantly governed by their interests, in so much that if you know what it is a man's interest to do, you can make a pretty good guess at what he will do. Now as men in power do not cease to be men by being in power, the same rules which govern the conduct of other men governs theirs likewise; and therefore when the interest of those who are placed under them clashes, as it is very apt to do, it is not difficult to see which must give way to the other.[8]

And, from the same speech:

Individuals have been known to make great sacrifices of their private interest to the good of their country, but bodies of men, never. When the glory of doing right and the shame of doing wrong are to be shared among so many that the share of each man is a trifle, no principle remains of sufficient strength to counteract the united force of the two great springs of human action, the love of money and the love of power.[9]

Later, when he came to work out his own views on the logic of the social sciences, the confident dogmatism of these generalizations was tempered and qualified.[10] But he never abandoned his father's reliance on certain alleged universal tendencies in human nature: indeed, he based his claim that sociology could become a science on its derivative relationship to the laws of individual psychology. And that his inherited beliefs on the subject were the raw material out of which his own conception of a science of society developed is well illustrated in a speech made in 1829:

. . . if there are any tendencies common to all mankind, and in particular if all the stronger tendencies of human nature are such, both those which require to be regulated, and those whose agency you must employ to regulate them, it is surely not an irrational subject of inquiry what are the laws and other social arrangements which would be desirable if no other tendencies than these universal tendencies of human nature existed. And this when ascertained merely constitutes *pro tanto* a universal science of politics, although before we apply it to any particular nation we must also ascertain what are the tendencies peculiar to that nation, and correct the abstract principles of the science by the modifications which those tendencies introduce.[11]

If there are these 'universal tendencies of human nature', if men in power 'do not cease to be men by being in power' and would, unless checked, act contrary to the interests of their subjects, then clearly a system of checks is crucial to the Benthamite goal of promoting the *general* interest. And among the checks on which James and John Stuart placed great emphasis was freedom of the press. We have already noticed how James Mill argued the case, and attention was drawn then to John Stuart's article on the same subject which drew heavily, with acknowledgement, on his father's essay. But before looking in detail at John Stuart's early writings on freedom of speech and publication we should turn first to what he said about 'checks' generally and, in particular, about the role of 'public opinion'— a matter which many consider to give its distinctive character to *On Liberty*.

One version of the doctrine of checks which James Mill had discussed in the essay on *Government* was the claim that the peculiar excellence of the British Constitution arose from its being a union of the three simple forms of government—monarchy, aristocracy, and democracy; that these three components balanced one another and by mutual checks ensured good government.[12] The elder Mill dismissed this theory as 'wild, visionary, chimerical', asking 'If there are three powers, how is it possible to prevent two of them from combining to swallow up the third?' From the principles of human nature which he took as foundations for his whole theory of government it followed that each of the three groups would attempt to acquire as much as possible 'of the means to the ends of human desire, namely, wealth and power'. Hence a combination whereby any two of the parties would swallow up the third 'appears as certain as any thing which depends upon human will'. Nor did he think that a stable alliance could exist between any two of them. Such an alliance presupposes that they are equal or they are not. The chances against an equality are extremely remote, 'as infinite to one'. If they are not equal then it would follow from the principles of human nature that 'the stronger will take from the weaker, till it engrosses the whole'. And if by some chance a 'little less than miraculous' they were equal, 'they would go to war, and contend till one or other was subdued'.

John Stuart took up the question several times in this early period and, since he was not writing an article for the *Encyclopaedia Britannica*, his language is on the whole less guarded and more polemical. In a speech on parliamentary reform he declared:

We all know, Sir, that the simple forms of government as they are called are three—monarchy, aristocracy and democracy. Each of these is universally allowed to have its advantages; each of them has also its disadvantages, and it has been pretty generally the doctrine of British statesmen and of British politicians that in every one of them the disadvantages preponderate. . . . All the simple forms being thus objectionable, the only chance for good government is to be found, they allege, in a mixture of the three, a mixture absurd indeed and inconsistent in theory, but which is said to be realized in the British Constitution . . .[13]

Mill went on to deny that a mixed government of this sort is possible and that the British Constitution in particular was an example of it. People speak of 'the balance of the Constitution', something which he finds mysterious. A metaphorical expression is invented and then people proceed to 'reason from it as if it was the name of something real, of something tangible. What is there that may not be proved in this way?' He continued:

Stripped of its metaphorical language the doctrine is that the British Constitution is a system of mutual checks; that each of the three branches when it oversteps its limits and attempts to do wrong is restrained by the other two. But why should the three branches check one another in doing wrong? Of three equal forces any two must be stronger than the third. May not two of them unite in doing wrong and overthrow the third if it opposes them? What is to hinder the monarchical branch and the aristocratical branch from uniting for the overthrow of the democratic? Not only is this probable but certain.[14]

The words 'balance' and 'equality', when applied to political forces, create an air of precision where none is really to be had.

For my part [he asserted] I never had much faith in these mathematical governments. The hopes and fears of men, the materials of which political power is made, do not admit of being cut out into equal parts, or measured out by a rule and a pair of compasses with geometrical precision. Besides, in the perpetual mutability of human affairs the nicest equilibrium of powers would require to be readjusted before it had been established a twelvemonth. And after all, if the balance be not really, what to me it appears, visionary and chimerical, it still remains to be proved that it would be good.[15]

Quite apart from the question whether or not a mixed form of government is possible, Mill was quite emphatic that the British Constitution, far from being mixed, was an aristocracy. A few persons control it, administer it, and conduct it wholly for their own benefit. Further:

. . . there is no check upon the conduct of those few which would not equally exist under an Oriental despotism, if the subjects of that despotism were equally wise, virtuous and enlightened with the people of Great Britain.[16]

It is generally admitted, he observes, that supreme power lies in Britain with the House of Commons. Yet two thirds of the members of the House were nominees of less than two hundred aristocratic families, so 'these two hundred families possess absolute control over the government'. Now, 'if a government controlled by two hundred families is not an aristocracy, then such a thing as an aristocracy cannot be said to exist'.[17] And the interests of the people must inevitably be neglected by such an unchecked aristocracy. It is, therefore, an undeniable deduction from the laws of human nature that a government of two hundred families must be a bad one. Moreover, is it not part of the theory of the British Constitution that unchecked power is always abused? Do we not have a House of Commons because we believe that the King, if he could, would act the tyrant? Why should we not impose the same check on the House of Commons? 'Have a hundred despots ever been found to be a less evil than one?'

But, it may be said, the people do exercise an indirect control over Parliament. Ministers dare not act against the declared wishes of the people and this prevents them from abusing their power. It is *public opinion* which constitutes the 'real checking power'; so what is apparently an aristocracy is in fact a mixed type of government uniting the advantages of all three simple forms. From this view Mill expresses his dissent:

If this be true, Sir, I say that we have no occasion for a Parliament. To resort to this doctrine is to give up the theory of the Constitution. The Constitution supposes that the House of Commons is a check . . . [and] if the governing body is neither elected by, nor responsible to, the people, and is only kept in awe by the partial and inefficient check of naked and disarmed public opinion, where is the use of keeping up a cumbrous and operose machinery to cheat the people by persuading that they really have some security in the Constitution of the House of Commons? . . . No, Sir, it is a cruel mockery to say that public opinion is a check upon the members of parliament when public opinion can neither remove them nor punish them. Carry this into practice and let any one consider how far he would be inclined to trust to public opinion for the prevention and punishment of theft and robbery. Yet a thief is far more unpopular than a bad member of parliament. How absurd to bid us trust for the security of our happiness and of our lives to a check that we would not confide in for the safety of a few shillings or pounds.[18]

On another occasion Mill maintained that the only security the British people possessed against the unlimited power of the aristocracy was its fear of a violent upheaval, and he put a very low value on this as a safeguard against misrule. Anything less than a general revolt posed no real threat to their hegemony, whereas 'those great convulsions which overthrow established governments' were such rare events that it cost them but little to avoid committing the flagrant acts of oppression which generally provoke rebellion. Let it be granted that they are 'ill at ease' when they suppose public opinion is against them. But when important interests are at stake they have no hesitation in defying it. Consider the obstinacy with which they hang on to the Corn Laws and the Game Laws, yet 'public opinion is unanimous on these two questions, or it never was unanimous upon anything'.[19]

It would be surprising were this all that John Stuart wrote about public opinion during the 1820s; perhaps less because of the way he dismisses the power of public opinion, *on its own*, to impose checks on the actions of rulers than the manner in which he apparently regards it as impotent to prevent immoral conduct by private persons. There is not the slightest hint in what he says here of one of the leading themes in *On Liberty*: the danger to individuality from an all-pervading public opinion. Moreover, it stands in sharp contrast to the important role assigned to public opinion by his father and Bentham. We saw, for instance, that James Mill considered 'the pains which are derived from the unfavourable sentiments of mankind' are a 'powerful agency for the prevention of injurious acts'. However, we must bear in mind the context of John Stuart's remarks, namely, that he was debating with the opponents of parliamentary reform, especially those who were content with the existing restraints on aristocratic power. He was not discussing the whole range of situations where public opinion operates and the use he makes of the case of theft—not the only occasion, incidentally—does allow for the effectiveness of public opinion when legal sanctions are inappropriate. And, indeed, there are times when even in relation to the control of governments he takes a more favourable view of its capacity to act as a check on rulers. For example, in another of his early speeches he makes this plea for the popular control of government:

Everything that there has been of good in any government has arisen from the share which the people have had in it. In every stage of society the governments in which the people have had most power have been the best governments which that stage of society has afforded. The Grecian and Roman governments are cases in point. As soon as the people ceased to have power the Grecian and Roman governments became the vilest governments in the world. . . . Our own government is an instance; it has become better and better just in proportion as the power of public opinion over it has become greater.[20]

The separate and apparently conflicting strands in his attitude to public opinion come together in one of the most considered statements Mill made at this time, in a speech on 'The British Constitution'.[21] Taking public opinion to include petitions, public meetings, and a free press, he argues that it does not amount to a sufficient check unless the public is 'allowed to act as well as speak'. Lacking the power to act, it has failed to abolish the Corn Laws and the Game Laws. It could not prevent the passing of the Six Acts; nor can it bring about the reform of our political institutions. The laws of England stand in need of much improvement and nothing but a reformed parliament would have the courage to do it. Mill goes on:

What is the influence of public opinion? Nothing at bottom but the influence of *fear*. Of what consequence is it to a minister what the public say, so long as they content themselves with saying? but when it comes to blows it becomes a serious matter. I do not deny the influence of character, of the opinion of others, even independently of fear. The opinion of others is a peaceful check upon every man, but then it must be the opinion of his own class. Experience has shown that there is no action so wicked that even an honest man will not do it if he is borne out by the opinion of those with whom he habitually associates. Was there ever a more unpopular minister than Lord Castlereagh? Was there ever a minister who cared so little about it? The reason was that although he had the people against him, the predominant portion of the aristocracy was for him, and all his concern about public dissatisfaction was to keep it below the point of a general insurrection.[22]

Mill's refusal to accept public opinion as an adequate substitute for a reformed parliament does not, then, imply a belittling of the power of public opinion to reinforce institutional safeguards against misrule. On the contrary, even a reformed parliament without a free press to provide a focus for public criticism would prove to be an insufficient check. On this issue he was, therefore, at one with his father and Bentham. Furthermore, he followed his father, despite a few signs of hesitation in believing that public opinion was a powerful factor in securing and promoting moral conduct. Evidence that he did so is far more substantial than the occasional manifestation of doubt about its potency. His commitment to this view comes out clearly in, but is not confined to, his 'Speech on Perfectibility'. This was delivered in May, 1828, i.e. over a year after the onset of his 'mental crisis', and when his mind had been opened to new trends of thought; but there can be no doubt that the central theme of the speech was very much a legacy of his father's teachings. As the title suggests, the speech was concerned with the question of how far human beings can be improved, morally and intellectually; and Mill sets out to establish the claim that:

. . . by all just rules of induction we ought to conclude that an extremely high degree of moral and intellectual excellence may be made to prevail among mankind at large, since causes exist which have been proved adequate to produce it in many particular instances.[23]

Turning first to the question of moral improvement, and on the assumption that his audience would accept as a fact that 'there are, and have been, persons who have possessed a very high degree of virtue', Mill goes on to ask what made them virtuous and offers the explanation in terms of education and public opinion. In the early years the 'influence of good moral education' is vital, and this must be consolidated and extended by 'the insensible influence of the world, of society, and public opinion upon their habits and associations in after life'. So, he contends:

. . . these two forces, education and public opinion, when they are both of them brought fairly into play and made to act in harmony with one another, are capable of producing high moral excellence . . .[24]

But moral virtue is not so widespread as it could be and Mill thinks the reason lies both in faulty education and the character of the values propagated by the insensible influences of society. (It is in the way he develops the latter point that we see unmistakable signs of the attitude to public opinion expressed in his better-known writings, especially the *Liberty*.) Education is faulty simply because there is 'sheer ignorance' of the means to produce good habits of conduct; and it is not fanciful to suppose that his remedy for this ignorance was the doctrine of education worked out by his father.[25] As to the educative pressures of the wider society, he laments that:

. . . almost everywhere the great objects of ambition, those which ought to be the rewards of high intellectual and moral excellence, are the rewards either of wealth, as in this country, or of private favour, as in most others . . . [and] the person who possesses these means . . . is the person who exercises influence over the public mind; he is the person whose favour is courted, whose actions are imitated, whose opinions are adopted, and the contagion of whose failings is caught by the mass of mankind.[26]

But, consistent with the belief in progress which he still held at this time, Mill declares his faith in the power for good of public opinion—'immense force that it is'. What is needed for its capacity to be realized is a proper system of education and that public opinion be 'well directed in respect of morality'. And to achieve this it is also necessary:

. . . to take men out of the sphere of the opinion of their separate and private coteries and make them amenable to the general tribunal of the public at large; to leave no class possessed of power sufficient to protect one another in defying public opinion, and to manufacture a separate code of morality for their private guidance; and so to organize the political institutions of a country that no one could possess any power save what might be given to him by the favourable sentiments, not of any separate class with a separate interest, but of the people.[27]

It must be admitted that there is little here which anticipates the alarm over the growing and illegitimate power of public opinion to be found in *On Liberty* apart from the remark about the inordinate search for material gain and the way it diverts the energies of men from more worthy pursuits. But before leaving the subject we should take note of some observations which, somewhat isolated though they were at this time, do suggest a readiness to assimilate ideas that Mill was to encounter in other writers before the end of the decade. Among these is the claim that men were unwilling, because afraid, to say what they really believed if it ran counter to the prevailing climate of opinion. In an article for the Morning Chronicle written as early as 1823 Mill asserts that 'the present time [is], on the whole, better than any former time'. There are more 'intelligent and enlightened men' in the country than at any time in the past. Yet he is aware of some disturbing features, and the one he singles out is 'the mental cowardice which prevents men from giving expression to their conviction, and the insincerity which leads them to express what they do not think'.[28] On another occasion, in a review of 'the present state of literature', he notes a movement toward uniformity among 'the vast majority of literary men', over whom 'the spirit of their age rules absolutely supreme, because they studiously endeavour to resemble it, and not only imitate but are apt to caricature its leading peculiarities'.[29] He goes on:

. . . the grand object of writers in general is success. The qualities most calculated to ensure success constitute the sole idea they have of merit: they cultivate in their own minds a habit of being pleased with that which they find pleasing to those to whom they address themselves: their aim is to be read and admired, and the degree in which that aim is successful, is the test by which they try their own merits and those of others. The weaker minds cannot resist the contagion of the common opinion or the common taste: and such of the stronger as prefer the honour and profit of pleasing others to the satisfaction of pleasing themselves, set the example to their numerous imitators of sailing with the stream.[30]

Perhaps more responsible than any other factor, in Mill's view, for the deplorable state of literature is the popularity of the periodical. This has a bad effect because, more than any other form of literature, the periodical is written 'for the day'.

II

In addition to the influence on John Stuart of his father and Bentham there were also a number of other strands of thought which contributed to his development. And among the influences which went to shape his emerging attitudes were Coleridge and Comte, Carlyle, and the Saint-Simonians. To the latter he was introduced by a young visitor from France, Gustave d'Eichthal, who was later to lead the first Saint-Simonian 'mission' to England. Comte was then numbered among the pupils of Saint-Simon, and his doctrine of the three stages also helped to provide Mill with 'a clearer conception than ever before of the peculiarities of an era of transition in opinion'. The articles Mill published in 1831 on *The Spirit of the Age*, with their insistence on the transitional character of the period, on the lack of correspondence between power and fitness as one of its main features, and on the need to restore the authority of the cultivated few, bear the unmistakable stamp of Saint-Simonian thought.

There is one aspect of Mill's relations with the Saint-Simonians which I propose to examine at greater length, along with other evidence available, in order to assess the importance of the various influences at work at this time in producing new attitudes to the problems he was later to discuss in the essay *On Liberty*. Now it is generally agreed that around 1830 he was forming the views we find expressed in his article on 'Civilization' (1836) and the first review of de Tocqueville (1835), views which anticipate some of the central contentions in *Liberty*. It has been pointed out that as early as 1832, in an article on 'Genius', Mill was complaining about the tendency of the age as one in which the 'march of the intellect' was rather 'a march towards doing without intellect, and supplying our deficiency of giants by the united efforts of a constantly increasing multitude of dwarfs'.[31] And it has been argued that the appeal for individuality made by Mill in this same article could not have come so soon after the expression of very different views to John Sterling only a year before had it not been for the influence of Harriet Taylor and her unpublished paper on toleration. Harriet's paper was written in 1832 and Mill met her for the first time in the summer of 1830. Mill became acquainted with a work written by a certain Dr W. E. Channing, published early in 1830, and was appealing to it in support of his dislike of the sectarianism of the Saint-Simonians in a letter of 6 March 1830—i.e. weeks before he had met Harriet. Channing's work was a much more emphatic precursor of those ideas in the *Liberty* which are partly foreshadowed in Harriet's essay. Moreover, in 1829 Carlyle's *Signs of the Times* had contained views similar to Channing's at a number of points. But before seeing just how Carlyle and Channing contributed to the formation of Mill's views let us see what Mill had written on the question of liberty before he began to feel the impact of their opinions.

In a series of letters to the *Morning Chronicle* in 1823 Mill discusses the arguments for and against toleration, with particular reference to religious toleration. He assumes there would be general acceptance of the principle that free discussion contributes to the propagation of truth and puts the burden of proof on those who want to make an exception in the case of religion. Even if it were true that there is a greater risk of making mistakes in religious matters, which Mill denies, the prohibition of free discussion increases the danger. To decide beforehand that only certain religious views should be freely ventilated means that the government would be allowed to choose our opinions for us. A government with this power is surely despotic since there is no conceivable opinion, true or false, which could not be made a religious doctrine or part thereof. To refuse discussion of any single religious doctrine is, logically, to refuse all discussions of religion. There can be no justification for banning just the atheists. Why should we be denied the right to examine thoroughly the contentions of atheism but no other point of view? Most people are, indeed, convinced of its falsehood. But, says Mill in a typical sortie, to bring this forward as a reason for preventing discussion is to say that people are better qualified to judge before discussion has taken place than after it: which is absurd, since before discussion, if their opinions are true, it is only by accident, whereas afterwards they hold them with a complete conviction and perfect knowledge of the proofs on which they are grounded. Now, if it is desired to preserve the doctrines of Christianity, the persecution of anti-Christian opinions is superfluous, for if the general belief that Christianity is true is itself true, Christianity cannot fail to prevail over falsehood in a condition of free discussion. Persecution can be defended only on the supposition that the people are stupid and quite incapable of distinguishing truth from error. Even were this so, the fact remains that men will favour the opinion to which they are already biased when they are presented with two opposed propositions. And most people are favourably inclined to religion. Then, in a comment on the trend of the times, Mill expresses the fear that though the number of intelligent and enlightened men in England is increasing there is a growing mental cowardice which prevents them from giving expression to their convictions and an insincerity which leads them to say what they do not really think. Several times in the remaining years of the decade Mill was to return to the benefits of free discussion. Not only was free discussion a means for ensuring the triumph of truth (like his father, Mill was unshaken in the conviction that when truth and error are allowed to compete freely truth never fails to prevail), but it constituted an important safeguard against the abuse of power by the rulers, a safeguard so important that without it all other safeguards were ineffectual.[32] Furthermore, along with education, discussion was an instrument for the culture of our intellectual faculties. And in these years Mill was already holding up as a goal of human endeavour 'the improvement of man himself, as a moral and intelligent being', or 'that higher state of cultivation, of which better opinions are the natural and almost spontaneous growth'.[33] In contrast to this ideal he found in England the worship of wealth and the material comfort it brought. In 1828, as we have seen, he was deploring the fact that 'almost everywhere the great objects of ambition, those which ought to be the rewards of high intellectual and moral excellence, are the rewards either of wealth, as in this country, or of private favour, as in most others'.[34]

To discuss any subject earnestly was to run the risk of ridicule. The English middle classes are so prejudiced and convinced of their wisdom that they have no wish to learn from others. Their one object in life is to ape their superiors upon whom they look with 'an open-mouthed and besotted admiration'. The idol of 'production' has so corrupted the national life as to make it virtually hopeless to inspire the people with any concern for the affairs of the intellect or the soul.

Although Mill believed that truth would prevail in the market of free competition in ideas he was constantly insisting during this period, as he was later to do in the essay *On Liberty*, that a man had to guard against assuming to be wholly false the opinions of those whose final conclusion was different from his, even if he had good grounds for holding that conclusion to be false. Truth would prevail, he argues, but men have to strive carefully to attain it. They should always allow for the possibility of being wrong and 'leave the means of correction in existence, even for the very remote chance of that very improbable possibility'. Equally important was it not to assume our own infallibility, an evil whether our opinions were true or false. In the case of Christianity, for example, to permit the denial of its truth is a public good; for without controversy over its tenets we should forget the reasons for believing it to be true, and religion without reason becomes a mere prejudice, losing its hold as a truth in so far as the reasons for its truth are unknown.[35] The good of mankind requires that all opinions should be questioned. Nothing should be believed until sufficient evidence has been adduced on its behalf, for we have no right to hold our opinions unless we have searched as far as we can in order to 'hold fast by that which is good'. Without this questioning of established opinions we do not hold our beliefs like rational beings.[36] Moreover, the great danger of our time is not so much error as half-truth, and men need to be supplied with the remaining portion of the truth, only part of which they have hitherto held. Exchanging one portion of the truth for another is not what men require, but combining them in order to attain as much as they can of the whole. To do this successfully we must avoid a mere head-on collision with established opinion and direct men's attention to what is good in it and try to draw them on from this, and through this, to something better.

I am averse to any mode of eradicating error [wrote Mill to d'Eichtal] but by establishing and inculcating (when that is practicable) the opposite truth—a truth of some kind inconsistent with that moral or intellectual state of mind from which errors arise. It is only thus that we can at once maintain the good that already exists, and produce more. And I object to placing myself in the situation of an advocate, for or against a cause . . . when I see any person going wrong I will try to find out the fragment of truth which is misleading him, and will analyse and expound that. I will suggest to his own mind, not inculcate in him as from mine, the idea which I think will save him. . . . In short, I do not insist upon making others give up their own point of view and adopt mine, but I endeavour myself to unite whatever is not optical illusion in both. When by this means, I shall have clearly embraced in my own view the entire truth, and shall be able to represent to others that whole of which they have before seen a part, I shall have great confidence in their ultimate adoption of it.[37]

Completely free though we may be to publish our views, might there not be some limit as to the manner in which they are presented? To this question Mill's answer was then, as later, a decided negative. Ridicule and invective make no difference to the long-run victory of truth. In the ultimate resort the balance of the argument wins through. Moreover, who is to judge what is invective and what is fair or moderate criticism? It must be left to the government, but there is no ruler who would not, if he could, suppress all hostile criticism. Now, all censure is either invective or equivalent to it and so it is impossible to control the mode of expression of the critics without at the same time silencing them altogether; without, in fact, 'prohibiting all discussion, or leaving it to rulers to decide what sort of discussion shall be punished, and what left free'. In much the same way Mill denies the validity of the distinction between liberty and 'licentiousness'. Those who have the power to decide what is liberty and what is licence have the power to determine what opinions the people shall hold. Allow our rulers to determine the limits of each and 'every thing will be licentiousness which implies censure of themselves, which involves any doctrine hostile to the indefinite increase and perpetual duration of their power'. So Mill insists that there is no medium between absolute freedom to express opinions and absolute despotism, for to grant rulers any power to suppress opinions is to grant them power to silence whomsoever they choose.[38]

Such, then, were Mill's views in the decade before he met Harriet Taylor. They clearly foreshadow many of the arguments which go to make up the essay *On Liberty*, though the fear that individuality might be crushed by the overweening pressure of a mediocre public has not reached the intensity it was later to assume. But the hints and suggestions are all there and were to receive their elaboration in the course of the decade following his acquaintance with Harriet. Describing the stage which the development of his thought had reached at this time (i.e. around 1830) Mill says:

The only actual revolution which has ever taken place in my modes of thinking was already complete. My new tendencies had to be confirmed in some respects, moderated in others: but the only substantial changes of opinion that were yet to come, related to politics, and consisted, on one hand, in a greater approximation, so far as regards the ultimate prospects of humanity, to a qualified socialism, and on the other, a shifting of my political ideal from pure democracy, as commonly understood by its partizans, to the modified form of it, which is set forth in my *Considerations on Representative Government*. This last change, which took place very gradually, dates its commencement from my reading, or rather study, of M. de Tocqueville's *Democracy in America*, which fell into my hands immediately after its first appearance.[39]

Mill goes on to observe that he was well prepared to receive the warnings uttered by de Tocqueville about government by the numerical majority. They undoubtedly gave an urgency to his thought largely absent from his earlier work, for in the articles he wrote soon after the appearance of de Tocqueville's book we find a more definite and vigorous anticipation of one of the main themes of *On Liberty*, namely, the importance of the free development of individual character in the face of the many obstacles modern society was putting in its way.

Mr Packe, in the passage of his biography of Mill, claims to see in the article on 'Genius' (1832) 'something quite unlike anything Mill had thought before . . . something foreshadowed in Harriet's *Toleration*' and to become fundamental to his political theory, that is, the idea that individual originality and independence of thought were in danger from the mediocrity of the mass.[40] He contrasts the views set out in the article on 'Genius' with some remarks made by Mill in a letter to John Sterling (October 1831) which show a great sympathy for the Tory belief that

it is good for man to be ruled: to submit both his body and mind to the guidance of a higher intelligence and virtue . . . the direct antithesis of liberalism, which is for making every man his own guide and sovereign master, and letting him think for himself, and do exactly as he judges best for himself . . . than which it is difficult to conceive a more thorough ignorance of man's nature, and of what is necessary for his happiness . . .[41]

In the article on 'Genius' Mill begins by referring approvingly to a previous writer in the *Monthly Repository* who had rated the promotion of the higher capacities of spirit and intellect as more important than great advances in the mechanical sciences with the consequent raising of material standards. He insists that there can be no genuine happiness without the development of our 'higher endowments' and expresses his disquiet at the tendency for a lower degree of intellectual attainment to spread itself evenly over large numbers at the cost of distinction in the few, carrying with it the dreadful prospect of the deficiency being eventually made up 'by the united efforts of a constantly increasing multitude of dwarfs'. Diagnosing the malaise, Mill points to education as the culprit, instilling its truths by formal repetition and absorption by rote rather than through a genuine understanding of the grounds of those truths. So widespread and entrenched has this procedure become that one is likely to incur the reproach of one's neighbour if one dares to work out one's views for oneself. It can therefore be a matter of no surprise that genius should have become so rare. In order to counter the danger we must change our educational methods and rely on the spontaneous use of the creative and analytical faculties: 'let all cram be ruthlessly discarded'. Let society, too, withhold its censure from those who would think for themselves and direct it rather to those who form their opinions hastily without trying to understand the views of those from whom they differ.

Now Mr Packe is right to say that Mill expresses ideas in this article very similar to those we find in Harriet's paper on toleration, and it cannot be denied that they were to become a vital component in the essay *On Liberty*. But as our summary of Mill's thought on liberty up to 1830 surely demonstrates, it cannot be said that they were 'quite unlike anything that Mill had thought before'.[42] But, it might be asked, how can one explain the letter to Sterling (1831) in which Mill pours scorn on the Liberal doctrine that each man should be allowed to think for himself? If we look back over the previous paragraphs of this letter we shall find the following sentence: 'In the present age of transition, everything must be subordinate to *freedom of inquiry*: if your opinions, or mine, are right, they will in time be unanimously adopted by the instructed classes, and *then* it will be the time to found the national creed upon the assumption of their truth'.[43] The letter to Sterling was written some months after the completion of the articles on the *Spirit of the Age*, and in the latter, as we have already noted, the Saint-Simonian influence was very pronounced. Together with the correspondence with d'Eichthal they show how Mill had come to approve of the Saint-Simonian idea of a 'pouvoir spirituel', 'a state in which the body of the people, i.e. the uninstructed, shall entertain the same feeling of deference and submission to the authority of the instructed, in morals and politics, as they at present do in the physical sciences. This, I am persuaded, is the wholesome state of the human mind . . .'[44] And Mill continued to uphold the authority of the intellectual élite, for whom he desired complete freedom of expression, at the same time as he looked upon the masses as incapable of reasoned thought and hence in need of instruction from the enlightened few. The amount of authority he would give the élite was never as much as Comte was prepared to confer on it and was more at this period than either before he came under Saint-Simonian influence or in the remaining years of his life. But there persisted an inner core of conviction that the masses needed guidance (cf. James Mill's attitude to the middle classes) and were largely incapable of arriving at reasoned opinions. How these apparently conflicting beliefs were held simultaneously by Mill is well brought out in *The Spirit of the Age*. He is discussing the extent to which the majority must accept the bulk of their opinions from the few who are able to devote themselves to study and 'make themselves thoroughly masters of the philosophical grounds of those opinions of which it is desirable that all should be firmly persuaded, but which they alone can entirely and philosophically know', and concludes that it is right that every man should 'follow his reason as far as his reason will carry him, and cultivate the faculty as highly as possible. But reason itself will teach most men that they must, in the last resort, fall back upon the authority of still more cultivated minds, as the ultimate sanction of the convictions of their reason itself.'[45] Moreover, in the same articles Mill welcomes the fact that the habit of discussion has spread in society and raised the level of intelligence of the lowest strata. Such progress as he is able to discern is, he claims, due to an increase of discussion. Perhaps no great extension of wisdom has occurred, but at least the amount of prejudice has declined, for 'to discuss and to question established opinions, are merely two phrases for the same thing'.[46]

The case, then, that I am trying to establish is that Mill's article on 'Genius' (1832) cannot be regarded as the first sign of those ideas which received their classic expression in the essay *On Liberty*, that it is not an abrupt change in his opinions of which the explanation is to be sought in the influence of Harriet Taylor. It might be argued that although these ideas are hinted at in earlier writings yet their greater degree of articulateness and the greater sense of urgency with which Mill puts them forward in 1832 are the result of his discussions with Harriet. But even for this more modest contention the evidence is inconclusive. Moreover, it leaves out of account the impact made on Mill at this period by ideas coming from other directions, from Carlyle, for example, and from a certain Dr W. E. Channing.[47] First Carlyle. Writing of the years immediately after his recovery from his mental illness, Mill refers to the new influences 'streaming in upon me' and mentions among them Carlyle's early articles in the *Edinburgh Review*. One of these had, as we have seen, attracted the attention of the Saint-Simonians, namely, 'Signs of the Times'. And it seems reasonable to assume that this is one that Mill had in mind when he wrote his *Autobiography*. From its contents no one can derive anything but a strong sense of the similarity of some of its ideas to what Mill was himself to put forward within the coming decade. The age, says Carlyle, is a mechanical one, but it is not only in the realm of physical things that mechanical processes are coming to prevail. Even in the sphere of the mind the old natural and spontaneous methods have given way and in their place is growing up a pervading mechanism, such that 'no individual now hopes to accomplish the poorest enterprise single-handed and without mechanical aids; he must make interest with some existing corporation . . . for in these days, more emphatically than ever, "to live, signifies to unite with a party, or to make one"' Individual endeavour and the striving for internal perfection have been forsaken for combinations and institutional arrangements. Man no longer loves truth for its own sake and he dares to proclaim it only with popular approval—'if there is a multitude huzzaing at his back . . .'. So, declares Carlyle,

we stand leashed together, uniform in dress and movement, like the rowers of some boundless galley. This and that may be right and true; but we must not do it. Wonderful 'Force of Public Opinion'! We must act and walk in all points as it prescribes; follow the traffic it bids us . . . or we shall be lightly esteemed . . . Thus, while civil liberty is more and more secured to us, our moral liberty is all but lost.[48]

Some months after the appearance of Carlyle's essay there was published in London in 1830 by W. E. Channing a pamphlet on the tendency for men to accomplish their aims by organized associations. That Mill came to read and approve of it is clear.[49] Mill's friend, Eyton Tooke, joined in the correspondence with d'Eichthal and criticized the Saint-Simonian 'apostles' for being sectarians who manifested those vices of sectarianism which had been recently described and condemned by Dr Channing. A few weeks later Mill, in March 1830, wrote to d'Eichthal and supported Tooke's reference to Channing's attack on sectarianism. Now, it is true that there is no reference to Channing in the section of the *Autobiography* where Mill acknowledges the various writers whose views ran along similar lines to his own, but a comparison of Channing's booklet with those published by Maccall and Warren in the 1850s would suggest that the reason why the latter two are specifically mentioned is largely due to the proximity in time of their publications to the writing of *On Liberty*. Certainly it cannot be held that Channing's argument is less similar than theirs to Mill's exposition in the *Liberty*.

Channing begins by looking for a principle to evaluate the activity of associations. The age, he says, is one in which the pressures of society are very great, threatening individuality of character, and with no compensating benefits. For this reason it is important to try to arrive at principles governing the activity of the associations that men are increasingly turning to for the attainment of their various ends in agriculture, manufacturing, science, and other walks of life. Our basic principle should be: social institutions are to be judged by the extent to which they promote and call forth 'intellectual and moral energy and freedom . . . inward, creative energy, is the highest good which accrues to us from our social principles and connections'. We know what we do because we are social beings, yet the individual mind must seek its own enlargement, especially in a cowardly and servile age like ours. Every person has a duty to develop himself in his own unique way, and though we may speak of a common human nature, human beings are capable of unfolding it 'in unbounded diversities' since it is 'rich enough for infinite manifestations'. Yet to this ultimate goal of self-development there has grown in our time a serious threat in the increasing pressure which society is constantly exerting on us, 'now open and direct in the form of authority and menace, now subtle and silent in the guise of blandishment and promise . . . what mighty power is lodged in a frown or a smile, in the voice of praise and flattery, in scorn or neglect, in public opinion, in domestic habits and prejudices, in the state and spirit of the community to which we belong!' From this all-pervasive influence there seems to be no escape, and so the cause of individuality is in danger of being lost; 'we are in great peril of growing up slaves to this exacting, arbitrary sovereign'. There is only one answer. We just have to resist it, to remind ourselves always that it is in individual action alone that virtue lies, in 'inward energy, in self-determination'. Nothing of true moral stature ever comes from mere imitation. Of course, the problem is complicated by the fact that we must, and should, derive constant help from our fellow social beings. To receive this aid without allowing society to impose a rigid pattern on our behaviour is the grand difficulty we face. There are, however, some encouraging and compensating trends working the other way, namely, the wider area of social contacts modern civilization offers to growing numbers of people, including the inhabitants of foreign lands.

When Channing finally turns to his specific problem, the role of associations, he echoes Carlyle in his estimate of them as poor substitutes for individual energy. A spontaneous individual action, 'performed from a principle within, performed without the excitement of an urging and approving voice from abroad, is worth more than hundreds which grow from mechanical imitation'. What we have to fear is that public opinion should express itself more and more through organized institutions, because 'when shackled and stimulated by vast Associations, it is in danger of becoming a steady, unrelenting tyrant, browbeating the timid, proscribing the resolute, silencing free speech and virtually denying the dearest religious and civil rights'.[50]

III

Although freedom of speech and publication were prominent among the securities for good government in Benthamite political thought, and although some of Mill's earliest journalistic efforts were produced in this spirit, by the time he came to write *On Liberty* the emphasis had changed. Indeed, the whole problem of liberty for him had gained new dimensions and in the forefront now was the fear that society would become increasingly hostile to the full and varied expression of individual character. For his watchword Mill took Wilhelm von Humboldt's assertion of the absolute importance of the rich and diverse development of the human personality, and it has seemed to some of his critics that by accepting this as his central theme he had abandoned the principle of utility. He himself however took care to say in his introductory chapter that his ultimate standard on all ethical questions was still utility; but, he insisted, 'it must be utility in the largest sense, grounded on the permanent interests of a man as a progressive being'.[51] We may assume that this formula was designed to embrace the more complex conception of happiness which distinguished Mill from the earlier utilitarians and, in particular, the repeated emphasis in the third chapter of the essay on the importance of the full flowering of individuality.

Mill's problem in the *Liberty* was partly generated by his realization that popular government was no guarantee of freedom. Tocqueville's account of democracy in America strengthened his misgivings about the Benthamite assumption that to identify the interests of rulers and ruled was a necessary and sufficient condition of good government. Not only could tyranny be exercised by a government based on the will of the people, but there was need to guard against the informal pressures of society, especially in England where the weight of public opinion was, in contrast with France, heavier than that of the law. The restrictions imposed on individuals, whether by law or opinion, ought to be based on some recognized principle rather than on the preferences and prejudices of powerful sections of the public, and Mill set himself the task of formulating such a principle, elucidating its nature and illustrating how it would work. He describes his principle in a number of different ways. Af first he permits social control only if it serves 'to prevent harm to others' or to deter a person from inflicting 'evil'[52] on someone else; and here the line of division is between conduct which 'concerns others', for which a person is answerable should it result in 'harm', and conduct 'which merely concerns himself' over which society has no jurisdiction at all.[53] But at other times it is the violation of 'a distinct and assignable obligation' or 'perceptible hurt' to an 'assignable individual'.[54] The variety of expression Mill used to determine the sphere of liberty has left his commentators the difficult task of finding an interpretation which would be consistent with his own words and at the same time conform to his undoubted intention of making the area of freedom as large as possible. Nor can an interpretation ignore Mill's clear recognition of the need for some restraint both as a condition of social life of any sort and as a safeguard of freedom itself. Furthermore, Mill did not recommend that we remain indifferent to conduct which though it did not violate the interests of others yet fell short of the accepted standards of private morality; but if we feel we should try to *persuade* a friend to give up his self-regarding vices we are not entitled to *coerce* him.

On Liberty is probably best known for the eloquent justification of liberty of thought and discussion contained in its second chapter. Mill contends that freedom of expression is no less necessary where an honest government is backed by the people than when the government is corrupt or despotic; and small minorities—even a single dissentor—have as much right to express their views as large or overwhelming majorities. His case, argued at length, rests on the claim that to suppress an opinion is wrong whether or not the opinion is true. For if it is true, we are robbed of the truth; if false, we are denied a fuller understanding of the truth from its conflict with error. And where, as often happens, the dominant view is part truth and part error we shall only know the whole truth by allowing the contesting opinions freely to circulate.

It should be noticed that Mill's argument here is strictly utilitarian, in terms of the social benefits to be derived from a policy of freedom and access to the truth. In his plea for individuality, however, he combines absolutist with instrumental arguments. The free development of individuality is indeed socially advantageous; it makes for improvement, progress, and variety in ways of living. But individuality is at the same time synonymous with men choosing to live their own lives in their own distinctive ways, and Mill insisted that a man's own mode of 'laying out his existence' is best simply because it is his own mode. Moreover, it is only by cultivating individuality that we can become well-developed human beings and 'what more or better can be said of any condition of human affairs than that it brings human beings themselves nearer to the best thing they can be?'[55] If then we ask whether Mill believed in liberty as good in itself or simply as a means to happiness and progress the answer must be that he believed both; and we should not forget that for him the ideas of happiness and progress were thoroughly infused with his conception of a freely choosing human agent.

III

On Liberty and its Early Critics

I

The work of the historian of political thought is incomplete without an account of the manner in which the classical texts have been received, their impact on public opinion, and on later political theorists. My object in this chapter is to offer a small and limited contribution in this field: it is, simply, to survey the opinions of Mill's contemporaries on his essay *On Liberty*, in particular the comment appearing between its publication in 1859 and Mill's death in 1873.

At first sight there would seem to be no room for disagreement about the extent of Mill's influence in nineteenth-century England. Most of us would concur in Mr Crane Brinton's judgement: 'Mill's political and moral standards are those professed by large numbers of his fellows. . . . You cannot get a more representative definition of the areas a good Victorian liberal thought should be sacred to the individual than John Mill's essay *On Liberty* . . . [he] stated as clearly as anyone has ever stated the central doctrine of nineteenth-century liberalism.'[1] Then there is the evidence of Frederic Harrison and John Morley, showing how powerful was Mill's hold on some at least of the young minds of the mid-century. 'I do not know', said Morley in later life, 'whether then or at any other time so short a book ever instantly produced so wide and so important an effect on contemporary thought as did Mill's *On Liberty* in that day of intellectual and social fermentation (1859).'[2] And Frederic Harrison is no less emphatic:

It is certain that the little book [*On Liberty*] produced a profound impression on contemporary thought, and had an extraordinary success with the public. It has been read by hundreds of thousands, and, to some of the most vigorous and most conscientious spirits amongst us, it became a sort of gospel. . . . It was the code of many thoughtful

This chapter first appeared as pp. 1–38 of *Mill and his early critics* (University of Leicester Press, 1956) with minor amendments.

writers and several influential politicians. It undoubtedly contributed to the practical programmes of Liberals and Radicals for the generation that saw its birth; and the statute book bears many traces of its influence over the sphere and duties of government.[3]

Yet Mr Michael Packe, in his recent biography of Mill, is able to say that the essay appeared at a time when the intellectual currents were hostile to the sort of message it had to give. It was, he agrees, widely read, but it was not accepted and applied because collectivism was on the march, and from many directions came the call for greater social solidarity—from the Tory, the trade-unionist, the Comtist, and the Christian-Socialist. If it did not, like Hume's *Treatise*, fall 'dead-born from the press', it was certainly delivered into an unfriendly atmosphere.[4]

I have not attempted to clarify what is involved in a dispute of this kind, still less to offer a definitive settlement. A good deal obviously turns on how representative were the circles in which Harrison and Morley moved and those to which Mr Packe refers. What the following pages surely indicate is that Mill's essay was more critically received in the journals of the time than we usually tend to allow, though they do not suffice to establish Mr Packe's claim that 'the whole intellectual climate was opposed to Mill'. For even among those who were critical of particular aspects of the work—and they were not calling for collectivism—some pay willing tribute to its qualities and imply that its influence was considerable. Fitzjames Stephen who, according to Morley, 'led the first effective attack on Mill's pontifical authority',[5] was at first in agreement with the general tone of the book and remarked of the second and third chapters: 'We know of nothing in English literature since the *Areopagitica* more stirring, more noble, better worthy of the most profound and earnest meditation. . .'.[6] And as late as 1872 a writer in *Fraser's Magazine* could say that the essay deserved the title some had bestowed upon it, 'the gospel of the nineteenth century'.[7] Very few are wholly depreciatory in the manner of the *Dublin Review*, which affirms that 'had Mr Mill's character depended on this essay alone he would never have acquired the reputation of "a logical consistent intellect"'.[8] On the other hand, Buckle is virtually alone in his almost unqualified praise for 'this noble treatise, so full of wisdom and of thought' by one whom he refers to as the most profound intellect in England since the seventeenth century.[9]

It will be noticed that although I have occasionally mentioned Fitzjames Stephen's *Liberty, Equality, Fraternity* it does not form part of the material I have drawn on for this survey. It was, of course, published before Mill's death and Mill had time to read and comment on it, but most of the points made by Stephen (besides a number of others) were anticipated in the reviews within two or three years of the essay's appearance. It might be true to say, as Morley did, that Stephen's was the first effective attack, because of the comprehensive character of the assault and the unity of thought on which the criticisms rested, yet the following pages show beyond question that 'Mill's pontifical authority' had been challenged and his central thesis called in question before Stephen had decided to fire his broadside.

Here and there I have seen fit to summarize the relevant parts of *On Liberty* and to draw attention to what some later writers have said about the issues discussed by Mill's contemporaries. But on the whole I have preferred to let the critics speak for themselves, either by quoting verbatim or by a précis of their arguments in language as close to the original as possible. That it has turned out to be largely a synopsis of hostile criticism cannot be helped, for, apart from a few introductory words of praise (and not always these), the reviews follow a similar pattern. They usually make serious reservations about the leading principles or question Mill's application of them. Their mood is typified by the able critic in *Bentley's Quarterly Review* who approaches the essay, as he would all things by Mill, with great respect, fully expecting to remember it as a landmark in his mental history. He finishes it with admiration unimpaired, yet disappointed. Disappointed because Mill has failed to provide him with any workable principles to further the ends which, to a great extent, they had in common.[10]

II

Mill's essay deals with one of the eternal questions of politics and is yet an endeavour to cope with the specific malaise of his time. For behind Mill's question—'What is the nature and extent of the power which society ought to exercise over the individual?' (one that had been raised many times before and has been asked many times since)—was his anxiety lest the tendencies which he claimed to see at work in the civilized world would eventually extinguish spontaneity in all forms of human conduct. Tocqueville had already pointed to some of the evils which he thought to be associated with the coming of democracy. The advent of democracy, he insisted, was the great problem of the time. Its central axiom—the sovereignty of the people—had been applied most consistently in America 'in which there is so little true independence of mind and freedom of discussion'.[11] Mill was impressed by these warnings. In a review of Tocqueville's book written in 1840 Mill was already complaining that the growing insignificance of individuals in comparison with the mass was a marked feature of English society. The fear of being eccentric and the unwillingness to be thought in any way original had penetrated to all classes, to such an extent that hardly anything depended on individuals, 'but all upon classes, and among classes mainly upon the middle class'. Tocqueville's analysis was masterly, says Mill, an example of the true Baconian and Newtonian method applied to society and government, but the effects of democracy had been confounded with the effects of civilization, for many of the features of American democracy were also present in Britain where the progress of equalization had not been so rapid. Tocqueville had in fact summed up all the various tendencies of modern commercial society under the one label, 'democracy', whereas the truth was that the moral and social influences producing a uniformity of habit and outlook were as fully operative in aristocratic England as in democratic America.[12] Later, in the essay *On Liberty*, Mill again traces the causes of the decline in individuality and his fears for the increasing loss in spontaneous behaviour have now assumed major proportions:

Individual spontaneity is hardly recognizable by the common modes of thinking as having any intrinsic worth . . . society has now fairly got the better of individuality . . . from the highest class of society down to the lowest, everyone lives as under the eye of a hostile and dreaded censorship . . . the general tendency of things throughout the world is to render mediocrity the ascendant power among mankind

. . . the only power deserving the name is that of masses, and of governments while they make themselves the organ of the tendencies and instincts of the masses . . . in the moral and social relations of private life as in public transactions. . . . Already energetic characters on any large scale are becoming merely traditional. There is now scarcely any outlet for energy in this country except business. The greatness of England is now all collective. . . .[13]

And the causes of these developments? The circumstances in which people live, says Mill, were becoming increasingly homogeneous. People were reading the same things, going to the same places, had the same rights and liberties. The spread of education was bringing more people under common influences, and improvements in the means of transport, in industry, and commerce were leading to greater contacts and to a general raising and standardization of material conditions. Most important of all, public opinion ruled supreme. Men of outstanding abilities and independent resources were disappearing, so that the power of resisting the opinion of the mass was gravely weakened. In such a climate the desire to stand up to public pressures would surely die and with it any support for nonconformity. 'The combination of all these causes', Mill concludes, 'forms so great a mass of influence hostile to Individuality, that it is not easy to see how it can stand its ground.'[14]

This is the background to Mill's problem, which he formulates in very general terms. The problem is to discover 'the nature and limits of the power which can be legitimately exercised by society over the individual', and the solution he proposes is to assign to society control over those actions which are chiefly of public concern, and to the individual freedom in those things that chiefly concern him and him alone. The respective spheres are marked out by the principle of self-protection, which asserts that interference with individual behaviour is justified only when the action prohibited would have caused harm to others. As he put it: '. . . the only purpose for which power can be rightfully exercised over any member of a civilized community, against his will, is to prevent harm to others. His own good, either physical or moral, is not a sufficient warrant.'[15]

It is important to notice that Mill limits the application of his principle to civilized communities. He does not intend that it should everywhere regulate both the dealings of governments with their subjects and the relations between individuals, though he is certainly recommending it for all advanced, democratic countries. As such it is a formula claiming general validity, a contribution to the endless debate on the manner of reconciling freedom with order. But, as we have maintained, the urgency of Mill's plea for the recognition of this principle derives from his belief that the threat to human freedom was becoming peculiarly grave. There was a time, he argues, when the struggle for liberty took the form of a contest between rulers and their subjects wherein the latter looked upon the former as being necessarily opposed to their freedom, and the attainment of liberty was regarded as being dependent on the restriction of the rulers' powers, either by compelling them to observe certain rights or by instituting constitutional checks. Eventually, however, it came to be thought that rulers were not destined to be in permanent opposition to the interests of their subjects. Some means might be devised of identifying the interests of both so that the people need not be 'protected against its own will'. But Mill was sure that the experience of democracy— 'elective and responsible government'—provided no grounds for thinking men in less need of securities for freedom than in the past. People might wish to oppress a part of their number. Had not 'the tyranny of the majority' come to be recognized as one of the dangers of the age? And this was a tyranny which manifested itself as much through the prevailing opinions of the masses as through the formal rules of law. Now, for Mill the development of individual character was the focal aim of social policy; hence his fear of an opinion which could fetter individual development more insidiously than the penalties of the magistrate. He believed that the danger was especially great in England where the informal pressures of convention had become far more oppressive than the law.

Thus the remedy Mill prescribes takes the form of a general principle which derived its urgency in his eyes from the particular circumstances of the time. If his audience was to be convinced of its truth he must persuade it of the correctness of his diagnosis, for the essay's reception would largely depend upon whether his contemporaries saw in his account of the decline of individuality something that accorded with their own experience. Very few of them, however, shared his anxiety about the impending eclipse of individual character. The majority of those who discussed the essay during his lifetime were either decidedly against him or strangely silent on an issue which he took to be so fundamental.[16] Furthermore, they demurred both in respect of the magnitude of the phenomenon he deplored and as to the causes of such evidences for it that they were themselves prepared to concede. Mill, they say, has written a melancholy book. In an obviously depressed frame of mind, he has allowed that mood to colour his conclusions. There is so much harping on the tyranny of society that, one writer boldly suggests, the shoe must have been pinching.[17]

It is widely agreed among the reviewers that custom, whilst it did lie heavily in some spheres of social life, was not more hostile to singular conduct and beliefs than in former ages. According to Mill, says the writer in *Bentley's Quarterly Review*, 'a dark shadow rests on the present and future of English society . . . [but] a generation which has produced, and which has listened attentively to Mr Carlyle, Mr Froude, and Mr Buckle, cannot be charged with shrinking blindly from independence of thought'.[18] A pamphlet written by 'Liberal' defends the middle classes against Mill's charge of intolerance. Where else are minorities so safe? Despite Mill's claim that the tyranny of opinion is so strong as to make eccentricity a reproach, eccentric people are plentiful in England. There are minorities upon almost all subjects and they are tending to increase rather than diminish.[19] The *London Review* agrees: 'There never was an age characterized by greater independence of thought and by a freer criticism of established truths.'[20] And even Buckle, so generally enthusiastic in his admiration of the essay, has reservations about Mill's claim. In religious matters at least, he contends, public opinion is becoming more liberal.[21] But Mill receives some support from the *Dublin Review*. It believes with him that society was pressing heavily upon individuality and that in all classes people were living under the eye of a dreaded censorship. However, as the reviewer candidly admits, 'the English public views this Essay very differently from ourselves . . . the great name of the author lends a sanction and an authority to notions which are the foundations of Protestantism, and the logical results of which have been obscured by the mist with which educational prejudice clouds the intellects of so many Englishmen'.[22]

Some of the critics try to explain why Mill should, as they considered, have been so seriously misled about the conditions of liberty in England. The *British Quarterly Review* is quite certain that Mill has been deceived. A sure sign that society is on the whole more tolerant nowadays is that our laws have become much more liberal than they have ever been. One can, like Mill, be tempted into thinking the opposite by the fact that culture, once a rarity, has in our own day become quite common. No great man stands alone in his greatness today because he is sure to have his equals. At best he can only be one of a class. And there is no need to be despondent about this, for society is no longer a plaything of its great men: it has in itself too many of the elements of greatness for that.[23]

The *National Review* grants that there is a tendency towards uniformity in social conditions, but not of a kind to endanger individual freedom. What is really happening is that class types are disappearing—'the country gentleman stands out no longer in that marked contrast to the tradesman or the man of letters which was observable in the days of Sir Robert Walpole; the dissenter is no longer a moral foil to the church man. . . .' But with all this the sphere of individual liberty is being enlarged. Englishmen were never more free to think and behave as they feel they ought to do, though this gain has been offset by the loss of some 'intensity of character'. Mill fails to distinguish the strength and intensity of an outstanding character from that individuality which is just allowed to develop on its own, perhaps not very remarkable, course. Mill is right to say that these are times without any marked character, but the cause is the weakening of the bonds of custom which, whilst it encouraged prominent types of character, did so at the expense of the individuality of those coming under their influence.[24]

According to the *Saturday Review* individuality is threatened at a number of points by some tendencies of the time, but Mill is blind to the 'immense scope for the development of individual character . . . afforded in one direction by the very social arrangements which forbid it in another . . . he seems to us to be distinctly wrong in asserting that, as a matter of fact, originality of character is ceasing to exist'. It is true that in dress, manners, conversation, and various other things, deviation from the accepted norms is visited with penalties sufficiently unpleasant as to amount to virtual prohibition. Thus there is a definite external uniformity about much of the Englishman's behaviour, and this applies to all classes of society. Furthermore, the tendency is for this to become even more rigid. But there is another side of the picture which Mill overlooks. This rigid code is far from being all-embracing in its compulsions, for in

this age of great cities, the isolation of every single person in his own house is as complete as if he lived in a Great Desert. What hat and what coat he shall wear, how far he shall express his opinions in mixed society, and in what manner, is settled for him by an inflexible law; but what he shall read, how he shall think, how he shall educate his children, whether or not he shall have any sort of religious creed, and take part in any kind of public worship, are questions which he is left to settle—not nominally, but practically—for himself. There probably never was a time when men who have any sort of originality and independence of character had it in their power to hold the world at arm's length so cheaply. The quit-rent which they have to pay for these privileges is not worth a thought.

The least educated part of the clergy does indeed manifest that intolerance towards opposite opinions against which Mill speaks so strongly. And it is an immensely powerful class. Moreover its influence is spreading, especially among the mercantile classes. But the same cannot be said of the lay professions or the men of independent means. These constitute a large enough proportion of society to secure a fair hearing for unorthodox social or theological views. Evidence of this is the great popularity of Buckle's *History of Civilization* which, in many respects, 'deviates fundamentally and irreconcilably from all the ordinary standards of orthodoxy'.[25]

Mill seems to be right, continues the writer in the *Saturday Review*, when he says that men are less disposed than formerly to hold heretical views. There is no doubt that philosophical and theological controversy have to a large extent vanished. But this does not mean that men no longer hold opposed opinions on these subjects. It has come to be recognized that many of the disputes which were at one time conducted so vehemently have led the contestants into a situation where the truth is now to be decided less by logical argumentation than by factual evidence. The clash between theism and atheism and, in ethics, between the upholders of conscience on the one hand and of utility on the other, are to be resolved less by logical analysis than by the fruits of empirical research—the results 'of a method in which history and criticism play a very important part'. This is the reason for the absence in the contemporary intellectual scene of dogmatic attacks upon received opinions and equally dogmatic defences of them. If, as Mill argues, fear of public opinion was the cause of the minority's silence we should expect the majority view to triumph. But this is not what has happened, since 'there is as little firing from the walls as from the trenches'. Logical controversy is just out of place at a time when, as we contend, it is widely realized that the results of current enquiries into the natural sciences, into language, and into history in all its forms, will produce results of the greatest significance for both moral philosophy and theology.[26]

One of the disputed matters in political theory is the true nature of freedom, and it is easy to dismiss this controversy, which has persisted through the whole modern phase of political thought, as a mere lexicographical disagreement and adjudicate in favour of those who conform to normal usage. But this would be to ignore the different conceptions of social policy and the divergent political goals that lie behind the war of words. It was no accident that the prevailing nineteenth-century view of liberty was a negative one, shared by philosophers like Mill and Spencer and a host of lesser figures ranging from pamphleteers to platform orators. And one of the classic expressions of this view is the essay *On Liberty*, where the term is employed in its normal sense, to mean absence of restraint. For Mill the appropriate region of human liberty comprised the 'inward domain of consciousness', the publication of opinions, and the framing of a plan of life to suit each person's character ('doing as we like'), so long as no harm was caused to others. Within this region we are to be free to do as we please and no person has a right to restrain us, by law or opinion. Now, it is well known that liberty was conceived in a different manner by a number of nineteenth-century thinkers, especially Green and

the Idealist School, writing in what Dicey has called the collec-
tivist phase of the Victorian era. What is more interesting is
that some of Mill's contemporary critics took a similar stand
and repudiated the central doctrine of the essay precisely
because it rested on a merely negative view of freedom. In its
deepest sense, says the *National Review*, liberty means more
than just absence of restraint. It has a positive signficance into
which enters the idea of individual conduct being influenced by
social or national thought.[27] And for the *London Review*, too,
Mill's conception is too narrow, because it seeks to keep society
at bay. It implies a rigid limitation of the sphere of government,
but the state is no mere umpire of society, maintaining a strictly
negative and neutral character. There may be men of high
character on whom the feeling of responsibility to society is a
needless restraint, but to the average man it is a necessary safeguard which we dare not weaken. Are we to regard the state as
only entitled to *punish* wrongdoers and having no right to *prevent*
crime?[28]

The *Southern Review* insists that there is no conflict between
liberty and authority as Mill imagines there to be.[29] It claims
that liberty instead of being abridged is rather introduced and
established by the state. Freedom in its true sense is the highest
achievement of man. It involves the harmonious and perfect
development of the three faculties of the soul—intellect, heart
and will. This is the freedom for which all other freedoms exist:
it is a moral state characterized by 'a deliverance of the *intellect*
from the dominion of ignorance and error, of the *heart* from the
reign of evil passions and propensities, and of the will from the
galling tyranny of vicious habits'. Personal, political, or civil
freedom is subordinate to it and even political despotism is legitimate if it serves to promote this moral freedom.[30] Hence
slavery may be, in certain circumstances, one of the means or
methods of freedom. And does not Mill admit this when he
allows despotism to be 'a legitimate mode of government in
dealing with barbarians, provided the end be their improvement . . .'?[31] But when it comes to modern communities Mill
adopts an entirely different principle—the sovereignty of the
individual ('Over himself, over his own body and mind, the
individual is sovereign'). The definition of liberty implicit in
this principle is wrong because it looks upon freedom as pursu-

ing our own good in our own way. This is not liberty, but license. Montesquieu was near the truth when he pronounced liberty to be the power of doing all that we ought to be allowed to do. Man may have the *power* but he certainly does not have the *right* to pursue his happiness in his own way: we should be free to do only what we *ought* to do. It is remarkable that Mill cannot see this, since it is really a corollary of the greatest happiness principle itself in that the common good may require the individual to do what he, personally, might not wish to do. What, for example, is to happen to the individual's sovereignty if he does not want to serve in the army? The fact is that Mill, despite his apparent adherence to utilitarianism ('mankind are greater gainers by suffering each other to live as seems good to themselves'), is attempting to limit the authority of society over the individual by recourse to what is really a doctrine of abstract rights.[32]

The object of this Essay [says Mill] is to assert one very simple principle, as entitled to govern absolutely the dealings of society with the individual in the way of compulsion and control, whether the means used be physical force in the form of legal penalties, or the moral coercion of public opinion. That principle is, that the sole end for which mankind are warranted, individually or collectively, in interfering with the liberty of action of any of their number, is self-protection. . . . The only part of the conduct of any one, for which he is amenable to society, is that which concerns others.[33]

A writer in *Fraser's Magazine* is satisfied that the principle gives 'approximately accurate results' and succeeds in dividing fairly 'the legitimate from the illegitimate objects of state interference'.[34] And another writer in *Meliora*, though doubtful about the application of the principle which Mill makes in some cases, is content with the principle itself.[35] But this is quite definitely a minority view. For the bulk of the reviewers the 'one very simple principle' is the main and decisive weakness of the essay: it will not work and it is based on a distinction between self-regarding actions and actions affecting others which cannot in fact be sustained. When Mill says that the only purpose for which power can be rightfully exercised over a member of a civilized community against his will is to prevent harm to others, how, asks Mr Joseph Parker, are we to understand the phrase 'prevent harm to others'? What sort of 'harm'? *Moral* harm, *physical* harm, or both? People disagree very considerably as to what constitutes 'harm'. Some moral reformers would argue that a man is doing harm to others by getting drunk. Mill, on the other hand, does not want us to interfere with mere drunkenness. Clearly a great deal here turns on the word 'harm', so it behoves us to assign a specific meaning to this very wide term. What, for example, would Mill say about the prevention of suicide? Would his doctrine, that the sole end for which interference is justified is self-protection, entitle us to stop a man from killing himself? It is unquestionably an immoral act, and for that very reason may it not be 'harmful'? Further, Mill says that the liberty of the individual must thus far be limited, he must not make himself a nuisance to others. But can we arrive at any precise notion of 'being a nuisance'? As Mill uses it, the term is so vague as to convey no definite idea at all. It is possible to be a nuisance to other people in countless ways; as the propagator of ideas, the smoker, or the swearer in mixed company. Again, Mill thinks the state ought to compel all its members to be educated even if it means imposing fines on those parents who fail to comply with the law. If Mill is arguing that the lack of education may be the occasion of 'harm to others' how widely are we to interpret 'education'? Could we not insist on knowledge of the Ten Commandments and other moral precepts? Would coercion of this nature be ruled out by Mill's principle?[36]

The vagueness and ambiguity of the principle is also criticized by the writer in *Bentley's Quarterly Review*. He foresees endless difficulties facing anyone who sets out to demarcate the respective spheres of actions which affect others and those affecting the agent alone. The limits to these areas are far from being as clear as at first sight they might appear to be, and they cannot serve as the basis for a sweeping generalization about the legitimate extent of social control. 'What concerns the individual only' is surely the very question that needs to be discussed before making pronouncements about human liberty.[37]

Another critic, Mr George Vasey, complains that Mill is quite inconsistent in the actual formulation of the principle. Mill first tells us that in the part of his conduct which merely concerns himself the individual ought to be free from any interference, but a few paragraphs later the original version is severely qualified by these words: 'When I say only himself, I mean directly, and in the first instance; for whatever affects himself, may affect others through himself. . .'. What Mill has done, says Vasey, is to erect a principle on the basis of distinction which is later openly abandoned—all within the same chapter. The category of self-regarding actions is made to consist of conduct which is *purely* self-regarding, along with actions which are admitted to affect others, albeit indirectly.[38]

Mill's zeal for liberty, says the *London Review*, has led him completely astray. There is no conduct whose impact is confined to the agent because 'no moral quality is limited in its action to the sphere of its possessor's own history and doings'. Such defects of character as idleness and ignorance are almost as harmful to others as to the individual himself. Since all vices are, more or less, crimes it cannot be denied that 'society has an interest, over and above that of mere self-defence, in the conduct of every one of its members. . . .'.[39] The writer in *Bentley's Quarterly Review* agrees, and insists that the interests of society are far too closely involved in those of individuals to allow that clean division which Mill's theory requires. The whole essay, he continues, rests on insecure foundations because there is no appreciation of the way in which 'by natural and inevitable laws, we *do* take account of the good of others, and feel ourselves bound to look after it and promote it . . . a theory of freedom, without also a theory of mutual action and influence, is but a theory of part of the social relations of men'.[40]

Mill was quite aware of some of the objections that could be made against his theory.

The distinction here pointed out between the part of a person's life which concerns only himself, and that which concerns others, many persons will refuse to admit. How (it may be asked) can any part of the conduct of a member of society be a matter of indifference to the other members? No person is an entirely isolated being. . . .[41]

These are Mill's own words, and he goes on to meet this objection with arguments which failed to satisfy his critics. When a person so behaves as to affect others adversely, 'both through their sympathies and their interests', and violates 'a distinct and assignable obligation to any other person or persons', then, Mill urges, the case falls outside the self-regarding category. But this does not apply to the merely contingent injury 'which neither violates any specific duty to the public, nor occasions perceptible hurt to any assignable individual except himself'. Society can safely afford to bear such an inconvenience 'for the sake of the greater good of human freedom', because, among various reasons, society has had control over the training and education of its members. If any community allows delinquents to breed in its midst it has only itself to blame. Thus Mill defends himself,[42] and his critics are unmoved. In view of what Mill says about the condition of present-day society how, asks Joseph Parker, can he really argue that society is competent to give all its members the required education? How can 'a community of fools rear a generation of philosophers'?[43] Mill, says George Vasey, is guilty of a *non-sequitur.* It does not in the least follow that because society has in the past been negligent in the training of its members it must therefore tolerate the wrongdoers of the present. What an impossible position we should be in if we were to condone crimes on the ground that our fathers did not know how to bring up their children. Every society has a duty to repress crime and evil conduct no matter who is to blame for the propensities of the agents, though it must at the same time tackle the sources of delinquency by providing the appropriate education for all its members.[44]

The frankness with which Mill stated the objections to his own thesis did not disarm his critics, and nowhere was he less successful in concealing the weakness of his case than in the attempt to reconcile the self-protection principle with his moving plea for freedom of expression. For words and deeds that affect others we are accountable to society, and surely there is no clearer case of conduct affecting others than the publishing of one's opinions. This was obvious to Mill, and he tries to meet the difficulty, on the one hand, by emphasizing the importance of freedom of expression, inseparable as it is from freedom of thought, and, on the other, by appealing to the distinction between the man who perpetrates the evil deed and the one who disseminates dangerous opinions. The critics claim that

Mill's theory cannot allow such a distinction, for if society has a right and duty to protect itself—as Mill admits it has—then it is surely entitled to suppress in their early stages those views likely to endanger social stability. It would be sheer folly to wait, they say, until the danger is upon us and the evil too great to be brought under control; and that Mill refuses to countenance the literal application of his principle to mischievous opinions is proof that his case for free speech is built on other grounds.[45] One subject on which the expression of opinion is of vital consequence is religion, and most governments, with perfect justice, regard religion as the foundation of social order. If we accept this view we cannot deny governments the right of imposing penalties on atheists who seek to win adherents to their side. Mill, however, wants us to be tolerant to atheists. In this, cries the *Dublin Review* triumphantly, he is being utterly inconsistent, for the *expression* of an idea is surely an *action* and Mill's central precept is that actions prejudicial to others may be subjected to legal penalties or the deterring force of public opinion.[46] 'Liberal' claims to see the same contradiction in Mill's remarks on tyrannicide. Mill, says 'Liberal', holds that no one should be punished for instigating another to commit the crime unless there has been an actual attempt at assassination. What a thoroughly pernicious doctrine! 'Imagine a man trying to induce another to commit a murder, and then get off without any punishment, simply because, at the last moment, the intending murderer relented, or was prevented by some accident from perpetrating the deed!' Yet how can Mill deny society the right to punish such a crime when it is so obviously covered by his own doctrine of self-protection?[47]

The application of a general principle to specific questions is notoriously a difficult task, and it is one which Mill attempts in the final chapter of the essay, seeking, as he says, not so much to offer solutions to contemporary problems as to illustrate his doctrine (though he could scarcely have doubted that its immediate application was both possible and desirable). In the literature covered by this survey one of the most frequent charges is that Mill's practical examples are not deducible from his principle at all. Mill, says George Vasey, has failed to bring forward a single example of an action whose effects are entirely confined to the agent. All his examples are of conduct teeming with results, results which are the inevitable consequences of the actions.[48] When Mill comes to consider examples of his maxim, says another writer, he provides what turns out to be very doubtful support. One can agree or disagree with Mill's views on the subjects of Sabbatarian legislation and the Maine Liquor Law but we cannot assume to be the case, as he does, that which is the very point at issue, namely, that the activities prohibited by these enactments fall into the class of conduct he terms 'self-regarding'. Moreover, the temperance reformer's remarks, which he strongly resents, are not so absurd as Mill makes out, for if the consequences of drink are really harmful then he has something of a case in claiming protection against the liquor trade.[49] In *Meliora*, too, the writer is disturbed by Mill's attitude to the sale of intoxicating drinks, the more so since he approves of Mill's general doctrine. He fears that the essay *On Liberty* will become a dangerous weapon in the hands of the free traders in alcohol. His argument follows the familiar pattern. Strong drink has a definite tendency to create conditions of insecurity, so prohibition is justified on the ground that society must safeguard the liberty and property of its members; and, since the sale of alcohol undermines people's intelligence and self-control, and contributes to the increase of crime and pauperism, it is impossible to deny the state's right to prevent the traffic in liquor. Indeed, such a measure would accord strictly with Mill's own dictum: 'The fact of living in society renders it indispensable that each should be bound to observe a certain line of conduct towards the rest . . . in not injuring the interests of one another . . . which, either by express legal provision or by tacit understanding, ought to be considered as rights. . . .'.[50]

A famous and much-discussed example given by Mill is of the man who is prevented in his attempt to cross a bridge known to others to be unsafe. Mill maintains that governments are entitled to prevent crimes before they are actually committed, and if the ordinary citizen saw someone about to commit a crime he could justly interfere. The same principle applies to accidents. If a person tries to cross a bridge we know to be unsafe we could seize him and turn him back 'without any real infringement of his liberty' provided there is no time to warn him of his danger, because, says Mill, 'liberty consists in doing what one desires, and he does not desire to fall into the river'.[51] 'Liberal' thinks this sort of reasoning undermines the rest of the essay, since it would sanction an amount of control over our behaviour which it is the chief purpose of the essay to denounce. What Mill is really implying in this passage, he contends, is that we may forcibly prevent a person crossing an unsafe bridge because we *know* that the bridge will not hold, something we could in fact never know for certain. If certainty in our knowledge is a precondition for interference of this nature we should never be justified in hindering others in carrying out their purposes, for none of us has the power of looking into the future. So Mill must either mean that we have the right to interfere even if the assumptions upon which we act fall short of complete certainty or he intends to confine interference to cases which could never occur, namely, when we can predict with absolute certainty. The latter alternative is sheer nonsense, and if we accept the former we shall be assenting to a veritable instrument of tyranny. Restrictions on the press could easily be justified in this way. A minister in a government has only to say to the newspaper editor: 'You do not desire disturbances or revolt, or to be punished for exciting such. If you have perfect liberty, these will be the inevitable consequences, therefore I shall not allow it.'[52]

The objections dealt with in the previous section all related to the principle of self-protection. But there is another sort of objection that Mill had to face. The principle might conceivably have been saved from these various attacks by suitable amendments, or a number of explanatory clauses could have been added in order to render more precise the qualifications it needed. Such measures as these would, however, prove of no avail if the possibility of discovering any general formula is itself precluded. The writer in *Bentley's Quarterly Review* suggests that not only does Mill fail to provide a clear guide for deciding between the claims of liberty and social control, but the very search for a formula of this kind is wasted energy. We must work out the problems of liberty by experience and discover the respective limits to authority and freedom by rule of thumb.[53] The *Southern Review* is even more emphatic. Mill seeks to demarcate the legitimate extent of public intervention, a project upon which many philosophers have embarked with equal confidence and just as little success. Moreover, Mill's solution to the problem is an old one, and quite false. Rousseau had already said that men should be permitted to do whatever does not cause harm to others. Although stated in different words Mill's principle amounts to no more than that, surely one of the most stale commonplaces of political philosophy. Mill makes the mistake of wanting one final answer to this question, one solution to serve for all ages and all places. But this cannot be had. Any claim to have found it can easily be shown to be unfounded, for the truth is that a search of this nature is a wild-goose chase. Sensible men as they were, the legislators of 1787 [the framing of the American constitution] recognized that the solution to the problem must depend on the particular circumstances of the time. If only Mill had followed up a suggestion made in his own work on *Representative Government*, where he maintains that a despotic form of government is the most appropriate for some peoples because 'institutions need to be radically different, according to the stage of advancement already reached', he would surely have abandoned the attempt to legislate in universal terms.[54]

Mill's doctrine of utility differed from the Benthamite version he learned from his father in at least one vital respect, namely, the overwhelming importance which he attached to 'human development in its richest diversity'. There were some critics who objected to what they considered an excessive concern for the fulfilment of individual personality on the ground that it would either weaken the social bond by encouraging contempt for the current standards of morality or promote a merely superficial eccentricity. Others denied that the means urged by Mill would succeed in attaining the end he desired. Mill, says the *National Review*, seeks to prevent public censure of all actions of a self-regarding nature, to 'emasculate public opinion, in order to remove one principal stumbling-block in the way of those who tremble to assert their own individual convictions in the face of that terrible tribunal'. In the past, however, strong individual characters emerged from the working of a powerful class opinion with its ideals of personal excellence, when there was a greater and more severe criticism of individual conduct than exists at present. The effect of Mill's plea for social indifference to individual behaviour must surely be not more vitality but mere apathy. 'Personal morality, once conscious that society has suspended its judgment, will grow up as colourless as a flower excluded from the light.' If it is Mill's purpose to foster distinctive types of character then he would do better to turn his attention to *improving* the judgements of society, by curing them of their one-sidedness, rather than by suspending them altogether.[55]

'L. S.', too, doubts whether independent and vigorous characters would be favoured if there were general unconcern about lazy and drunken habits of behaviour. Are not, he asks, the self-regarding virtues just as important to social well-being as those virtues which directly impinge on others? Would not a general indolence do as much damage as a general brutality? To expect men to become more vigorous 'by simply removing restrictions, seems to be as fallacious as the hope that a bush planted in an open field would naturally develop into a forest tree'.[56]

The manner in which Mill would have met these criticisms can be judged from his attempt to distinguish between the sorts of penalty to be visited for conduct harmful to others and actions of a self-regarding nature. In the first type of case we have a right to control the offender and we may feel it necessary 'to make him uncomfortable', but in the second we must confine ourselves to expressing 'our distaste', or to standing aloof from him. But 'L. S.' is not convinced. He does not think it possible to hate a particular manifestation of a bad quality without also hating the quality in which it is rooted. Yet Mill would have us pity the person who habitually gets drunk in his private room and express anger and resentment if he is a soldier on duty.[57] Fitzjames Stephen was later to make the same kind of point when he doubted whether there was any difference in principle between the, in Mill's words, 'inconveniences which are strictly inseparable from the unfavourable judgment of others' and similar ones defined and inflicted as part of a legal process.

This organization, definition, and procedure [Stephen argued] make all the difference between the restraints which Mr Mill would permit and the restraints to which he objects. I cannot see on what the distinction rests. I cannot understand why it must always be wrong to punish it by the infliction of those consequences which are strictly inseparable from the unfavourable judgment of others.'[58]

It is the moving plea for liberty of thought and expression in the second chapter of the essay that has most impressed readers of *On Liberty*, and it is sometimes said that the principle of self-protection might be completely discarded without impugning the great value of what is undoubtedly the finest modern statement of the liberal ideal of human freedom. It is of this section of the work that one reviewer says, 'since the *Areopagitica* of Milton, our language has produced no nobler or more eloquent vindication of the right of free discussion . . .'.[59] Yet much of Mill's argument here was assailed as vigorously as any part of the essay. Mill, it will be remembered, denies the right of any government or of public opinion to control the expression of opinion on the ground that any such coercion 'is robbing the human race; posterity as well as the existing generation; those who dissent from the opinion, still more than those who hold it'. If the opinion is true, the suppression of it prevents us from learning the truth: if it is false, we are denied something equally important, namely, 'the clearer perception and livelier impression of truth, produced by its collision with error'. And, of course, we can never be certain that the opinion we try to suppress is false. Any attempt to stop others deciding the question for themselves is to equate our own conviction with *absolute* certainty. 'All silencing of discussion is an assumption of infallibility.'

This conclusion does not frighten one writer, who boldly refuses to deprecate all who assume themselves to be infallible. No one should be condemned for believing it to be absolutely true that the three angles of any rectilineal triangle are equal to two right angles and no man is to be blamed for 'assuming himself to be infallible in asserting the existence of God', for there are truths, besides mathematical truths, of which we can be completely sure. Further, when Mill says that we ought not to decide the question for others he is confusing the issue, since we can assume our belief to be absolutely true without committing others to it. There is an important difference between stifling an opinion opposed to our own and being sure that the opinion is false.[60]

Another of Mill's reasons for advocating freedom of expression is that even if we could be sure of the entire truth of our opinions it would still be desirable for them to be vigorously and earnestly contested', otherwise they would come to be held as mere prejudices, with no understanding of the reasons which make them true. But, says Joseph Parker, this is assuming that the degree of conviction with which we hold our opinions depends on the amount of opposition they encounter, and this is surely false. There is no reason to think that, because controversy develops excitement, unanimity would paralyse conviction. Men have hitherto spent so much time and energy counteracting error that they have had but little chance of showing how they would behave if controversies were all to be settled.[61] 'L. S.', too, is certain that mere controversy is no index to conviction. The man with the most confidence in his opinion is little moved by the fact that others think differently. That two plus two equals four is probably believed more strongly than any doctrine subject to genuine controversy. It is thus important to distinguish the strength of an opinion from the enthusiasm it generates: the strength, *ceteris paribus*, increases with the number of people holding it, but the enthusiasm grows in proportion to the size of the opposition.[62] Disagreement of a different kind is expressed by the *Dublin University Magazine*, which claims that the contradiction of one's beliefs does not necessarily fortify them. Although 'hardy plants be all the hardier for the nip of frost . . . there be plants, not worthless, which the nip of frost kills outright'.[63]

The mass of people, Mill complains—even 'ninety-nine in a hundred of what are called educated men'—have no real understanding of their own beliefs. They have never considered carefully what can be said against their opinions, hence they do not, 'in any proper sense of the word, know the doctrine which they themselves profess'.[64] Seeing all sides of the question is so essential to the understanding of 'moral and human subejcts' that it would be necessary to invent opponents of the accepted opinions of the day if they did not already exist. The *London Review* wonders whether this is a justified complaint, since for ordinary men the alternatives are not groundless beliefs on the one hand against considered opinions and rational beliefs on the other. It sees the real choice as between unverified convictions or no convictions at all. How many people are capable of weighing the evidence relevant to their accepted ideas? To expect the average person to question the grounds of his own convictions would merely be to bewilder him. 'We do not say that this is a noble or lofty state of mind, but it is the inevitable condition of thousands . . . the truth is, that intellectual independence, however theoretically desirable, is practically unattainable in the vast majority of cases.'[65] The writer in *Bentley's Quarterly Review* argues in the same strain. What Mill says may be perfectly appropriate for those who have the capacity and responsibility of forming opinions for themselves, but the masses would be in a desperate condition if each man had to rely on what he could think out for himself. It is as impossible as it is undesirable that men should inquire into the very foundations of their moral beliefs. Men, in general, need to take many things for granted: they cannot be always hesitating between conflicting opinions.[66] And, in any case, 'L. S.' maintains, what *can* be known is so vast that we simply have to accept nine-tenths of our beliefs on trust.[67] Nor is any great harm done when society comes down strongly on those who pretend to be original, because it usually succeeds in exposing the imposter. The conventional opinions of a society are not produced at random: there are usually good reasons for them. Without a powerful sentiment in favour of certain standards society could not survive. True, unusual views may be harshly treated and many mistakes made, but on the whole things work out well. The able few are always with us to prevent stagnation and to ensure improvement. And in England, at least, this intellectual élite does have the necessary freedom to perform its function. Some hostility to new opinions is unavoidable, indeed, in many cases, highly desirable; because in the long run an argument, if it is sound, will carry the day. Men cannot afford to be the victims of every change of weather in the intellectual climate. The real absurdity lies rather in treating all opinions as if every man were an original thinker, since it presupposes a society in which men do not think and feel together, without common principles, stable beliefs, and accepted norms of conduct. Moreover, has not Mill himself written elsewhere in persuasive terms of the importance of *national* character, of the necessity for a common sense of allegiance to some fundamental principle and a strong bond of cohesion among the members of each national community?[68] Here, in the essay *On Liberty*, he takes too little account of the needs of society. He fails to draw that vital line 'between questions which are open to the schools, and those which society must close or go to pieces'. It is far from obvious that men were happy in those days 'when the rage of free discussion of difficult questions invaded those who were manifestly unfit for it . . . when the mysteries of freewill and grace were the daily subject of metaphysical wrangles at the tables of hard-headed Puritans'.

For Mill's proposal that we should invent counter-arguments to the prevailing opinions when they are insufficiently contested the *Dublin University Magazine* has nothing but contempt.

Toleration of devil's advocates [the writer exclaims] is a different thing from institution of them. Would Mr Mill conceive it to be advantageous to the formation of his maid-servant's enlightened opinion upon the excellence of chastity, that she should be invited to spend her Sunday afternoon in earnest controversy upon the matter with a profligate dragoon from Kensington barracks . . . ?[69]

Many of Mill's readers were antagonized by his citing of Christianity as an example of a creed which had become little more than a formal profession of faith due to the lack of free and vigorous discussion of its tenets. Unless it is constantly and energetically criticized, contends Mill, even the noblest belief will degenerate into a prejudice, held 'with little comprehension or feeling of its rational grounds'. The meaning of the doctrine will be either lost or seriously weakened, with no practical influence on human behaviour. Thus Christianity has fallen into decay, and not one Christian in a thousand 'guides or tests his individual conduct by reference to . . . the maxims and precepts contained in the New Testament'. Mill also gave offence when he referred to Christian morality as a negative rather than a positive code, with the emphasis on 'thou shalt not' rather than 'thou shalt'; and when he claimed that the Calvinistic version of Christianity did not consider the decline of individual spontaneity to be an undesirable feature of civilized life. For Calvinism, declared Mill, the suppression of human capacities is no great evil.[70]

All this, as one should expect, provoked a chorus of indignant protest, so much so that if vehemence and volume were to be accepted as the criteria of importance we should have to devote more space to this topic than to any other single question. But it can be dealt with quite briefly. Mill's representation of Calvinism, it is asserted, is a sheer caricature. Why, in giving an altogether false estimate of Christian morality, should Mill choose Calvinism as the paradigm of Christianity? Another claims that Mill's appraisal of the social influence of Calvinism is patently false. Calvinism, so far from suppressing energetic individual behaviour, is

notoriously the creed of the most vigorous and least submissive nations in the world. A theory must be strangely wrong which proves that the Scotch in the seventeenth century ought to have been a slavish pusillanimous people, with no marked characters amongst them . . . if it were possible to effect a detailed comparison between families in which what Mr Mill describes as 'Calvinism' does and does not prevail, it would be found that, *ceteris paribus*, the former had a larger share of originality of character than the latter.[71]

The *Dublin Review* asks what Mill has to offer in place of the Christianity he assails. It alleges that he has nothing better to propose than a 'return to the hopeless Eleatic scepticism'. According to Mill an *approach* to truth is the best we can hope for; but if he is so sure that certain knowledge is unattainable why should he delude his readers with talk about principles, rights, truth, and utility? He should have started his essay with a frank declaration that his whole system is a mere guess, that he really *knows* nothing of what he is about to write. And as to the arguments he deploys in the essay itself, the briefest examination is enough to suggest that they rest on no solid foundation. Take first his maxim that we ought not to interfere with any action unless it causes harm to others. This would seem to be an important principle, but we are later told that utility is the ultimate appeal on all ethical questions and that this utility is itself founded on the permanent interests of man as a progressive being. So what do we have? An ultimate appeal based on something as unsubstantial as 'permanent interests', which are never explained in any greater detail than that they are themselves derived from the progressive character of human nature. The structure of Mill's doctrine therefore turns out to be this: we begin with a very simple principle, which is to govern *absolutely* the dealings of society with the individual, resting on the vague notion of utility, itself deduced from 'permanent interests'—an even vaguer concept—but in turn based on a knowledge of human nature. That this last idea must be thoroughly vague follows from Mill's own assertion that we can never be sure an opinion is false. Thus, when subjected to close scrutiny the whole theory is revealed as unintelligible, and we do not shrink from admitting

our inability to understand this fabric without a basis, this lever without a fulcrum, this progress from no starting-place and towards no goal, this knowledge begotten of doubt, this logic without premisses and without conclusion, or rather let us say, this ocean of hypothetical propositions which yields before us and closes behind us, as though the whole intellectual life and activity of man were one infinite and eternal If.[72]

Historians of English political thought have often contrasted the individualistic premises of the early Utilitarians with the conception of society as an interdependent whole characteristic of Green and the Idealists, and Mill is commonly represented as an interlude between these two types and phases of liberal theory, breaking away from, but never completely shaking off, the narrow Benthamite view of the relation between the individual and the community. Thus Sir Ernest Barker writes of Mill: he was 'the prophet of an empty liberty and an abstract individual . . . he had no clear idea of that social whole in whose realization the false antithesis of "state" and "individual" disappeared'.[73] So it was left for Green to complete the revision of the foundations of liberalism hinted at in Mill, with a more realistic account of the social process and the individual's place in it. From this familiar account of the significance of Mill's social philosophy it might be inferred that the understanding of social relations implicit in the essay *On Liberty* passed unchallenged by Mill's contemporaries.[74] No such conclusion is warranted. On the contrary, the burden of a good deal of the early criticism is precisely that Mill carries individualism to excess and in so doing is committed to a false judgement of the respective spheres of authority and freedom.[75]

Mill, says the *National Review*, thinks of society as a mere aggregate of independent units, a profoundly mistaken view because there is a common life and a common conscience in society. To shut the individual up in a private sphere, from which social life is to be jealously excluded, would be fatal to that very development of individuality which Mill so forcefully advocates. What Mill lacks is the insight which reveals any national society as essentially organic in nature.

An aggregate of individually free minds, if they are to be held asunder from natural social combinations by the stiff framework of such a doctrine as Mr Mill's, would not make in any true or deep sense a free society or a free nation . . . [for] if it be in reality a far truer mode of thinking to conceive individuals as members of a society, rather than society as pieced together of individuals, it is certain that true liberty demands for the deepest forms of social thought and life as free and characteristic an expression as it demands for the deepest forms of individual thought and life.

Mill's remedy for social intolerance is 'to erect, by common consent, every individual mind into an impregnable and independent fortress, within the walls of which social authority shall have no jurisdiction'. It could only succeed at the cost of that social unity and cohesion which is alone responsible for the diversity of individual character developing through contact with other characters. How could the moral and intellectual experience of society be enriched if its constituents are excluded from living relationships with each other? It is not surprising that from this false individualist premiss Mill is led to consider those who break the moral rules of a society as mere *invaders* of that society from *outside*, and to estimate their guilt in terms of the harm caused to *others*, thus artificially separating the consequences of their actions from their own developing personalities. Individuals who flout the moral authority of society are none the less parts of the social organism. They are rebels, not invaders. It is from a fear of a monotonous uniformity of behaviour that Mill recommends his self-protection doctrine and wishes to impose a vow of complete silence on public opinion in all matters touching the individual alone; but the individual will become nothing more than a loose atom of eccentricity if he is not made to feel and acknowledge the influence of the common life in society. 'Society has, and ought to have, a common life, which sends its pulses through every individual soul.'[76]

In his zeal to encourage originality and spontaneity, insists another critic, Mill supposes the entire argument to lie wholly on one side and overlooks the value of restraints; whereas in the realm of moral conduct the influence of collective opinion is in general beneficial. Individuals gain more in happiness and worthiness than they lose, 'by subjecting themselves to the moral standard of an ordinarily enlightened and civilized community'. Moreover, concerned as he is to foster variety of character Mill is in danger of encouraging a merely frivolous eccentricity. Proper individuality must never be confused with eccentricity.[77]

IV

Modern Critics

I

IT is easy to see how someone familiar with the story of Mill's intellectual development as told in the *Autobiography* could be tempted into formulating a thesis of 'two Mills'. And, without using precisely this expression, quite a number of studies of Mill's thought have taken the view that his philosophy is composed of ingredients that cannot be fitted together into a coherent whole. On the other hand, if there are to be as many Mills as there are components in his mature philosophy which it is difficult to reconcile with each other it may be more appropriate to talk of, say, five or seven Mills rather than just two. The case for limiting the number to two would be that before his 'mental crisis' he adhered to a system of beliefs taught him by his father and that he then went on to absorb various currents of thought which he tried to accommodate within the inherited framework. The tussle between the old and the new is reflected throughout his mature writings in tensions and conflicts which derive from the attempt to combine two incompatible philosophical positions.

It needs to be said, however, that Mill himself did not see the matter like that. He believed he had managed to produce a coherent synthesis, for he records in the *Autobiography*:

I found the fabric of my old and taught opinions giving way in many fresh places, and I never allowed it to fall to pieces, but was incessantly occupied in weaving it anew.[1]

Moreover some of the most distinguished of Mill scholars have accepted that verdict and the most notable attempt to show in detail the underlying unity of Mill's thought, John M. Robson's *The Improvement of Mankind*, is an important challenge to all those who wish to advance the thesis of two (or more) Mills.

This section first appeared as 'The Thesis of the Two Mills' in *Political Studies*, Vol. XXV, No. 3, 1977.

Nevertheless, the thesis continues to be asserted and three books which have appeared in recent years are concerned with the conflicts in, rather than the unity of, Mill's thought. Two of them have Mill as their principal subject and the third draws inspiration from him in a sustained attack on certain influential trends in the philosophy of science. I refer to Gertrude Himmelfarb's *On Liberty and Liberalism*, Bruce Mazlish's *James and John Stuart Mill*, and Paul Feyerabend's *Against Method*. [2]

Mazlish covers much wider ground than Himmelfarb and Feyerabend in an effort to show how Mill's thought can in some sense be illuminated or explained in terms of a father–son conflict. Central to his argument is a psychoanalytic interpretation of the mental crisis and the claim that Mill's ready assimilation of new currents of thought corresponded with a need to assert his independence of a father who had dominated his life, emotionally and intellectually, up to that time. I do not wish to enter here into the controversial question whether psycho-history can add to the knowledge supplied by the conventional historian of ideas, but it is important to notice that the tensions and conflicts in Mill's philosophy for which Mazlish seeks to offer an explanation had already been thoroughly charted in the considerable body of scholarly literature that now exists on Mill. I shall restrict myself to two of the many examples that could be cited.

The first is Charles Douglas's book, *John Stuart Mill* (1895), written very much in the spirit of English Idealism. [3] One important aspect of this philosophical tendency was the comprehensive assault it launched on some major doctrines of the Utilitarians, especially their epistemology and ethics. Mill was therefore one of their principal targets, but it was recognized, particularly by Green, that Mill's movement away from raw Benthamism brought him, on some issues at least, close to the philosophy of the Idealists. All this is reflected in Douglas's study.

Mill, says Douglas, was an individualist in both his epistemology and his ethics. This was his inheritance and serves to place him emphatically within the tradition of British empiricism. Yet his philosophy 'contains elements that are almost explicitly at variance with his inherited creed'. [4] These elements manifest themselves in a number of important themes 'which are idealistic in spirit and temper' and hence incompatible with empiricism.[5] But Mill never recast his theory of knowledge in order to accommodate these ideas. In places he gives an account of social life and the role of moral principles in it which assumes an individual self made up of more than 'transient states of consciousness'; and his attachment to a conception of individual worth takes him beyond Benthamite hedonism. In this sense, Douglas is saying, there were two sides to Mill's philosophy; or, as some would prefer to say, 'two Mills'.

My second example is R. P. Anschutz's *The Philosophy of J. S. Mill* which appeared in 1953.[6] Here, probably better than anywhere else, we find the case argued that Mill's philosophy contains incompatible elements. All Mill's theories, claims Anschutz, 'are extremely complex and unstable structures, prone to fall to pieces at the first inconvenient question'. He is a romantic

in the eagerness with which he seeks out and endeavours to assimilate every last exotic line of thought which shows any signs of vitality. . . . Somewhere or other in his writings you can discern traces of every wind that blew in the early nineteenth century.[7]

Whereas Mill seemed confident that he had kept the fabric of his opinions intact after the absorption of new ideas, Anschutz contends that in the process of 'weaving it anew' he failed to harmonize the materials into a coherent whole. The root of the inconsistencies in Mill's thought, according to Anschutz, lies in the conflict between two views of human nature which are expressed in different parts of his philosophy. Mill's writings, he says, are 'spotted with reminders of the inconsistency between these two views of man'; and the conflict is illustrated in Mill's treatment of the free-will *versus* determinism problem.

Given the universal law of causation it follows that every person's character is shaped by circumstances. Human behaviour is thus determined by the 'causes called motives according to as strict laws as those which exist in the world of mere matter'.[8] On this view, claims Anschutz, a human being cannot possess any more individuality than a physical object. But Mill also believes that every man has, 'to a certain extent', a power of altering his own character and this commits him to seeing man as something quite different from a physical object whose behaviour can be explained simply and entirely by the principle of the composition of physical forces. Mill's exposition of the naturalistic or scientific view of man is to be found mainly in the *Logic*; the romantic or self-formative view can be found, among other places, in the *Liberty*.

It is worth pausing for a moment to consider whether what Anschutz alleges to be an incompatibility does not depend on a particular viewpoint in the ongoing debate over 'reasons and causes' and the problem of free-will. There are philosophers who maintain that Mill's belief in a power to shape our own characters, 'if we wish', is consistent with an acceptance of the universal law of causation; just as there are those who would argue that the assimilation of motives and intentions to causes does not preclude the possibility of giving an account of human actions which allows for what is distinctive in individual personality, e.g. its capacity for decision and moral choice. In the same sort of way it has been said that Mill was both an élitist and a democrat, and that the confusions in his political thought derive from the attempt to combine incompatible doctrines. But here again it may be that what are taken to be mutually exclusive doctrines rest on a disputable view as to the nature of democracy. Perhaps there can be a form of democratic theory which embodies élitist tendencies. If, therefore, we try to construct a 'two Mills' thesis out of the supposed conflicts highlighted by Anschutz we leave ourselves open to the reply that given a different set of philosophical assumptions the conflicts disappear. I do not mean to claim that Mill's thought is free of tensions and conflicts, but only to emphasize that the criteria in terms of which they are identified may not all receive universal assent. And to be fair to Anschutz, he says in the very last paragraph of his book that the issue over which Mill struggled to combine a naturalistic view of man with a belief in self-development and individuality 'is still an open question'.

Himmelfarb is concerned with a much more restricted range of Mill's thought than Anschutz, Douglas, or Mazlish. The case she puts forward is a fully elaborated version of a thesis she advanced over ten years earlier in the introduction to a collection of Mill's writings entitled, *Essays on Politics and Culture*, where she said:

John Stuart Mill is thought of today as the archetype of the liberal, the author of that classic of liberalism, *On Liberty*. But there is another John Stuart Mill, who wrote in quite a different vein and was anything but the perfect liberal. The drama of Mill's life was the alternation of these two Mills.[9]

There are some interesting differences between the two versions of the thesis which it would be beyond the scope of this chapter to discuss in detail, but one or two points ought to be brought out because they have a bearing on the validity of the later version. In 1962 the contrast betwen the Mill of *On Liberty* and the 'other Mill' is made to depend mainly on certain important differences between what Mill says in the well-known essay and the group of articles written in the period 1836–40 which are included in Himmelfarb's collection, i.e. 'Civilization', 'Bentham', 'Coleridge', and two articles on Tocqueville. These essays, says Himmelfarb, represent 'his most imaginative, independent, and spirited work'. After 1840 Mill's work reflected increasingly the influence of Harriet Taylor—he was 'dominated' by her—and the chief products of that period (up to Harriet's death in November 1858), *Utilitarianism, Political Economy*, and *On Liberty*, are grouped together as the output of their partnership. Now this periodization suggests that these three major works whilst not covering the same ground, would at least be in harmony with each other and that where there is important common ground they would express a uniform outlook. And it implies that the revisions to *Utilitarianism* and *Political Economy* which were made after Harriet's death would manifest the new phase that Mill is then said to have entered. The 1974 version, however, broadens the scope of 'the other Mill' to take in *most* of his other writings, among them *Utilitarianism* and *Political Economy*, and the passages from the former which are set against the *Liberty* do not appear only in the later, revised, editions. But more of this presently. The 1974 version also adds substance to 'the other Mill' by specifying what makes him 'other' and identifying the tradition to which he belongs, i.e. 'the tradition of Montesquieu, Burke, the Founding Fathers, and Tocqueville'. Himmelfarb goes on:

It is a tradition that is eminently modern and yet resonant of classical thought. It is also a genuinely liberal tradition, although its liberalism is very different from that of *On Liberty*. It does not belittle the importance of liberty; on the contrary, one of its purposes is to make liberty more secure by buttressing it with other principles essential to a good life and a good society. If it denies the absoluteness of liberty, it does so to ensure the integrity and viability of liberty. It is a temperate, humane, and capacious liberalism, a philosophy that can accommodate liberty together with such other values as justice, virtue, community, tradition, prudence, and moderation.[10]

This is central to the 1974 version of the 'two Mills' thesis, the 'absolute' nature of liberty advocated in *On Liberty* to the detriment of other values and their moderating effect. Moreover, this is the kind of liberty championed by the modern liberal which leads to the harmful results catalogued in the later section of the book in matters relating to censorship and pornography. And it is this feature of her argument with which I shall be mainly concerned.

Himmelfarb's opening attack on the Mill of *On Liberty* is nicely calculated to appeal to an audience distrustful of 'the one true principle' approach to moral and social questions, whether made so by the repeated and calamitous failures of the messianic left or by the refinements of modern analytic philosophy. She quotes the remark in the *Autobiography* in which *On Liberty* is described as 'a kind of philosophic text book of a single truth' and then the passage in the first chapter of *On Liberty* where Mill states the purpose of the essay as being 'to assert one very simple principle' to govern 'absolutely' the way that society exercises control over the individual. And it strikes her as 'remarkable' that one could entertain the idea that all 'the dealings of society with the individual in the way of compulsion and control' can be subject to a principle which is 'single', 'simple', and 'absolute'. 'Remarkable' both because anyone who is sensitive to the complex realities of social life would recoil from the suggestion that they could properly be regulated by such a principle and because Mill had shown himself to be fully aware of the dangers of basing 'an entire philosophy upon a single principle'.

Now when the charge is put in this general form I fancy it will strike a responsive chord in many of Himmelfarb's readers, but it is my view that if subjected to closer scrutiny it loses much of its appeal. And this requires that we look at it in more detail. Take first the statement in the *Autobiography* about *On Liberty* being 'a kind of philosophic text-book of a single truth'. What this 'truth' is Mill explains just two lines later:

. . . the importance, to man and society, of a large variety in types of character, and of giving full freedom to human nature to expand itself in innumerable and conflicting directions.[11]

There is nothing in this passage which can rightfully be construed to mean that variety and individuality are the *only* important values. Important they certainly were for Mill, extremely important in view of what he took to be the prevailing climate of public opinion, but not exclusively so. For the freedom to cultivate individuality was to operate within certain limits (perhaps not well-defined limits), namely, such as to avoid infringing the rights and interests of others or, in its most brief form, so long as there is no 'harm' to others. Exactly what this qualification amounts to has been much debated and Himmelfarb's contribution to the discussion seems to me to be very slender. This is a matter to which we shall have to return.

It was, says Himmelfarb, 'the absolute value of liberty, the absolute sovereignty of the individual, that distinguished *On Liberty* from Mill's other writings and from the liberalism of his contemporaries'.[12] For '. . . anything short of absolute liberty (except for the qualification about injury to others) was an infringement on each person's sovereignty, a denial of his individuality, an impediment to his full development as a human being . . .'.[13] Mill's principle 'governs "absolutely", and the independence of the individual is "absolute"'.[14]

It is true that in the opening statement of his doctrine Mill does say that his 'one very simple principle' is to 'govern absolutely' the relations between society and the individual 'in the way of compulsion and control'; and it is true that he goes on to assert that in matters which merely concern himself the individual's 'independence' is 'of right, absolute', that 'over himself, over his own body and mind, the individual is sovereign'. But one crucial question here is what difference it makes to this 'absolute' principle that Mill should have insisted on the 'qualification' which Himmelfarb puts in parenthesis. However, we need first to consider the sense, or senses, in which Mill's principle may be said to be 'absolute'. Himmelfarb uses

'absolute' or 'absolutely' in relation to the principle in more
than one way and this could well lead to confusion. It could, for
instance, serve to conceal the important difference between
saying that a principle to regulate liberty is to be applied 'absolutely' and saying that the liberty itself should be 'absolute'.
For it certainly does not follow from the fact that a principle is
to regulate liberty 'absolutely' that the liberty it allows is 'absolute', i.e. in the sense of being completely unrestricted. Indeed,
would there be any point to a principle which is to regulate
liberty if it did not restrict it? Which, of course, is not to deny
that the nature and extent of the restriction is vital. If a principle, to be applied 'absolutely', left very *little* liberty, would
Himmelfarb still wish to talk of 'absolute liberty'? The expression she sometimes uses—'the absolute nature of the principle
of liberty'[15]—therefore contains an ambiguity. Is it because the
principle is to be applied without exceptions, in all circumstances, that we say it is 'absolute'? Or is it on account of
the extent of the liberty it secures? Himmelfarb also talks of the
'absolute value of liberty' and this phrase seems to convey the
suggestion that Mill put liberty at the very top of his scale of
values, that all other values were subordinate to it. But this
hardly squares with her admission that causing 'harm' or 'injury' to others can justify the restriction of liberty, especially if
we take account of what Mill intended to cover by these terms.

In her discussion of what sorts of restrictions on 'absolute'
freedom were imposed by the notion of 'harmful' or 'injurious'
conduct Himmelfarb says at one point that although Mill's
language is vague and imprecise his general intention was to
confine the limitation to physical and material rather than
moral or spiritual harm. This makes it sound as if an action
would not be counted as harmful unless it threatened to, or
actually did, result in physical damage. But there is too much
in *On Liberty* (and elsewhere) which goes against this suggestion
for it to be taken seriously. For example, when she is discussing
Chapter 4 of *On Liberty* Himmelfarb has to record that the
notions of 'rights' and 'interests' are stated to be constitutive of
the restrictions placed on freedom of action; and these certainly
cannot be defined in purely physical or material terms nor
limited to cases where material possessions or physical injury
are involved. What is most lacking, however, in her treatment

of this problem, crucial for the interpretation of Mill's principle of liberty, is any sign of recognition of how Mill's discussion of 'harm', 'rights', and 'interests' in *On Liberty* is related to what he says about these concepts in the final chapter of *Utilitarianism*. This is particularly damaging to her thesis of 'two Mills' when it is realized that the discussion takes place in the course of an analysis of 'justice'—a value which, she claims, is either belittled or neglected by the Mill of *On Liberty*. When she does invoke *Utilitarianism* it is in order to underline the contrast between the 'two Mills'. Thus, after pointing to certain passages in it which strike her as being in conflict with *On Liberty*, she concludes:

> The primary goods in *Utilitarianism* were morality and a sense of unity; the primary goods in *On Liberty* were liberty and individuality.[16]

We have already noticed how in the 1962 version of the 'two Mills' thesis *Utilitarianism*, along with *Political Economy* and *On Liberty*, were grouped together as works produced during the period of Harriet's greatest influence. *Utilitarianism* was first published in 1861, i.e. after Harriet's death, but Mill had written essays on Justice and Utility when she was still alive. These were embodied in one 'little manuscript treatise' soon after her death and thoroughly revised in 1860. If one wanted to stick to the 1962 version one would have to contend that the passages in *Utilitarianism* which are held to be out of accord with *On Liberty* were introduced by Mill in 1860 when he is supposed to have entered 'a new phase'. So far as I know we do not have the evidence which might substantiate such a contention. Hence we are left with the claim made in the 1974 version that the published text of *Utilitarianism* contains passages which conflict with *On Liberty* and thus represent 'the other Mill', but the passages which Himmelfarb cites do not seem to me to be capable of bearing the weight she wants to put on them.

Himmelfarb thinks the distinction between self-regarding and other-regarding actions is undermined by 'the other Mill' when he says in the *Logic* (Book VI, Chapter IX) that 'there is no social phenomenon which is not more or less influenced by every other part of the condition of the same society'. And she believes it is undermined in a similar way in *Utilitarianism* by the account Mill gives of 'the social feelings of mankind' which produce a sense of unity among the members of a society such that each person comes to see the interests of others as his own. By means of 'laws and social arrangements', of 'education and opinion', this social feeling could be fortified to such an extent that every person would become possessed of the habitual motive 'to promote the general good'. In *Utilitarianism*, therefore, 'Mill clearly gave to society a large and positive role in the promotion of morality', whereas in *On Liberty* 'so far from seeking legal and social sanctions . . . to promote morality, to develop the social sense, Mill would have withdrawn such sanctions as currently existed (apart from those required to prevent injury)'.[17]

Himmelfarb is so anxious to present Mill as speaking with two voices in *Utilitarianism* and *On Liberty* that she fails to include among the quotations she makes from the former his remarks about Comte. After saying that this feeling of unity with one's fellows could, as Comte had shown, acquire 'the psychological power and the social efficacy of a religion', Mill immediately goes on to express the fear that it should become 'so excessive as to interfere unduly with human freedom and individuality'. This suggests that, in Mill's eyes at least, it was possible to have both a strong sense of social solidarity and respect for freedom and individuality. I am not convinced that Himmelfarb has shown Mill's belief to be groundless, far less that it must have been another Mill who wrote these passages in *Utilitarianism*.

The contrast drawn by Feyerabend is between Mill as philosopher of science and Mill as libertarian humanist or, more strictly speaking, between the *Logic* and *On Liberty*. The distinction is not made expressly in *Against Method* (1975) but what remains there as an unstated assumption is rendered explicit in an article published in the same year. ' "Mill" always means the Mill of *On Liberty*', says Feyerabend, 'not the Mill of the *Logic*: Mill was one of those rare individuals who can be persuaded by argument to completely change their point of view'.[18]

In the *Logic* Mill lays down certain rules for the conduct of scientific enquiry. There is, in other words, a 'scientific *method*'. These rules can be regarded as both descriptive and prescriptive, for they are based on the way science *has been* carried on in the past and they also stipulate how it *should* proceed in the future. Scientific method, thus understood, consists of certain canons of induction and a definite view of what constitutes a scientific explanation. This side of Mill belongs to a tendency in philosophy of science which Feyeraband sets out to criticize and which he had been attacking for years before the publication of *Against Method*. A few words about this tendency, albeit brief and oversimplified, will help set things in context.

Books on the methodology of political science, mainly but not only those written in the United States, frequently assume, when they discuss the question whether politics can be studied scientifically, that the proper model for a scientific explanation is that advocated by Hempel and Popper and widely known as the covering-law model. Now Hempel and Oppenheim, in a famous article setting out the details of the model, specifically mention Mill among those who anticipated their account and refer to a passage in book III of the *Logic* where he states the conditions of a scientific explanation.[19] This model has, of course, come under heavy fire in recent years. Not only has the claim that it is applicable to history and human actions been challenged, but its validity even in respect of the natural sciences has been impugned. Scriven, Hanson, and Achinstein are among those who have questioned its credentials, but perhaps the most radical critic of all is Feyerabend. And Mill plays a double role in the elaboration of Feyerabend's case. Most of the time he quotes him admiringly; but, as we have seen, his enthusiasm is for *On Liberty*, not the *Logic*, for it is in the latter that Mill went astray.

It is scarcely necessary to add that Feyerabend, unlike Himmelfarb and Mazlish, has not written a book about Mill. Nor has he set out to show that there is a major inconsistency in Mill's philosophy; this is only incidental to his main aim. His interest for us here is that he does claim there is a conflict between the *Logic* and *On Liberty* which, if substantiated, is clearly a matter of importance for the understanding of Mill. Moreover, if there were such a conflict it might well have a bearing on the arguments of Anschutz and Himmelfarb, who both assign a special place to *On Liberty* in Mill's thought, taking it to represent a 'romantic' phase in his intellectual development.

Feyerabend's purpose, as I have said, is to attack certain prevailing orthodoxies in the philosophy of science, particularly some dogmas of empiricism and positivism—terms which are to be construed broadly enough to include Popper. The Mill of the *Logic* stands indicted, along with Popper and others, for holding that there is a method, a set of firm and binding principles, for carrying on scientific activity. According to Feyerabend the history of science shows that there can be no such method; there is only one principle that can be defended in all circumstances and that is the principle—'Anything Goes'. It is *possible*, though, by a process of simplification to portray the history of science as if it had conformed to definite and rigid principles, 'a tradition that is held together by strict rules'. But is this *desirable*? No, says Feyerabend, because it would mean transferring to such a tradition 'the sole rights for dealing in knowledge', ruling out of court the results produced by any other method. He states two reasons for taking this stand. First, the world we seek to know is still largely unknown, so all possible roads to knowledge should be kept open. Secondly, and here he cites Mill, because such a tradition goes against the free development of human beings, 'the cultivation of individuality'. But though Mill is specifically quoted in *Against Method* in support of the second reason it is clear from the earlier version which appeared as a lengthy paper with the same title in 1970 that Feyerabend finds both reasons in favour of a 'pluralistic methodology' stated in *On Liberty*.[20] As he put it in the 1970 version, '. . . methodological and humanitarian arguments are intermixed in every part of Mill's essay, and it is on *both* grounds that a pluralistic epistemology is defended, for the natural as well as for the social sciences'.[21]

Although it is true that the principal themes of *On Liberty* are not rigidly confined to distinct chapters, nevertheless the 'methodological' argument is mainly to be found in Chapter II and the 'humanitarian' one in Chapter III. Mill's plea for freedom of thought and discussion in the second chapter rests on the contention that it is a necessary condition for attaining the truth and understanding its grounds. The case for individuality in the third chapter rests on a mixture of utilitarian and non-utilitarian considerations. There is an intrinsic value in a society of well-developed and varied human beings, 'for what more or better can be said of any condition of human affairs than that it brings human beings themselves nearer to the best thing they can be'? But it is also useful to society that there should be 'different experiments of living; that free scope should be given to varieties of character'. Now, the important question that Feyerabend raises is whether these arguments can be reconciled with the position Mill took up in the *Logic*.

In tackling this problem we need to separate the issue of whether Mill himself recognized *On Liberty* to be an abandonment of certain views in the *Logic* from the question of whether the two works are in fact at odds with each other—on certain matters at least—irrespective of how Mill saw them to be related. The way Feyerabend puts it in the Lakatos article—Mill was persuaded by argument completely to change his point of view—can well be taken to mean that Mill saw *On Liberty* as a substantial revision of the relevant parts of the *Logic*. This is, we might say, the 'surface meaning' of Feyerabend's remarks. On the other hand, in his 1970 paper Feyerabend says that Mill was 'free and inventive enough not to restrict himself to a single philosophy, but to pursue different lines of thought'[22] (a statement, incidentally, with which Anschutz and Himmelfarb would heartily agree) and this could allow for the possibility that Mill was not fully aware of the extent to which the various strands in his thought were at odds with each other. 'Not *fully* aware' because there are places where he admits that he had taken certain lines of thought too far, e.g. in reaction against his youthful Benthamism.

Let us consider first what I call the 'surface meaning' of Feyerabend's claim. What must count against it, and surely amounts to a conclusive objection, is the fact that the editions of the *Logic* which were published after *On Liberty* give no hint of a completely changed point of view. Although the *Logic* first appeared in 1843 and *On Liberty* came out in 1859—a long enough interval for Mill to have changed his mind—the former went through several editions up to a final, eighth, edition in 1872; four of these editions being later than *On Liberty*. Given that Mill took pains to see that successive editions of his major works (apart from *On Liberty*) incorporated any changes in his opinions which had taken place one would expect to find some indication of such an important shift of opinion as that which is supposed to be represented by *On Liberty*. The Toronto edition of Mill's *Collected Works* contains all the variations in the different editions of the *Logic* and it is a relatively simple task to determine the nature and extent of the revisions Mill made. They do not bear out the surface interpretation of Feyerabend's claim, so we must turn to the more interesting, and also more difficult question, namely, whether the *Logic* and the *Liberty* are in conflict.

One might be tempted to say that the two arguments from *On Liberty* to which Feyerabend appeals cannot have the same critical impact on the *Logic* because it would seem perfectly feasible to have a society of diverse and well-developed individuals sharing a common standard for validating scientific theories, whereas the principle of freedom of discussion could be applied to that standard itself, making it the subject of critical debate and hence loosening its potential rigidity. And though Feyerabend claims that the two arguments are intermixed in all parts of the essay, the claim assumes that there are *two* arguments. So we are led to enquire whether they can stand independently and whether they have equally damaging implications for the doctrines of the *Logic*.

What does Mill's idea of individuality include? As the idea is expounded in the third chapter of the *Liberty* it combines elements of Benthamite Utilitarianism with what he calls the 'Greek ideal of self-development'. Because human beings differ in their tastes, aspirations, and aptitudes they should be allowed and encouraged to follow pursuits of their own choosing. 'Individual spontaneity' is said to have 'intrinsic worth'. But there is a benefit to society in that free scope for each person facilitates 'experiments in living' which in turn enables us to adopt 'better modes of action'. Moreover, the pains and pleasures individuals experience have no uniform source, hence if each is to have his 'fair share of happiness' there must be a 'corresponding diversity in their modes of life'. At the same time, though Mill set his face against coercion as a means of inducing men to cultivate their higher faculties—there is value in doing what one has freely chosen to do—it was his view that we should strive to become the best that we have it in ourselves to be, 'to grow up to the mental, moral, and aesthetic stature of which our nature is capable'. However, it needs to be said again that whilst Mill's idea of self-development relates to 'desires' and 'impulses' as well as the 'understanding', and favours the 'energetic' and the 'original' as opposed to the 'indolent' and the 'hidebound', there must be no 'encroaching on the rights of others' or gratifying one's inclinations 'to the injury of others'; for 'to be held to rigid rules of justice for the sake of others' is not only a justifiable restriction in itself but it 'develops the feelings and capacities which have the good of others for their object.'

Feyerabend's contention that the 'methodological' and 'humanitarian' arguments in the *Liberty* are 'intermixed' surely gets support from our sketch of Mill's doctrine of individuality because that doctrine cannot be stated independently of a commitment to liberty. Being free to engage in activities, including intellectual pursuits, of one's own choosing enters as a constitutive element into the notion of self-development. And this comes out even more clearly from Mill's endorsement of von Humboldt's remark that freedom and variety of situations are two 'necessary conditions of human development'. But the question remains, how far does all this run counter to the *Logic*? Would it be fanciful to maintain that just as there must be 'rigid rules of justice' operating as a framework within which individual spontaneity can flourish, so also must there be standards in scientific enquiry which serve as criteria of success or failure in the search for knowledge? Moreover, it could be granted that we might disagree over what precisely the rules of justice are, or how they should be interpreted in specific circumstances, in the same way that we might (and do) disagree over what constitutes 'scientific method', but there are limits such that not anything can count as a rule of justice or as a scientific procedure. Might this not be the sort of relationship that obtains between the *Logic* and *On Liberty*? Perhaps we can shed further light on the problem by studying what Mill says about freedom of discussion in the second chapter of the *Liberty*.

'No one pretends', says Mill, 'that actions should be as free as opinions'. So the crucial qualification, treated as of minor importance by Himmelfarb, about respecting the rights and interests of others would therefore seem not to apply to 'opinions'. And this appears to be confirmed by the statement in the opening chapter where Mill is defining 'the appropriate region of human liberty' and declares that there should be 'absolute freedom of opinion and sentiment on all subjects'. He goes on to say that though expressing and publishing opinions 'belong to that part of the conduct of an individual which concerns other people' (is not this tantamount to saying that it is an 'action'?) it should nevertheless be similarly unrestricted because it is of almost equal importance as, and 'practically inseparable' from, 'liberty of thought'.

It is only in passing that I can record my sense of uneasiness over Mill's use of the distinction between 'actions' and 'opinions', for in the context in which he makes it he is talking about the *expression* of an opinion and it is difficult to see how that is to be marked off from an 'action' (physical movement cannot be the criterion because 'forgery' or 'obtaining by false pretences' need involve no more in the way of bodily motions than, say, the publication of defamatory statement). Of greater significance for our present concern is the problem of what Mill intended to cover by 'opinions', whether he meant to advocate complete absence of restraint on statements of any sort whatever, whether the freedom which he clearly accords to opinions on moral, political, philosophical, religious, and scientific questions is to extend to such matters as 'contempt of court', libel, official secrets, or 'invasion of privacy'. It may be difficult, perhaps impossible, to draw a precise and uncontentious line between these two 'areas', but there is nothing absurd or inconsistent in allowing freedom in the former and imposing restrictions in the latter. Freedom of discussion on the topics which figure prominently in the second chapter of the *Liberty* need not be affected by, say, legal prohibitions on what the press may publish before and during criminal trials. None of this, however, can be made to count against Feyerabend's thesis. But Mill's case for freedom of opinion may permit us to differentiate among the subjects which mainly engage his attention in *On Liberty* such that on some questions it would be artificial and pointless to encourage a variety of opinions. For instance, Mill treated the 'mathematical and physical departments of speculation' as a special category, and since they form a substantial part of the *Logic*'s terms of reference this limitation should make us hesitate to set *On Liberty* in opposition to the *Logic*.

I am therefore inclined to the view that the subjects on which Mill was anxious to encourage freedom and diversity of opinion form a limited class. I do not suggest that he wanted to impose a ban on topics outside that class but rather that he thought to stimulate discussion of them would be pointless, partly because there would be nothing to be said on the other side, partly because they were not opinions of sufficient importance, and partly because they were really not 'opinion' at all. There is a revealing remark in the passage dealing with 'doctrines' (it is no accident that this word is used so often in the second chapter of *On Liberty*) which 'share the truth between them'. He makes it clear that he is not concerned there with 'popular opinions, on subjects not palpable to sense', implying that where there is conflict on matters which can be settled by an appeal to sense experience there is only room for one 'opinion'. The subjects that receive his attention, overwhelmingly, are 'ethical doctrines and religious creeds', the question of belief in God and the 'commonly received doctrines of morality'. His ideal is an 'intellectually active people' who have no dread of 'heterodox speculation' and have not adopted a 'tacit convention that principles are not to be disputed'. His warning examples are the condemnation of Socrates, the crucifixion, the persecution of the Christians under the Roman Empire, and of 'truth put down by persecution' in the cases of Luther, Savonarola, and the Hussites. And when he comes to stress the importance of learning the grounds of one's opinions by having to defend them against objections he hastens to add that in a subject like mathematics 'there is nothing at all to be said on the wrong side of the question . . . there are no objections, and no answers to objections'. It is in subjects like morals, religion, politics, and 'social relations' that there is room for a diversity of viewpoint and where it is vital that we should put ourselves into the position of those who differ from us.

There is no support in our summary of the relevant parts of Mill's argument, so far at any rate, for a *Logic versus Liberty* thesis. But there are passages which could be interpreted as going the other way; indeed they might look as if they undermine completely what we have already quoted Mill as saying about the special character of science and mathematics. They are obviously crucial to Feyerabend's case. The first passage runs as follows:

If even the Newtonian philosophy were not permitted to be questioned, mankind could not feel as complete assurance of its truth as they now do. The beliefs which we have most warrant for have no safeguard to rest on, but a standing invitation to the whole world to prove them unfounded.

The context for this statement is indicated by the second sentence, i.e. the importance of keeping the lists open, for it is only when beliefs are always subject to scrutiny that we can hope to find, if there is one, 'a better truth'. Now it seems to me that although the passage quoted appears to jar with what Mill says later in the same chapter about 'the mathematical and physical departments of speculation' there is a perfectly reasonable way of accommodating it within the framework of the *Logic*. If Newtonian physics were challenged, how would we proceed to meet the challenge? The answer of the *Logic*, very briefly, is that if it survives the tests prescribed by the canons of induction, if it is confirmed by observation and experiment, and if its rivals fail to measure up to these standards, then our belief in its truth is well-founded. For Mill there could be no other sense to the assertion that a scientific theory was true or superior to available alternatives than that it conformed to certain principles of scientific mehod. This is an answer, of course, which Feyerabend's work in the philosophy of science claims to show is seriously inadequate, but that is not the issue here. The question is whether *On Liberty* goes back on that answer: Mill's remarks about the 'Newtonian philosophy' surely do not require that we give an affirmative answer to the question.

The other extract which might be construed to favour Feyerabend's contention occurs in the passage where Mill contrasts mathematics with controversial subjects like morals, religion, and politics. In the former there is, as we have noted, only one side to the question, which is obviously not the case in the latter. And of the natural sciences he says:

Even in natural philosophy, there is always some other explanation possible of the same facts; some geocentric theory instead of heliocentric, some phlogiston instead of oxygen; and it has to be shown why that other theory cannot be the true one: and until this is shown, and until we know how it is shown, we do not understand the grounds of our opinion.

I can see nothing here to suggest that Mill gave up the position he maintained against Whewell in the *Logic*. Although he admits there are other explanations of 'the same facts' this is consistent with holding that only one explanation is the true one and, further, that the procedure whereby we can show it to be true is set out in the *Logic*. There he agrees with Whewell (Book III, Chapter II) that different descriptions of the facts can all be true but denies Whewell's claim that this could also apply to *explanations*. If the doctrine of vortices, for instance, 'had been only a Description, it would, no doubt, have been reconcilable with the Newtonian theory', but as explanations the one 'absolutely excludes the other . . . it is impossible that both opinions can be true'.

It might be urged that despite the lack of formal contradiction or obvious conflict between any specific assertions in the *Liberty* and the doctrines of the *Logic* there is nevertheless a fundamental incompatibility between the two works and that the real strength of Feyerabend's case lies in bringing out this vital fact, namely, that it is against the whole spirit of 'keeping the lists open' to exempt mathematics and science from the critical approach which Mill calls on us to adopt toward all other spheres of intellectual enquiry. (And was there not the example of Whewell in Mill's own day to serve as a warning against the belief that scientific research can be characterized in terms of precise and agreed rules?)

But if there is a conflict of this kind it is one that appears *within* the *Liberty* rather than between the *Logic* and the *Liberty*. What is alleged to follow from the principle of keeping the lists open collides with the assertion clearly made in *On Liberty* that mathematics and physics do not, can be expected increasingly not to, manifest the diversity of opinion typical of certain other subjects. However, must it be assumed that there is a conflict? Can we not say, as Mill does, without subscribing to all the particular features of his philosophy of science, that science is a special sort of enquiry in that the conditions for declaring a scientific theory to be true differ from those obtaining in ethics, religion, and philosophy? (In his introduction to the Everyman edition of *On Liberty* Acton prefers to put it like this: 'Mill . . . distinguishes mathematical truth and error from the truths of the empirical sciences, and scientific truth generally from what is attainable in matters of religion, morality, and politics. He does not think that "true" means something different in each of these spheres, but rather that they each have a different degree of evidence or cogency.')[23] It may not be a conclusive reason of itself, but it would be a remarkable and puzzling phenomenon, were there not this difference between the subjects, that scientists in Delhi, Los Angeles, Moscow, and Tokyo should share in common a set of concepts and procedures despite the enormous variety in their cultural backgrounds, philosophies, religions, and political opinions. The idea of keeping the lists open needs to be qualified by what it is reasonable to suppose can be kept open. On the other hand, if we grant that Feyerabend is right in saying that the *Logic, or any similar type of philosophy of science*, does violence to the history of science, to the way scientific research has often been conducted—and he is on strong ground in thinking that there is much in *On Liberty* which would have us allow that he may be right—then the conclusion that follows is that the lines drawn in *On Liberty* between the various branches of knowledge were wrongly drawn and that the critical scrutiny of accepted beliefs has a wider application than Mill thought possible. Whether or not we are drawn to that conclusion will depend on how far we are prepared to go along with Feyerabend as a philosopher of science.

II

If anyone has given classic expression to the case for liberty it is surely Mill. Such is the dominant view. And even if we make full allowance for the several divergent lines of thought which he strove from about 1826 to unite into a single fabric he still emerges by common consent as the most eminent advocate of individual freedom. Over recent decades a number of writers have shown his thought to be more complex than popular myth likes to permit and to contain ingredients which are not

This section first appears as 'Was Mill for Liberty?' in *Political Studies*, vol. XIV, number 1, 1966.

ally associated with liberalism. Gertrude Himmelfarb, for example, has suggested that the drama of his life consists in the alternation of two Mills: the author of *On Liberty* and the Mill 'who wrote in quite a different vein and was anything but a perfect liberal'. But it is no part of her case that Mill always (or almost always) had leanings toward 'moral totalitarianism'; that even the plea for individuality in the essay *On Liberty* was 'designed to detract from human freedom, not to maximize it'. Mr Cowling, however, thinks a study of Mill's writings can amply substantiate such a charge.[24] Moreover, it is an accusation he believes to be based on the better-known works and not artificially derived from occasional passages of some early essays or letters and other relatively obscure pieces. In his judgement the true picture of Mill is certainly not one of an unqualified exponent of freedom; nor is it one of a thinker with two incompatible sides in constant tension with each other. Rather it is one of a single-minded 'proselytizer of genius' whose mission was to persuade man to discard Christianity and adopt the Religion of Humanity—'a peculiarly exclusive, peculiarly insinuating moral doctrine' and one which would be quite as effective as Comte's 'in proscribing large ranges of conduct'. For Mill's aim, despite appearances to the contrary, was not diversity of opinion as such but 'diversity of opinion within the limits of a rationally homogeneous, agreed, social consensus' and this means that the individuality he wanted to see flourish had to confine itself within the bounds set by his lofty yet constricting conception of happiness and under the direction of a clerisy whose claims to exercise influence were based both on their knowledge and their capacity to develop their higher feelings and sensibilities.

In support of his general charge Cowling explores in detail several aspects of Mill's thought which seem to him to be either directly or indirectly hostile to freedom. In an early work, which he never disavowed, Mill had characterized his own age as one of transition from a world in which the Church had supplied men with a widely accepted set of fundamental beliefs about the universe and their own place in it; an age which had not yet succeeded in working out a stable system of values appropriate to the state of knowledge men had reached; and an age in which there was a singular lack of concern and self-consciousness about first principles. Mill consistently looked to philosophy and sociology to do what the priesthood had done in medieval times, and regarded his own task as helping to furnish a new system of thought to supplant a long-decaying Christianity, to create a new religion, a Religion of Humanity. He believed that no society could really be healthy unless its members were bound together by a universal consensus in certain vital beliefs and values, and he relied on an intellectual élite to provide an agreed body of knowledge and principles which all rational and reflecting men would recognize as true and binding. In contrast with Comte, Mill saw the élite acquiring its position of authority by persuasion and education but, Cowling insists, he hoped it would 'succeed, without coercion or compulsion, in making the same sort of impact on society as Comte's Spiritual Power was designed to make *with* them'.

Cowling feels that Mill's assumption of a basic homogeneity among all educated and rational persons, coupled with his desire to see established an intellectual élite propounding 'a body of commanding doctrine' for all members of society, is a sure sign of authoritarian, even totalitarian, leanings. There are other features of Mill's philosophy which Cowling treats as further evidence of such leanings, but we should look first at one or two details in the argument thus far.

Cowling repeatedly refers to the beliefs and principles which Mill upheld, and wanted to see prevail generally in society, as 'binding'. At times he uses stronger language. At one point he says that Mill wished to 'impose' his doctrine of 'disinterested utilitarianism' in place of those creeds which rational criticism would cause to be discarded. He refers to Mill's religion of humanity as 'the destiny to which all men should be committed' and as 'providing rationally binding chains' which will 'free men from the arbitrary finiteness of their condition'. Perhaps without intending it, Cowling creates the impression, in the choice of such language, that Mill was prepared to see stringent measures adopted in order to secure the supremacy of his favoured principles. But as Cowling himself admits, especially when contrasting Mill's attitude with Comte's, this would be an utterly baseless charge. There are occasions when Mill too writes of the 'binding force' of moral standards, but only in the sense that such standards are felt to be obligatory. If this is all that Cowling intended to convey he could have prevented doubts from arising had he selected words and phrases less likely to generate an air of authoritarianism.

According to Cowling, Mill's scheme to secure a general consensus of beliefs and values rests heavily on universal education. Unless education were compulsory, he says, the impact of the clerisy (i.e. the intellectual élite) would not be great; Mill wished the 'spiritual consensus' to grow by '*rational* persuasion and *rational* argument based on *rational* education'. Yet he fails to inform his readers of Mill's strenuous opposition to a uniform and monolithic system of education. There is, for example, a passage in Chapter V of *On Liberty* where Mill denounces the idea that the whole or any large part of education should be in state hands. He fears that a state monopoly of education would tend to cast people in the same mould and, in so far as it was efficient, to establish a despotism over the mind. Precisely because he attached overwhelming importance to individuality and diversity in general conduct and opinions he requires that education too be diverse. Although the state should insist on certain levels of achievement in matters of fact, parents might still, if they chose, have their children 'brought up either churchmen or dissenters as they now are', since 'all attempts by the state to bias the conclusions of its citizens on disputed subjects are evil'.

Mill's central principle, Cowling maintains, is not liberty but utility, and the latter is 'less practically libertarian in implication than is often supposed'. The principle of utility asserts that happiness is the sole desirable end of human action. In Mill's version, however, the idea of happiness is a restrictive one and 'greatly limits the range of acceptable action'. By happiness Mill 'means not any happiness that individual happens to desire, but the sort of elevated happiness men should desire . . . the happiness that *rational* reflection would approve, not *any* pleasure a man happens to pursue'. Cowling concludes from this that liberty is for Mill just instrumental, a means to promoting mental cultivation and a necessary condition for attaining the truth. Liberty as such, without regard to its consequences, is not a proper end of social action. The diversity of opinions which Mill appeared to cherish for its own sake is less extensive than surface judgement suggests because, Cowling contends, the goal to be reached is diversity within the limits of an ultimate consensus itself shaped by rational and high-minded human beings.

Like many before him, Cowling finds Mill's attempted proof of his principle of utility inadequate. He thinks, however, that Mill tried to reinforce the justification offered in the *Utilitarianism* by the elaborate plea for accepting the 'normative authority' of philosophers and sociologists which he understands him to make in Book VI of the *Logic*. According to Cowling, Mill believed that the combined contribution of philosophy and sociology would 'free politicians from the limitations of the empiricism by which they tend to be confined', and this is a belief which Cowling rejects and which he seems also to regard as evidence of Mill's qualified attachment to liberty. Whether sociology is, or ever will become, a body of knowledge like engineering or medicine is a controversial question on which Cowling takes the side of the sceptics. He duly makes a number of important points, though he would claim no originality for them, against the pretensions of sociology and also against the claim that philosophy can, or should try to, offer guidance on principles to politicians, or to anyone else for that matter. Of Mill in particular he complains that he is recommending the supersession of one style of politics (i.e. empiricism) by another which involves deference to those possessing the appropriate kind of knowledge, whilst on Mill's own admission that knowledge is still at a rudimentary stage. What Cowling does not make explicit is the connection between all this and his claim that Mill is not so libertarian as he seems. He appears to imply that anyone who looks forward to the social sciences playing a large part in political policy and decision—as Mill certainly did—must necessarily be committed to an authoritarian scheme of things; that no one can really value liberty and at the same time hold that a science of politics is both possible and desirable.

But Cowling must surely allow for the possibility that someone could be genuinely attached to liberty and yet also welcome the prospect of the social sciences being widely used in the course of governmental action. Such a person might see no necessary threat to freedom from the growing prestige of the scientific study of society. He could, of course, be mistaken but

the matter is by no means settled. To argue that because Mill
was a champion of the claims of sociology to be a major source
of political decision he must therefore be written off as a true
lover of liberty is to assume both what needs to be proved and
that Mill would not have concerned himself with finding safeguards against the dangers which Cowling takes to be insur-
mountable. If it came to choosing between liberty and giving
total power to a scientific élite to control our lives Mill's answer
was clear; his attitude to Comte's proposals puts the issue
beyond doubt.

Cowling has, of course, other arguments to support his
charge that Mill was in fact an authoritarian and they are
generally of a more direct nature; it is therefore in relation to
them that we should mainly judge his thesis. Up to this point
the most he can claim to have established is that against the
essay *On Liberty* should be set Book VI of the *Logic* and the
Utilitarianism, and such other writings as express the same
ideas. On the one side we have a deep conviction in freedom,
on the other a vision of society under the sway of superior
minds possessed of the moral and scientific knowledge to pursue and attain noble ends. These two ideals, Cowling seems to
argue, are in conflict. If this is what he wishes to maintain it
would not necessarily show Mill was less for liberty than we
generally have supposed him to be. For Mill might have said,
as indeed he does at times, that everything must be subordin-
ated to liberty, or at least to the amount of liberty his principle
of self-protection would permit, that all social schemes,
whether involving the application of a fully developed social
science or not, are to be judged by their capacity to protect and
extend individuality and diversity in both thought and action.
To meet this possible objection Cowling resorts to the more
radical course of denying that the essay *On Liberty* itself is really
concerned to promote freedom. In this way he is able to present
Mill's thought as all of a piece; *On Liberty*, the *Logic*, and *Utilitarianism* all preach the same gospel and the plan for a social
science is but one method of securing to the learned the power
they need to produce a new set of socially accepted beliefs and
values. It is therefore important to Cowling's argument that
the essay *On Liberty* should be fitted somehow into his scheme of
interpretation.

At first sight, says Cowling, the essay *On Liberty* is libertarian. But, when we come to realize that 'individuality' stands for 'less than all the ends to which men might want to move' we shall more readily be able to appreciate that Mill's principle of individuality is 'designed' to limit rather than enhance human freedom. Cowling accepts the view that the principle is based on 'interests' rather than 'effects' but claims this version is 'more definitively inquisitorial' than the old one because, as Mill uses it, the interest of a man 'is his interest as a progressive being—a progressive being with an obligation to be concerned for the well-being of society as a whole'; and this implies that men must follow their higher natures, be disinterested and defer to superiority of intellect. So Cowling argues that social control of individual conduct would, according to Mill's prin- ciple, be justifiable if it served to promote happiness in Mill's special sense, i.e. the cultivation of our higher natures; for 'if the interest of others is taken to lie in producing the greatest amount of higher happiness possible' and 'if interference with individual liberty can be justified on the ground that interfer- ence is in the interest of others' then Mill's purpose is clear.

What makes Cowling's argument unacceptable here is the shift from 'interference is justifiable only if actions harm the interests of others' to 'interference is justifiable if it promotes the interests of others'—i.e. elevates their characters and minds. Mill can be construed in the former sense but not the latter; and Cowling is perfectly well aware of the passages which would support my criticism, since his next concern is to place a construction on them consistent with his general thesis. I do not think he succeeds in doing this: moreover, his very attempt carries implications at odds with the argument just considered. The passages in question appear in the fourth chapter of the essay. Mill restates and elaborates the principle announced in the first chapter; 'as soon as any part of a per- son's conduct affects prejudicially the interests of others, society has jurisdiction over it'. He goes on to stress that the principle does not preach selfish indifference to other people's conduct but, on the contrary, is consistent with 'a great increase of dis- interested exertion to promote the good of others'. However, the means we should employ to influence others, except when interests are harmed, are 'conviction and persuasion' because we have no right to prevent another from doing 'with his life for his own benefit what he chooses to do with it'. For self-regarding deficiencies, therefore, the individual is not liable to social penalty but only to 'the inconveniences which are strictly inseparable from the unfavourable judgment of others'.

Cowling admits that what Mill says here 'might seem to make his principle more libertarian than we are suggesting', but goes on to argue that Mill allows so much liberty not because he is in favour of diversity of character as such but on account of 'the good of mankind' or 'the greater good of human freedom'. When, therefore, we remember that such freedom is merely instrumental and is valued by Mill because it promotes general social utility in the special sense of inducing men to cultivate their higher natures, then the import of his doctrine, Cowling claims, is far more restrictive than it appears. Mill favoured freedom, save where assignable damage is done to the interests of others, because he thought men are more likely to maximize utility this way than 'by preventing the damage a free man may do by perversely misusing his freedom'. He did not want his 'rational consensus' by force and relied on freedom, coupled with a 'rational education', to produce it. So, concludes Cowling, it is not diversity in itself that Mill was after but 'diversity informed by the rationally agreed education the clerisy alone can provide'.

We should notice that although Cowling began by denying the libertarian nature of Mill's doctrine on the ground that he would allow liberty to be restricted if the restrictions were in the interests of others (i.e. served their higher development), he is forced later to recognize that Mill does not wish to punish men for self-regarding deficiencies. By recognizing this Cowling is, in effect, being forced to repudiate his original view that Mill's principle is designed to *promote* the 'higher' interests of society by coercing people into the right sorts of happiness rather than to *prevent* injury to the interests of others. The difference is important. According to the former view society would be entitled to force men to improve themselves, under the latter it would restrict itself to the protection of rights and interests. By insisting on education and persuasion rather than legal or social coercion to raise the level of human cultivation Mill was choosing the way of freedom. That he did at times play with the idea of the clerisy (though *not* as an authoritarian ruling élite) should not tempt us to get things out of focus. Whatever meaning one should assign to 'the good of mankind' it still remains the case that Mill sought to achieve it with the weapons of freedom. Moreover it is less than the whole truth to say that Mill did not value diversity and individuality for their own sakes. 'To give any fair play to the nature of each', he says in the third chapter of *On Liberty*, 'it is essential that different persons should be allowed to lead different lives'. And later in the same chapter: '. . . nor is it only persons of decided mental superiority who have a just claim to carry on their lives in their own way. There is no reason that all human existence should be constructed on some one or small number of patterns. If a person possesses any tolerable amount of common sense and experience, his own mode of laying out his existence is best, not because it is best in itself, but because it is his own mode'.

Mill, of course, preferred that men should make good use of their freedom. Certainly he wanted men to develop, and to encourage others to develop, their higher natures, both because this would be good in itself and because it had beneficial consequences for the quality of social life and for the advancement of knowledge. But were men to abuse their freedom they should not be brought under the jurisdiction of society until their conduct encroached on the rights and interests of others.[25]

Mill's attitude to Comte is especially interesting in this connection. On more than one occasion he refers to Comte's proposals for social reform in a highly critical tone, largely because they would inevitably stifle freedom. Cowling, to be sure, does not try to hide this. Yet he tends to understate the radical contrast between them. In his fourth chapter Cowling quotes at length from the *Utilitarianism* with the aim of showing that Mill's principle of utility has some of the qualities of a religion. Mill is arguing that a utilitarian morality which stresses concern for the interests of others could come to be felt with the force of a religion. Comte, he says, had 'shown the possibility of giving to the service of humanity, even without the aid of belief in a Providence, both the psychological power and the social efficacy of a religion'. But, he cautions (within a few lines of the point at which Cowling ends the lengthy quotation), 'the danger is, not that it should be insufficient, but that it should be so excessive as to interfere unduly with human freedom and individuality'. And the difference here is not just that Mill considered coercion to be ineffective, which is how Cowling presents the matter, but rather that freedom and individuality were values in themselves, quite apart from the good to society which springs from a jealous regard for their protection and growth.

Cowling's thesis is in error therefore at two crucial points. He oversimplifies Mill's case for liberty by denying the fact that Mill valued freedom and diversity for their own sakes. Moreover, even assuming Cowling to be right that freedom for Mill was merely instrumental, it would not follow that his principle is less libertarian than it is generally taken for. Its being instrumental says nothing about the nature and scope of the freedom it would ensure to individuals. The reasons Mill advanced in support of the principle may have been largely connected with his special conception of happiness, but if it really seeks to maximize liberty as a necessary condition of individuality it cannot therefore be said to detract from freedom. There is, on the contrary, ample evidence that Mill comes down on the side of liberty whenever any question of conflict arises between the requirements of a rational social consensus and 'pursuing our own good in our own way'.

What leads Cowling to regard Mill's plea for liberty as 'less practically libertarian' than we normally suppose is partly his belief that the central concern is not liberty but utility, and utility conceived in terms of an élitist and limited form of happiness. Accordingly, if we can interpret *Utilitarianism* as an essentially authoritarian work we should then set the *Liberty* in that framework, especially when we recall that Mill specifically affirms that his argument for liberty is not to be regarded as an appeal to abstract right but derived from 'utility in the largest sense, grounded in the permanent interests of a man as a progressive being'. Since the ultimate goal is 'the sort of elevated happiness men *should* desire' it would seem to follow that conduct incompatible with that goal will be discouraged—though by education and persuasion, not coercion, as Cowling readily agrees. But why should utility in this sense be thought authoritarian? Mill does not say that men will be coerced or pressed into a life of higher cultivation of the mind. He certainly implies that it is better to enjoy Bach and Plato than lower forms of art and literature; nowhere does he suggest that men should not be free to do otherwise. Indeed, he insists that the development of the individual personalities of men is compatible with a wide diversity of character and modes of life; and if a man should choose what Mill would consider a depraved form of life he is to suffer no more than 'the loss of consideration' and 'the inconveniences strictly inseparable from the unfavourable judgment of others'.

I have said that it is wrong to think of Mill's concern for liberty as being due solely to its instrumental value. To talk of liberty as a means to some higher value can often be very misleading and it is especially so in Mill's case. We might say that Mill valued freedom because it enabled men to develop their higher capacities. But this way of putting it hides the sort of relationship Mill had in mind. We would be seriously mistaken if we thought that liberty was one of several alternative methods for achieving fulfilment, as, say, boat, plane, or train were alternative ways of getting from Swansea to Glasgow. How we get there is not going to change Glasgow, but it would be absurd to suppose that the sort of fulfilment or happiness Mill talks about could be achieved except through freedom. Liberty was a *necessary element* in Mill's conception of happiness. The measure of Cowling's failure to enter sympathetically into Mill's scale of values is reflected in just this persistent use of 'instrumental' to characterize the relationship between liberty and Mill's idea of the good life.

In a well-known passage in the *Autobiography* Mill says that after his 'mental crisis', which began in 1826, he found the fabric of his ideas constantly giving way and in need of repair. To some degree most commentators on Mill have been aware of the variegated assortment of materials that went to patching up the garment and a true insight into the resulting complexity of his thought must accept the conflicts and tensions between the different strands which Mill collected from almost all the significant intellectual trends of his time. Cowling resolves the problem by converting Mill into a single-minded propagator of a new religion of humanity. His ethics, his sociology, his social philosophy, and his political theory are all made to serve the same end and therefore to form a consistent whole. I do not find this unity. To insist on it at the cost of distorting Mill's persistent and deeply felt zeal for liberty is surely to get things out of proportion. On the other hand Cowling brings to our notice again those elements which do not fit too easily together with his basic moral and political values. How we are to reconcile Mill's interest in the clerisy and the attraction a homogeneous set of social beliefs had for him with those values lies outside my task here, but it would seem more accurate and more just simply to face up to the fact that any attempt to reconcile them is going to be extremely difficult, if not clearly impossible to achieve, than to strive after what must turn out to be an artificial and precarious unity.

V

The Principle of Liberty

I

MY aim in this chapter is to discuss what Mill was trying to do in his essay *On Liberty*. Or, to put it more precisely, to consider whether the commonly accepted version of 'the very simple principle' asserted in the essay is a fair account of Mill's intentions. Before setting out what I take to be the traditional version and giving my reasons for questioning it, we ought to remind ourselves of the general purpose Mill had in publishing his work.

In his *Autobiography* Mill describes the essay as 'a philosophic text-book of a single truth . . . the importance, to man and society, of a large variety in types of character, and of giving full freedom to human nature to expand itself in innumerable and conflicting directions'.[1] The book deals with one of the recurring questions of politics but was written in circumstances which gave that question a new significance. For behind Mill's question—'What is the nature and extent of the power which society ought to exercise over the individual?'—was his anxiety lest the tendencies which he claimed to see at work in the civilized world would eventually extinguish spontaneity in all the important branches of human conduct. 'Society has now [the manuscript was completed in 1857] fairly got the better of individuality . . . in our times, from the highest class of society down to the lowest, every one lives as under the eye of a hostile and dreaded censorship.'[2] The essay had, therefore, the practical aim of helping to ward off the dangers which the trends of the age seemed to carry with them and, in particular, to counter 'the general tendency of things throughout the world to render mediocrity the ascendant power among mankind'.[3] The work, Mill tells us, was conceived and written as a short essay in

This chapter first appeared as 'A Re-reading of Mill on Liberty' in *Political Studies*, Vol. VIII, No. 2, 1960.

1854.[4] In a letter to Harriet from Rome in January 1855 he wrote:

On my way here cogitating thereon I came back to an idea we have talked about, and thought that the best thing to write and publish at present would be a volume on Liberty. So many things might be brought into it and nothing seems more to be needed—it is a growing need too, for opinion tends to encroach more and more on liberty, and almost all the projects of social reformers of these days are really liberticide—Comte's particularly so.[5]

But Mill's fears and anxieties go back long before this period. They were clearly expressed in an essay on 'Civilization' published in 1836 and there are definite signs that they were taking root in even earlier years.[6]

One of the tasks Mill set himself in *On Liberty* was to fix a limit 'to the legitimate interference of collective opinion with individual independence'.[7] This seemed to him to be at least as important as 'protection against political despotism', for the 'yoke of opinion in England is perhaps heavier, that of the law is lighter, than in most other countries of Europe'.[8] The preservation of individuality and variety of character was possible, he believed, if a principle were observed whereby every person was accorded an area of liberty in thought and action. His father and Bentham had argued the case for representative government, but its practical consequences, whether in the United States as revealed by Tocqueville or experienced in England since the Reform Act, were in his view by no means wholly favourable to liberty.[9] And even more menacing than the now apparent weaknesses of a system of government whose establishment was the great aim of the orthodox Utilitarians were the informal pressures of society that the coming of democracy tended to strengthen and make still more relentless. Progress and the attainment of the truth were, as Mill saw it, the work of a select few; and to promote and safeguard the conditions for the distinctive activity of this élite in face of the growing power of the mediocre mass was a result he hoped his essay would help to achieve. Yet to a number who have shared his aspirations the specific principle he offered has always seemed defective. Mill's attachment to liberty has been admired on all sides and the many eloquent and moving passages he dedicates to its virtues have been widely acclaimed as classic utterances on behalf of one of the most cherished of western ideals, but, it has been generally said, the principle he advances for its protection cannot do what is expected of it. My purpose here is to look again at that principle and to discuss whether it has been properly understood by its critics.

II

The object of this Essay [says Mill] is to assert one very simple principle . . . that the sole end for which mankind are warranted, individually or collectively, in interfering with the liberty of action of any of their number is self-protection . . . to prevent harm to others. . . . His own good, either physical or moral, is not a sufficient warrant. . . . The only part of the conduct of any one, for which he is amenable to society, is that which concerns others. In the part which merely concerns himself, his independence is, of right, absolute.[10]

This passage appears in the first chapter of the essay. In the last chapter, where Mill offers some examples of how his principle might be applied in practical cases, he restates

the two maxims which together form the entire doctrine of this Essay . . . first, that the individual is not accountable to society for his actions, in so far as these concern the interests of no person but himself. . . . Secondly, that for such actions as are prejudicial to the interests of others, the individual is accountable, and may be subjected either to social or to legal punishment, if society is of opinion that the one or the other is requisite for its protection.[11]

A study of the comments on Mill's essay during the century since its publication shows that the principle just stated has been widely criticized because it appears to rest on the possibility of classifying human actions into two categories—actions which concern only the agent and actions that concern others besides the agent. The distinction between these two categories, it has been repeatedly argued, is impossible to sustain. As one of the critics has put it: 'The greater part of English history since his day has been a practical commentary on the fallacy of this distinction. No action, however intimate, is free from social consequences. No human being can say that what he is, still less what he does, affects no one but himself.[12] The crucial point in this criticism is clearly the supposition that Mill's principle depends for its validity on there being some actions, including some important ones, which are free from social consequences, i.e. that they affect no one but the agent himself.[13] I shall argue that this assumption on the part of the critics is false and that it derives from a failure to observe the form of words which Mill often employs in the text and to take at its full value Mill's firm assertion that actions of the so-called 'self-regarding' variety may frequently affect, even harmfully, persons other than the agent. Before elaborating this claim I want to pass briefly in review the evidence for my contention that the traditional account of Mill's principle makes just this assumption about his classification of human actions.

I begin with a commonly made criticism, drawn from among the first reviews of *On Liberty*. There is no conduct whose impact is confined to the agent, said the *London Review* in 1859, because 'no moral quality is limited in its action to the sphere of its possessor's own history and doings . . . society has an interest, over and above that of mere self-defence, in the conduct of everyone of its members'.[14] Fourteen years later, Fitzjames Stephen, whose *Liberty, Equality, Fraternity* has set the pattern for much of the criticism directed against Mill up to the present time, asserted with characteristic vigour that 'the attempt to distinguish between self-regarding acts and acts which regard others, is like an attempt to distinguish between acts which happen in time and acts which happen in space. Every act happens at some time and in some place, and in like manner every act that we do either does or may affect both ourselves and others . . . the distinction is altogether fallacious and unfounded.[15] Further, in defence of the attitude of a temperance reformer whom Mill had attacked in the *Liberty*, Stephen remarks: 'It is surely a simple matter of fact that every human creature is deeply interested not only in the conduct, but in the thoughts, feelings, and opinions of millions of persons who stand in no other assignable relation to him than that of being his fellow-creatures. . . . A man would no more be a man if he was alone in the world than a hand would be a hand without the rest of the body.'[16] The view of human relations expressed in this last passage was, of course, shared by the Oxford Idealists, and we should expect from them too a decided lack of sympathy with

Mill's principle. Thus Ritchie considers the conception of the individual implied in Mill's doctrine to be abstract and negative, for the individual finds his true self 'not in distinction and separation from others, but in community with them'.

We may very well doubt [he continues] whether any acts, nay, even thoughts, of the individual can, in the strictest sense, be merely self-regarding, and so matter of indifference to other individuals. . . . The more we learn of human society, the more we discover that there are no absolute divisions, but that every atom influences and is influenced by every other. It may be very inexpedient to meddle with particular acts, or it may be practically impossible to do so; but we can lay down no hard and fast line, separating self-regarding acts from acts which affect others.[17]

And Bosanquet: '. . . every act of mine affects both myself and others. . . . It may safely be said that no demarcation between self-regarding and other-regarding action can possibly hold good.'[18]

Closer to our own day, MacIver in his *Modern State* remarks of Mill's principle:

This statement has a form which suggests that the full significance of the interdependence of social beings is hardly realized by Mill . . . he thinks of man as in certain categories social, but in others wholly 'individual'. But if we realize that the nature of man is a unity, that in every *aspect* he is a social being at the same time that he is also autonomous and self-legislating, so that his sociality and his individuality cannot belong to two different spheres . . . we can no longer be content with an abstract doctrine of liberty.[19]

In similar vein Sir Ernest Barker says that Mill's assumption of the existence of two different spheres of conduct is open to the criticism that Mill separates the inseparable. 'The conduct of any man', maintains Sir Ernest, 'is a single whole: there can be nothing in it that concerns himself only, and does not concern other men: whatever he is, and whatever he does, affects others and therefore concerns them.'[20] Finally, to conclude with a quotation from one of the best studies of Mill's philosophy that has appeared in recent decades, here is the view of Professor R. P. Anschutz. He is commenting on Mill's principle of self-protection ('the argument for insulation' as Anschutz calls it) and says: 'It is a completely untenable as well as a completely impracticable doctrine. It is quite impossible to distinguish between that part of a person's behaviour which affects himself and that part which also affects others; and there is nothing to be gained by attempting to make the distinction.'[21]

This, then, is the case which has been built up against Mill over the last hundred years. The essential point in the criticism is, as I have said, that Mill wrongly assumes some human actions to be free of social consequences. But if we look carefully at the two passages quoted at the beginning of this section, where Mill is explicitly stating his principle, it will be noticed that, although in the first case he writes of conduct which 'merely concerns' the agent and of conduct which 'concerns others', he introduces the word 'interests' in the second passage. He says that the individual is to be held accountable only for those actions which 'are prejudicial to the *interests* of others'.[22] Elsewhere in the essay both types of phrase appear, with a number of variations within each type. Thus we find on the one hand: 'what only regards himself', 'conduct which affects only himself', 'which concerns only himself', 'things wherein the individual alone is concerned'; and on the other: 'concern the interests of others', 'affects the interests of no one but himself', 'affect the interests of others', 'damage to the interests of others'. Traditional commentary has assumed that all these expressions were intended to convey the same meaning and that Mill's distinction was simply between actions which affect no one but the agent and actions which affect others. My case in this chapter is that we ought not to gloss over these different modes of expression, that there is an important difference between just 'affecting others' and 'affecting the interests of others', and that there are passages in the essay which lend support to the view that Mill was thinking of 'interests' and not merely 'effects'. As a first step I wish to support my claim that there is a significant difference between saying, on the one hand, that an action affects another person and, on the other, that it affects his interests.

It seems to me quite clear that a person may be affected by another's behaviour without his interests being affected. For example, when we speak of a man's equilibrium not being affected in trying circumstances we are not thinking of his interests. Indeed a man's interests may well be seriously injured without his equilibrium being affected to any marked degree. And even if it were, there would be two things affected, not one. Similarly, if we heard of someone's outlook on life being fundamentally affected by an event such as a religious experience we should not have to conclude that his interests had likewise been affected. True, a religious convert has an interest in religion that he did not have before, but we are not speaking of interests in that sense. My interests in literature can undergo a radical change without anything like business, professional, or property interests being affected to the slightest extent. To bring out the distinction I am trying to make between interests and effects, but with no pretence at offering a definitive account of the nature of interests, one might say that interests—and I do not wish to imply that they are necessarily legal—depend for their existence on social recognition and are closely connected with prevailing standards about the sort of behaviour a man can legitimately expect from others. A claim that something should be recognized as an interest is one we should require to be supported by reasons and one capable of being made the subject of discussion. On the other hand I could be very seriously affected by the action of another person merely because I had an extraordinarily sensitive nature and no claim to have others respect these tender spots would be recognized as amounting to an interest. How one is affected by a theatrical performance depends partly on one's tastes, but the interests of a businessman would be affected by a tax on business property no matter what his tastes or susceptibilities; just as the interests of a university are affected by a scheme to establish a research institute in the same area (in a common subject of course) whether the university authorities welcome the idea or not. Moreover, 'effects' is a concept applicable to plants and animals as well as human beings, but no one talks about the interests of plants. Crops are affected by fertilizers or drought in much the same way as a certain drug would have an effect on, say, chronic lassitude. And dogs are affected by thunder in the kind of way that I might be affected by the news that my favourite football team had been beaten in the cup-final. There are no interests necessarily at stake here, though drought could affect my interests as well as the crops, and gamblers stand to win or lose by a result that could also leave them dismayed. Apart from really trivial actions—which we can ignore in this context—it is probably true that what I do or am like affects other people.[23] Any principle which rested on the assumption that other people are not (or may not be) affected would be open to precisely the objections brought against Mill. But deciding whether interests are affected is another matter and a principle that seeks to limit social interference to cases where interests are involved cannot be attacked because it fails to recognize the truth that 'every atom influences and is influenced by every other' or to realize that 'the nature of man is a unity'.

It might be objected at this stage that Mill does not consistently adhere to the term 'interests' and that one is not entitled to assume from its appearance in some passages, coupled with the employment of such phrases as 'conduct which concerns only himself', that there is one unambiguous doctrine running through the entire essay. Our objector might well concede the distinction between a principle based on interests and one based on mere effects, but he feels we are not justified in attempting to produce a coherent theory when, from the variety of the terms used in the relevant passages, there is clearly not one there to extract. My answer to this objection, for the moment at least (whether one can find a single consistent principle running through the whole work I discuss below), is that if Mill is really trying to maintain two (possibly more) principles, and moves from one to the other at different points of the essay without really knowing what he is doing and hence with no warning to his readers of what he is about, then to recognize this fact is at least to notice something which commentators on Mill have, so far as I know, failed to discern in the past. But it need not necessarily follow that because Mill uses phrases like 'conduct which concerns only himself' along with 'conduct which affects the interests of no persons besides himself' this must be regarded as conclusive evidence of an unwitting affirmation of two distinct and potentially incompatible principles. For though the word 'concerns' has sometimes no more force than 'has reference to' or 'affects', with no implication that interests are being referred to or affected, it can also mean 'is of importance to' and could in some contexts carry with it the suggestion that interests are involved. Thus when Mill says that social control is permissible only in cases when one's conduct 'concerns others' we are not compelled to assume that he means actions which just have 'effects' on others. Hence it may well be that the ambiguity of the word 'concerns' is responsible for concealing a coherent theory based on 'interests' rather than 'effects' and that we can so interpret the passages where the term 'interests' is not specifically used as to yield a single consistent principle.

However that may be, it should be observed that there are statements in the essay suggesting that Mill was quite aware of the manner in which individuals are constantly affecting one another. And so forthright are they that one wonders how it ever came to be thought of Mill that he wished to declare a whole area of human behaviour 'self-regarding' because the actions so named had no 'effects' on others (as opposed to 'affecting their interests'). Thus in the fourth chapter of the essay Mill discusses a possible objection to his principle in these terms: 'How (it may be asked) can any part of the conduct of a member of society be a matter of indifference to the other members? No person is an entirely isolated being; it is impossible for a person to do anything seriously or permanently hurtful to himself, without mischief reaching at least to his near connections, and often far beyond them. . .'. And Mill concedes to this objection 'that the mischief which a person does to himself may *seriously affect*, both through their sympathies and their interests, those nearly connected with him and, in a minor degree, society at large'. But he goes on to insist that only when conduct of this sort (i.e. conduct affecting others) violates 'a distinct and assignable obligation to any other person or persons' is 'the case taken out of the self-regarding class, and becomes amenable to moral disapprobation'. A little farther on in the same chapter Mill speaks of a person preventing himself 'by conduct purely self-regarding, from the performance of some definite duty incumbent on him to the public' and thus being guilty of a social offence, but where the conduct 'neither violates any specific duty to the public, nor occasions perceptible hurt to any assignable individual except himself; the inconvenience is one which society can afford to bear, for the sake of the greater good of human freedom'.[24] It is surely obvious that Mill would be contradicting himself here in the most flagrant manner if we were to interpret 'purely self-regarding' to mean those actions which have no impact (i.e. no 'effects') on other members of society. And the case against this interpretation becomes even more conclusive if we consider Mill's remarks in the opening chapter where he is elaborating the central principle of the essay. He writes: '. . . there is a sphere of action in which society, as distinguished from the individual, has if any, only an indirect interest; comprehending all that portion of a person's life and conduct which affects only himself . . . when I say only himself, I mean directly, and in the first instance; for whatever affects himself, may affect others through himself . . .'.[25] Further, in the fourth chapter, Mill talks of the 'self-regarding deficiencies' which a person may manifest and which 'render him necessarily and properly a subject of distaste, or, in extreme cases, even of contempt'. For vices of this kind, he says, a man may 'suffer very severe penalties at the hands of others for faults which directly concern only himself'. Here, then, is a clear affirmation that what he calls, perhaps misleadingly, 'self-regarding conduct' can have effects on others. Even to the extent that those affected can retaliate with '*very severe penalties*'!

Mill's critics, Fitzjames Stephen among them, have wondered how the division of human conduct into two spheres could be sustained if self-regarding actions might suffer severe penalties at the hands of others. Mill attempted to maintain the distinction, which is, of course, crucial for the viability of his principle, in these words: '. . . the inconveniences which are strictly inseparable from the unfavourable judgment of others, are the only ones to which a person should ever be subjected for that portion of his conduct and character which concerns his own good, but which does not affect the interests of others in their relations with him. Acts injurious to others require a totally different treatment . . . these are fit objects of moral reprobation, and, in grave cases, of moral retribution and punishment.' And as if to meet the objections of the sceptical Stephen, who could not see how 'inconveniences strictly inseparable from the unfavourable judgment of others' could be differentiated from the 'moral retribution' to be visited when other people's interests were harmed, Mill went on to show why this distinction was not merely nominal, in his eyes at least. In the former case the offender incurs a loss of consider-

ation by reason of his imprudence or lack of dignity, whereas in
the latter reprobation is due to him 'for an offence against the
rights of others'.[26] And, claims Mill, people will react differently if the conduct of which they disapprove is such that they
think that they have a right to control the agent. Whether Mill
makes his point or not I do not wish to discuss further, but the
words 'for an offence against the *rights* of others' raise a very
important question and seem to introduce a new element into
the principle. Nor is this the sole occasion when 'rights' are
mentioned.[27] In the same chapter from which I have just been
quoting, specifically devoted to discussing 'the limits to the
authority of society over the individual', and therefore concerned to elaborate and give more detailed consideration to the
principle mentioned and briefly treated in the opening chapter
—it is in this fourth chapter that we should, I think, look for
pointers to Mill's intentions—Mill attempts to demarcate the
area of conduct for which we are to be made responsible to
society. 'This conduct', he says, 'consists in not injuring the
interests of one another; or rather certain interests which,
either by express legal provision or by tacit understanding,
ought to be considered as *rights*.' Nor is this the complete extent
of social control, for conduct may harm others 'without going
to the length of violating any of their *constituted rights*'. In
those cases punishment is inflicted by opinion rather than the
law. Then, to sum up, Mill adds: 'As soon as any part of a person's conduct affects prejudicially the interests of others, society
has jurisdiction over it', but no such question can arise 'when
a person's conduct affects the interests of no persons besides
himself . . .'[28]

The paragraph from which these extracts have been taken,
coming as it does at a crucial stage in Mill's argument, is of
some significance for the interpretation of his leading principle.
It serves, incidentally, as further proof of my claim that it is
'interests' rather than 'effects' with which Mill is concerned.
But its main significance for us at this stage is the appearance
in it of the term 'rights' and the relationship Mill seems to suppose that term to have to the idea of 'interests'. From Mill's
wording it is certain that the rights he has in mind are legal
rights ('constituted rights'), for he envisages the law, rather
than opinion, protecting some interests and these interests are

then to be considered as rights. Other interests will not receive legal protection, though Mill does not exclude the possibility that these might be regarded as rights, though not legal ('constituted') rights. Certainly Mill is not saying that rights and interests are the same things, synonymous terms (and of course they are not), but he does seem to imply that they are very closely related to each other. It would be consistent with what he says here to suppose that when a person can be thought to have interests he is thereby possessed of a right, though not necessarily a right to the unqualified protection of his interests; perhaps only a right to have his interests taken into account. Moreover, by linking interests to rights in this way Mill leaves us with no excuse for confusing the notions of 'interests' and 'effects', which must now be seen as belonging to quite different categories. It may be true that because of the element of vagueness attaching to rights and interests (i.e. as to what a man may legitimately, I do not mean *legally*, account his rights or interests) the concepts would be much more difficult to operate as part of a principle of liberty than the relatively simple notion of effects, but that ought not to blind us to the difference it makes to a principle to have the one rather than the other type of concept as a component.

III

The case I have been trying to make out is that Mill's principle of self-protection rests on a division of conduct into actions which either do or do not affect the interests of other persons rather than on what has generally been supposed to have been the division, namely, into conduct having or not having effects on others. This interpretation does not rely on the evidence of only one or two isolated passages where the word 'interests' appears. In fact the word appears at least fifteen times in the course of the essay and some of the passages where it is used are of the greatest importance in assessing Mill's intentions.[29] Furthermore, there is also the evidence I have already cited which shows how freely Mill admitted that what have commonly been thought of as literally self-regarding actions did have their effects on other persons. But having said that, I would be

seriously misleading the reader if I failed to mention a number
of difficulties which stand in the way of this interpretation, or at
least suggest that Mill was not always clear in his own mind as
to what he wanted to say. The first difficulty arises out of a
passage previously quoted in another context: '. . . there is a
sphere of action in which society, as distinguished from the
individual, has, if any, only an indirect interest; comprehending all that portion of a person's life and conduct which affects
only himself. . . . When I say only himself, I mean *directly, and in
the first instance*; for whatever affects himself, may affect others
through himself . . .'.[30] And we find phrases similar to the one
italicized here in other parts of the essay; for example, 'things
which do not *primarily* concern others' and 'the part of life in
which it is *chiefly* the individual that is interested . . . [as opposed
to] the part which *chiefly* interests society'.[31] This seems to me
a difficulty because if we are to take this passage seriously (and
the repetition of like phrases elsewhere suggests it is not merely
a case of careless writing) we should, on the account I have
been giving, have to say that when Mill writes here of 'conduct
which affects only himself' he means to say 'conduct which
affects only his own interests'.[32] Further, since what affects my
interests may also affect the interests of others, we should have
to allow that 'self-regarding' conduct could affect the interests
of others, though not 'directly' or 'primarily'. Hence the distinction Mill was attempting to make in his use of the self-
regarding and other-regarding categories would seem to resolve
itself into a division between (i) actions which primarily affect
the interests of the agent but may affect the interests of others
too, and (ii) actions which primarily affect the interests of
others, though the agent's own interests may also be involved.
It requires little imagination to foresee the immense complications that would be bound to arise in the application of such a
formula. Nothing could be less appropriately described as a
'very simple principle'—Mill's own characterization in his
opening chapter. Yet we should have to interpret these passages in some such manner or else admit, which is quite possible, that Mill falls occasionally into the language of 'effects',
without realizing that he thereby allows a second principle to
peep through from time to time while adhering mainly to a
doctrine based on 'interests'.

IV

Assuming, then, that Mill's doctrine involves the idea of 'interests' rather than 'effects', is it, interpreted thus, a useful working principle of liberty in the way that the traditional version is patently not? The revised version would read something like this: 'Social control of individual actions ought to be exercised only in cases where the interests of others are either threatened or actually affected.'[33] But how to decide when interests are affected? What are interests? Is there any commonly accepted criterion, or set of criteria, of an interest? Mill's principle, as reformulated, must inevitably provoke questions like these and its value will obviously depend on the answers to be given to them. They cannot be fully treated here and all I shall attempt are some preliminary and tentative remarks.

As it is commonly used, the concept of 'interests' is an elusive one. There is no precise and generally acceptable definition. As Mr Plamenatz observed, the idea of 'interest', compared with notions like 'right' or 'duty', is extremely vague.[34] But there are many important concepts in our language which evade exact description and they remain none the less indispensable. Failure to bring the notion within the confines of a neat definition ought not to be a sufficient reason for rejecting out of hand a theory to which the concept is central. Moreover, there are sociologists and jurists for whom the term occupies an important place in their theories. MacIver, for example, conceives human activity through the two concepts 'interest' and 'will'. There is, he says, 'no will without an interest and no interest apart from a will'. And by an interest he means 'some object which determines activity', though it is more than mere desire; it has 'a certain permanence and stability'.[35] Another definition of interest he offers is, 'the object of consciousness . . . anything, material or immaterial, factual or conceptual, to which we devote our attention'.[36] Roscoe Pound, too, employs the word with the same kind of wide meaning. For him an interest is a *de facto* claim and he draws up a comprehensive classification of interests which covers a vast field, ranging from individual claims to privacy to the social interest in free science and cultural progress. Among other writers the term is confined to certain kinds of consciousness or a particular class of attitudes such as, for example, those based on needs; and an appropriate list is provided of the bodily and spiritual needs which are to count for this purpose.[37] How are these uses of the word related to the normal sense of the term? Indeed, is it possible to identify an 'ordinary' use of the word? There would seem to be some grounds for saying that in a normal context an interest should not be construed as just a claim, far less any sort of claim. Rather it seems to be the condition in which a person's claim to, or title to, or share in something is recognized as valid by others, or at least is regarded as worthy of consideration. That is to say, there is an objective element about it which precludes any fanciful demand from being an interest. For interests are things we would generally look upon as deserving protection, to be prejudicially affected only by advantages likely to accrue in another direction. Certainly we feel that they ought not to be ignored even if there are compelling reasons for subordinating them to what we think are more important considerations. Interests, then, are not just arbitrary wishes, fleeting fancies, or capricious demands, though some of them may well have developed from forms to which these terms might have been particularly apposite at the time.

Mill does not say much to indicate how he understood the notion of interest, but there is nothing in the essay to suggest that he uses the term in any exceptional manner. There is a passage, however, which points to some of the problems inseparably connected with the idea of interests. The secretary of an association formed to secure prohibition had claimed a right to be protected from the consequences of the liquor trade which, he argued, 'destroys my primary right of security, by constantly creating and stimulating social disorder. . . . It impedes my right to free moral and intellectual development, by surrounding my path with dangers, and by weakening and demoralising society, from which I have a right to claim mutual aid and intercourse.' Mill repudiates with indignation such a sweeping claim, amounting, as he saw it, to 'the absolute social right of every individual, that every other individual shall act in every respect exactly as he ought' and conferring on everyone 'a vested interest in each other's moral, intellectual, and even physical perfection'.[38] Mill and the prohibitionist are disputing what may legitimately be claimed as rights and what is to count as an injury to a person's interests. According to the standards prevailing in Mill's day, and certainly by those current in our own time, the secretary's claims appear ludicrously excessive and there would be no point in taking his case seriously. But what is of importance is the very fact of disagreement as to what a man may hold to be his interests. The prohibitionist could have submitted the relatively modest claim that a man's interests are prejudicially affected by the noisy behaviour of groups of people gathering outside a public house adjoining, or close to, his home. If the noise became such a nuisance as to lower the value of the property it could not be denied that interests had been affected. But apart from depreciation of value, has a man's interest been adversely affected by the mere fact of disturbance of his privacy? He could be the tenant of the house and suffer no personal pecuniary loss, yet he might find the behaviour of the publican's clients extremely annoying and might set a high monetary value on its cessation. Is it part of a man's interests to be free from interference of this sort? From the noise of the radio in his neighbour's flat or from the machines on the airfield near his house? If we are going to say 'no' to the claim that interests are affected by interference such as noise, as opposed to monetary loss caused by noise, then this would seem to prevent Mill's principle from operating in spheres in which he clearly wanted it to work. But it is obvious that people can differ about what are to be regarded as interests, since standards and values enter into what will be recognized as interests (or what will *not* be recognized) at any given time in a way that they do not in the case of 'effects'.[39] Consequently, whether one takes a wide or narrow view of interests, the principle of self-protection must necessarily harbour value-ingredients which will inevitably render its use a controversial operation. That a drug affects a certain disease is a strictly empirical matter. There are objective procedures for tracing its 'effects'. It is true that there are also cases when it would be a relatively simple matter to decide if my interests have been affected: legal interests for example. But there are also occasions when, because standards differ, people will disagree about what their interests are. And this is likely to make a principle based on 'interests' rather than 'effects' difficult to apply in many situations. For not only is the concept 'interest' in itself vague: what are to count as interests, even supposing there were a commonly accepted definition, would be an open question in an indeterminate number of cases. Had Mill formulated his principle in terms of rights rather than interests he would have met the same difficulty precisely because what a man's rights are is a question which can be reasonably answered in more than one way.

Mill's principle raises yet another problem. Social interference, he says, is justifiable only when the interests of others are affected but, he adds, 'it must by no means be supposed, because damage, or probability of damage, to the interests of others, can alone justify the interference of society, that therefore it always does justify such interference'.[40] Evidently the principle is not intended to absolve us from deciding cases on their merits even when interests have actually been affected. We should have to weigh up the advantages and disadvantages of social interference on each occasion. As Mill puts it: '. . . the question whether the general welfare will or will not be promoted by interfering with [another person's conduct], becomes open to discussion'.[41] One of the examples he gives is the unsuccessful candidate in a competitive examination.[42] Others have gained at his expense, but no one would have it otherwise. A recent example would be the publicity given to statements warning of the harmful effects of heavy smoking. No one would wish to suppress information about the relation between smoking and lung cancer merely because it affected the interests of the tobacco firms. However, says Mill, in the case of conduct which affects no person's interests but one's own there can be no question of permitting social control and restraint: 'in all such cases, there should be perfect freedom, legal and social, to do the action and stand the consequences'.[43] So the principle provides us with a clear directive only when we can be sure that other people's interests are *not* involved; where interests *are* affected we are left with a margin of discretion and are advised to consider whether the general welfare is or is not likely to be promoted by interference in each particular instance. Hence the range of matters covered by the 'automatic' application of the rule is limited to those occasions on which it can be said that no one's interests have been injured. And it seems to be assumed that the question of interests being injured or not is one that can be readily determined.

It would be uncharitable to reject Mill's principle out of hand merely because it fails to provide an automatic and definite solution in an extensive range of cases (i.e. actions which *do* affect the interests of others). For how many of the principles we constantly wield in everyday life supply us with quick and certain answers? From Mill's point of view the important thing was to check the growing tendency to interfere in cases where intervention should be totally banned, and for this purpose what had to be done was to demarcate the area of non-intervention from that in which a prima facie right to control could only be overridden by an appeal to the 'general welfare'. We have seen that with all its indefiniteness Mill's principle is emphatic on one point, namely, that when the interests of others have *not* been affected society should not intervene. But even here a serious doubt emerges. Are there not some actions we should want to control or prohibit which do not seem to injure the interests of others? Take the case of obscenity. It may be that some acts and some kinds of publications which the present law in the United Kingdom prohibits would be permitted in a more enlightened society, but there are certainly many which are, and ought to continue to be, prevented. Mill, too, seems to take this view. He refers to 'offences against decency', acts which, when done publicly, violate good manners, and places them 'within the category of offences against others' and therefore to be prohibited. But he remarks that offences of this nature 'are only connected indirectly with our subject'.[44] Why this should be so he does not explain and it is difficult to see what reasons he could have for saying it. Perhaps he realized that to prohibit offences against decency on the ground that they caused harm to other people's interests would involve a dangerous extension of the conception of 'interests'. For whose interests are threatened or injured by the appearance of obscene publications (or the sale of opium, to take an example from a related field)? The interests of those who concern themselves with public morality? Or the social interest in maintaining standards of public decency? But if we are allowed to bring in considerations of this sort, how could Mill have maintained his opposition to a prohibition on the eating of pork in a predominantly Muslim country?[45] Measures against the dropping of litter or the emission of black smoke from chimneys in specified areas are taken in order to protect the *public interest*, not because they affect the interests of particular persons. That Mill recognized the claims of the general interest is clear enough from his discussion of the case of the person who instigates or counsels others to do acts which if done of one's own free and unaided will would be 'blameable' but not subject to social penalties because 'the evil directly resulting falls wholly on the agent.[46] On the one hand, argues Mill, people must be allowed 'to consult with one another . . . to exchange opinions, and give and receive suggestions', but the question becomes 'doubtful only when the instigator derives a personal benefit from his advice' and is gainfully occupied in promoting 'what society and the State consider to be an evil'; for we would then be faced with a class of persons having an interest 'opposed to what is considered as the public weal'. Mill has in mind such people as the pimp and the keeper of a gambling house. He fails to come to a definite conclusion about the justifiability of prohibiting these activities, remarking that 'there are arguments on both sides'. What is interesting in Mill's discussion here is—apart from the confirmation that his principle can yield no clear directive in questions of this kind—his appeal to 'the public weal' as a factor we have to take into account before deciding on the legitimacy of social control. Does he intend that we should classify actions as being harmful to the interests of others if it could be shown that they are contrary to 'the public weal'? We are thus led back to the problem of how widely (or narrowly) we are to construe the notion of interests. Are we to interpret interests so narrowly as to exclude the public interest or so widely as to involve consideration of the general interest and social morality? On the former interpretation we should find ourselves unable to prohibit activity we should want to prohibit; on the latter we should be able to prohibit actions that Mill would certainly wish to be left unrestrained. And if standards and values enter into what we conceive to be a man's interests even in a restricted sense of the term, *a fortiori* they will shape what we take the public interest to require.

VI

Liberty and Justice

Justice and liberty are the central concepts of social and political thought. The ideological differences between political parties depend largely on differing interpretations given to the ideas of justice and liberty, and on the comparative weight attached to each when we have to choose between them.

So writes Professor David Raphael.[1] I agree that they are *central*, yet I would hesitate to say that they are *the* central concepts of social and political thought. But my aim in this chapter is less to dispute the matter than to explore the relationship between liberty and justice in the writings of J. S. Mill. In particular, to consider what bearing his discussion of justice in *Utilitarianism* might have on the interpretation to be put on his principle of liberty. First, however, I want to look more generally at the concept of justice, before examining Mill's position in detail.

Immediately after the passage I quoted from Raphael, he goes on to remark that there is often a real conflict between liberty and 'the equalitarian aspect of justice'. But justice also serves to protect the rights of the individual against the demands of the public interest. In this respect, he argues, there is a basic identity in the aims of justice and liberty which derives from the Kantian idea of persons as ends-in-themselves.

That both 'equality' and 'rights' enter into the notion of justice is a common assumption among recent writers on the subject. And indeed they play a prominent part in Mill's account of justice. Furthermore, there is a certain plausibility in the suggestion that, depending on which one the emphasis is put, the relation of justice to liberty can be either one of conflict or harmony. Perhaps the best known argument for the view that an *egalitarian* conception of justice is hostile to freedom is that advanced by Hayek.

Since his famous, or notorious, attack on the drift to collectivism and state planning in *The Road to Serfdom*,[2] which came out in 1944, he has restated and refined the thesis that the well-intentioned search for what is called 'social justice' leads to totalitarianism and tyranny. The second volume of his most recent work on the theme is, significantly, subtitled, 'The Mirage of Social Justice'. In it Hayek argues that there are limits to what can be called just or unjust. Nothing that is not subject to human control falls within the area of justice. It is only through an anthropomorphic misuse of language that we could consider nature to be just or unjust. The actions of individuals, and also of organizations—including governments—may be just or unjust. *Society*, however, is not an organization and 'though the order of society will be affected by actions of government, so long as it remains a spontaneous order, the particular results of the social process cannot be just or unjust'.[3] Thus, if it has turned out that *A*, a person or class of persons, has great wealth, influence, or prestige whilst *B*, a person or class of persons, has little, or none, then this state of affairs—though some may wish to deplore it—cannot be called just or unjust unless it is the intended result of someone's action. So, Hayek concludes, what is termed 'social' or 'distributive' justice is strictly meaningless when applied to the workings of a spontaneous social order—it has meaning only within an organization.

Among those who have contributed to the widespread misuse of the concept of justice, by using the expression '*social* justice' and thereby interpreting the results of the spontaneous social order as if some thinking being had deliberately produced them, Hayek singles out J. S. Mill. He quotes this passage from the final chapter of *Utilitarianism*:

. . . society should treat all equally well who have deserved equally well of it, that is, who have deserved equally well absolutely. This is the highest abstract standard of social and distributive justice; towards which all institutions, and the efforts of all virtuous citizens, should be made in the utmost degree to converge.[4]

His complaint is that Mill, when he surveys the various meanings, or applications, of the term 'justice', seems not to have appreciated the crucial difference between justice as applied to individual conduct and when it is used in connection with a state of affairs which need not be the result of 'deliberate human decision'. When Mill says, for instance, that it is unjust to break an agreement, or disappoint expectations, at least when we have knowingly raised those expectations; or that it is unjust to be partial, to show preference in matters in which preference is inappropriate, then he is dealing with rules or principles that relate to individual conduct. The situations when these rules are typically invoked are entirely different from those to which 'social justice' is assumed to apply. Mill, claims Hayek, seems to have been wholly unaware of this important difference. Nor did he realize that this conception of 'social justice' leads straight to full-fledged socialism.[5]

One has to be on one's guard here against falling into confusion over the relation between equality and justice. The passage from Mill quoted by Hayek runs close to Aristotle's famous contention, namely, that justice consists in treating equals and unequals unequally, but in proportion to their relevant differences. But even if one were to accept the Aristotelian formula as a guide to social policy the question is left as to how egalitarian its application has to be. For, as so many commentators have asked, what are to count as relevant differences? To favour merit rather than need is commonly thought to be 'élitist' and to produce highly inegalitarian results. Yet Hayek would seem to believe that a concern for justice in this sense, with its extremely diluted interpretation of 'equality', endangers liberty. At the same time he also advances the more common claim that *material* equality and liberty are irreconcilable. And, indeed, if the former were true the latter would appear to be even more securely so. His contemporaries at the LSE, Tawney and Laski, both held that substantive equality was the means of achieving a genuine and wider freedom; and their beliefs were one of his obvious targets. It is surely far from self-evident that the arguments he directed against them are sufficient to convict Mill as well of being, despite himself, an enemy of liberty.

II

I now wish to turn to some aspects of Mill's discussion of justice and their connection with his doctrine of liberty.

He opens the final chapter of *Utilitarianism* with these words:

In all ages of speculation, one of the strongest obstacles to the reception of the doctrine that Utility or Happiness is the criterion of right and wrong has been drawn from the idea of Justice. The powerful sentiment, and apparently clear perception, which that word recalls with a rapidity and certainty resembling an instinct, have seemed to the majority of thinkers to point to an inherent quality in things; to show that the Just must have an existence in Nature as something absolute, generically distinct from every variety of the Expedient . . .[6]

Mill's attempt to surmount this obstacle must be reckoned a failure in at least one sense, namely, that many philosophers since his time have remained unconvinced; for the opinion is widespread among contemporary philosophers that utilitarianism *cannot* provide a satisfactory account of justice because, so it is asserted, a rule or principle which served to promote great pleasure among the vast majority would be unjust if it deprived a small minority of the basic conditions of a decent life. But my concern is less with the potential conflict between considerations derived from justice and those from utility than, to repeat, the relationship between justice and liberty; though the two sets of relationships are not unconnected. For if there is a problem of reconciling justice with liberty and, so Mill maintains, the case for liberty is based on utility, albeit in the 'largest sense', then prima facie at least the connection between liberty and justice is likely to be far from straightforward. That Mill envisaged a persistent tension between the claims of each would seem to be implicit in the way he champions the idea of individual self-development.

It is not by wearing down into uniformity all that is individual in themselves, but by cultivating it, and calling it forth, within the limits imposed by the rights and interests of others, that human beings become a noble and beautiful object of contemplation . . .[7]

Then, a little later in the same paragraph—of the essay *On Liberty*—he continues:

As much compression as is necessary to prevent the stronger specimens of human nature from encroaching on the rights of others cannot be dispensed with; but for this there is ample compensation even in the point of view of human development.[8]

Mill's point is that when self-development is achieved at the expense of others, by gratifying one's inclinations to 'the injury of others', it is the selfish rather than the social part of one's nature which is being exercised. Hence, 'to be held to *rigid rules of justice* for the sake of others, develops the feelings and capacities which have the good of others for their object'.[9]

The argument, in brief, is that restrictions on liberty are justifiable only if they are designed to prevent injury to others. Furthermore, the restraints imposed benefit those whose freedom is curtailed because it encourages their social rather than their selfish qualities. But the prevention of injury to others is a *necessary* condition for restricting liberty; the beneficial side-effects are never, taken by themselves, a reason for doing so.

However, what I want to single out from this paragraph is the use of what I take to be certain key expressions—'the rights and interests of others', 'the rights of others', and 'rigid rules of justice'. In saying they are key expressions I imply that Mill did not use them casually. On the contrary, what he calls the 'rules of justice' constitute precisely that set of rules which secure the members of society from harm, hurt, or injury: three words frequently used by Mill to present and explain his principle of liberty in the essay *On Liberty*, but also in *Utilitarianism* in his account of justice (not a conclusive consideration, I agree, but nevertheless significant). How 'rights' and 'interests' fit into the account will appear presently. For the moment it will be enough to point out that one of the chief reasons Mill had for writing *On Liberty* and advocating his principle of liberty was the danger to individuality which came from, as he saw it, the growing and stifling power of a mediocre public opinion. Instead of being at the mercy of the likings and dislikings of informal social pressures which acquire their shape and content from a 'narrow theory of life', the individual should be free to act within the limits set by such notions as 'harm to others' or respect for the 'rights and interests of others'. Both these notions find a place in his analysis of justice.

Before going on to justify this claim I should like to draw to your attention certain other passages, outside *On Liberty* and *Utilitarianism*, where Mill ventilates these ideas. And I also think it worth repeating the extent to which the framework of his thought on the subject had already been shaped by his father and Bentham, a matter which has received, so it seems to me, far too little attention from the scholarly commentators. As pointed out in Chapter I, John Stuart drew on the writings of his father and Bentham for the essay *On Liberty*, although the general view is that it was exactly there where he departed most from the opinions of his teachers, and surely James Mill and Bentham gave no sign that they were concerned about the crushing of individuality by an all-pervasive public opinion. Nevertheless, I maintain that important ingredients in John Stuart's position are clearly foreshadowed by the elder Mill and Bentham.

First, consider this statement in *Auguste Comte and Positivism* which came out a few years after *On Liberty* and *Utilitarianism*:

There is a standard of altruism to which all should be required to come up, and a degree beyond it which is not obligatory, but meritorious. It is incumbent on everyone to restrain the pursuit of his personal objects within the limits consistent with *the essential interests of others* . . . to keep all individuals and aggregations of individuals within them, is the proper office of punishment and of moral blame.[10]

It is the phrase, 'the essential interests of others' which I draw attention to in this extract. Mill goes on to say that conduct which does remain within the limits consistent with 'the essential interests of others' is 'conduct necessary to give all other persons their fair chance', that is, 'conduct which chiefly consists in not doing them harm, and not impeding them in anything which without harming others does good to themselves'. The similarity of thought and language between this passage and certain parts of Mill's treatment of justice in the *Utilitarianism* is striking. We should also notice the reference to punishment and moral blame as the means of protecting the 'essential interests of others', which corresponds to the way Mill states the purpose of *On Liberty* early on in the essay, that is, to lay down a principle for regulating the exercise of social control over the individual, whether by legal penalties or the 'moral coercion of public opinion'.[11] The only reason that can justify the use of these sanctions is 'self-protection', 'to prevent harm to others'.

It is perhaps unnecessary to go on adding examples to support my case. I cannot, however, refrain from citing one more, partly because it appears in a somewhat unlikely place, namely, in the course of a long editorial comment in the edition of his father's *Analysis of the Phenomena of the Human Mind* published in 1869, i.e. four years after the essay on Comte; and partly because it is a very compact statement of Mill's position on the role of punishment in the protection of what in the essay on Comte he calls 'essential interests'. The general context here is 'the Association theory of the moral sentiments' and the particular problem, the difference between having a duty or obligation to do something and merely regarding it as useful. What marks the difference, says Mill, is the idea of punishment. He puts it like this:

No case can be pointed out in which we consider anything as a duty, and any act or omission as immoral or wrong without regarding the person who commits the wrong and violates the duty as a fit object of punishment. We think that the general good requires that he be punished, if not by law, by the displeasure and ill-offices of his fellow-creatures . . .[12]

The feeling of indignation with which we react to misconduct of this kind is, Mill claims, 'a case of the animal impulse . . . to defend our own life or possessions, or the persons whom we care for, against actual or threatened attack'. He continues:

All conduct which we class as wrong or criminal is, or we suppose it to be, an attack upon some *vital interest* of ourselves or of those we care for, (a category which may include the public, or the whole human race): conduct which, if allowed to be repeated, would destroy or impair the security and comfort of our lives.

What are described here as 'vital interests' Mill also goes on immediately to refer to as 'paramount interests'. The desire that punishment be inflicted when one of these is attacked, closely bound up as it is with the idea of the act which has *hurt* us, is not, Mill insists, in itself a moral sentiment. It only becomes that when it is accompanied by the conviction that punishment would be for the general good.

What then are these special interests which Mill variously describes as 'essential interests', 'paramount interests', or 'vital interests'? Well, a small pointer to their nature is provided in the same passage when he contrasts the way we react if someone steals something from us with that when we are simply irritated or annoyed by someone smoking tobacco in our presence. In the former case the ideas of obligation and of injury (or harm) are involved, whereas in the latter it is a question of our disliking something that is disagreeable to us. More important, however, is the fact that Mill should talk of them as 'essential' or 'vital' interests rather than merely as 'interests', which he generally does in *On Liberty*. If affecting an interest prejudicially is taken to be a prima facie ground for the exercise of social control and no criteria are supplied for identifying the sorts of interests which require to be protected by legal or moral coercion then, as it has been rightly argued, Mill's doctrine can be falsely construed as relativistic; that is, interests are seen as being constituted by the norms or values current in a specific society at a particular time, and since societies vary greatly in this respect so also would what are regarded as 'interests'. Interests in this sense would 'depend for their existence on social recognition' and would be 'closely connected with prevailing standards about the sort of behaviour a man can legitimately expect from others'.[13] Moreover they can range from the important to the trivial, whereas the interests which Mill has in mind, and which he associates with 'harm' or 'injury', are *essential* or *paramount* because they turn on such crucial matters as *security*—'to everyone's feelings the most vital of all interests . . . security no human being can possibly do without; on it we depend for all our immunity from evil . . . [it is the] most indispensable of all necessaries after physical nutriment . . .'[14]

Now Mill is clearly not limiting the application of his remarks to Britain in the mid-nineteenth century. The complaint against attributing to him a relativistic interpretation of interests is therefore well founded; for Mill emphasizes that security is something 'no *human being* can possibly do without'. And he has in mind the *human* condition when he says that the rules and institutions which provide for our security, and the conduct which conforms to these rules, go to make 'safe for us the very groundmark of our existence'. To see how security, this most vital of the 'essential interests', is related to his account of justice we need to look more closely at the course of the argument in Chapter V of *Utilitarianism*.

'Justice', he maintains, 'is a name for certain classes of moral rules, which concern the essentials of human well-being more nearly, and are therefore of more absolute obligation, than any other rules for the guidance of life . . .'. And then, by way of explaining what these rules are,

The moral rules which forbid mankind to hurt one another (in which we must never forget to include wrongful interference with each other's freedom) are more vital to human well-being than any maxims however important, which only point out the best mode of managing some department of human affairs . . . they are the main element in determining the whole of the social feelings of mankind. It is their observance which alone preserves peace among human beings . . .[15]

Now it is 'these moralities' which according to Mill, 'compose the obligations of justice', primarily at any rate. They are the moral rules designed to prevent the infliction of harm by others, 'either directly or by being hindered in one's freedom of pursuing one's own good'. When he proceeds to cite examples of injustice, or the infliction of harm, security features again in his list, though it would be stretching the term very widely indeed to make it cover all the cases he mentions: 'acts of wrongful aggression', 'wrongful exercise of power over some one', 'wrongfully withholding from someone something which is his due'—all of which Mill puts into the category of 'inflicting a positive hurt'.[16]

So far the connection between 'justice' on the one hand and 'hurt' or 'injury' on the other has been obvious. Another of Mill's rules of justice, 'good for good', seems less obviously related to the idea of harm. He insists, however, that the connection in this case is no less real because it is inseparable from what he regards as one of the more important evils, namely, disappointment of expectation; for 'he who accepts benefits, and denies a return of them when needed, inflicts a real hurt, by disappointing one of the most natural and reasonable of expectations'. What brings it within, or close to, the province of 'security' is the fact that something on which we have 'habitually and with full assurance relied' is removed just when it is needed.[17]

Mill claims that most of the precepts of justice currently accepted in his day are simply ways of implementing the principles he has already enunciated. That one should only be held responsible for *voluntary* actions or omissions; that no one should be condemned without his own case being heard; that the degree of punishment should be related to the gravity of the offence—all these and other similar maxims serve the purpose of 'inflicting punishment when due, and awarding to each person his right'. In saying this Mill shows that he shares the widespread conviction that justice requires that everyone should receive what he deserves; and that a central case of injustice 'consists in taking or withholding from a person that to which he has a *moral right*'.[18]

We have noticed that Mill distinguishes justice from other branches of morality. It comprises 'certain moral requirements' which, he maintains, 'stand higher in the scale of social utility, and are therefore of more paramount obligation, than any others'.[19] How, apart from their supreme importance, do we identify the rules of which it consists? Mill's answer is that the rules of justice can be distinguished from the other obligations of morality by the fact that its obligations give birth to 'a right'. It is this feature, 'a right in some person, correlative to the moral obligation [which] constitutes the specific difference between justice, and generosity or beneficence'. 'Justice', he declares, 'implies something which it is not only right to do, and wrong not to do, but which some individual person can claim from us as his moral right'. Hence, 'wherever there is a right, the case is one of justice'. To deny that this is the distinguishing feature of justice can have no other consequence than 'to merge all morality in justice'.[20]

I am less interested in the question whether Mill may have gone astray here in asserting a conceptual link between justice and rights than in seeing how the violation of *rights* along with—so we have noticed—damage to *essential interests* fall within the area which Mill defines as injustice. Early on in this chapter I pointed out that the principle of liberty sought to secure freedom of action within certain limits, alternatively described as 'being held to rigid rules of justice' or 'the limits imposed by the rights and interests of others'.

We are now in a position to appreciate what these expressions signify and the way Mill saw them to be related to each other. Among the deductions one may be tempted to make is that justice, so far from being in conflict with, or limiting, liberty serves to support it. I mean that there is in both the idea of a right and in the notion of essential interests a bias, to put it at its lowest, in favour of freedom. For, as Hart has argued, if there are any moral rights at all, it follows that there is at least one natural right, namely, the equal right of all men to be free.[21] If we combine this with Mill's claim that an essential interest is damaged when there is wrongful interference with a person's freedom, then we would seem compelled to locate liberty on both sides of the liberty versus justice dichotomy.

III

It is time to take stock. Mill's principle of liberty specifies that 'harm to others' is the only reason for restricting individual human conduct. Ever since the publication of the essay *On Liberty* in 1859 questions have been asked about the meaning of and scope of this restriction. What constitutes *harm*? Let us confine ourselves to three of the several possible answers.

(1) Given that Mill was a self-professed utilitarian, harm = pain;
(2) Harm is used in a non-technical, normal sense of the word;
(3) Harm = violation of the rules of justice.

I think that the first can be eliminated. To say that something is harmful is not the same as saying that someone may be pained or distressed by it. Someone may be distressed by the revelation of an unwelcome truth or pained by getting the worse of an argument, but in neither case would admit to his being harmed. Moreover, we may do harm to someone without causing him any pain, e.g. by over-indulgence. We judge an action to be harmful in terms of certain standards. It is not a simple matter of empirical observation—as painful effects would be. John Stuart saw it as an advantage of utilitarian ethics that it appealed to an external consideration whereas likes and dislikes were merely internal reactions. Bentham and James Mill similarly distinguished between genuine moral condemnation and disapproval based on 'mere' antipathy.

A 'consistent utilitarian' can surely discount some pains— e.g. the pains involved in the extraction of a rotten tooth or the distress experienced by the mass-murderer at being caught and imprisoned. (John Stuart gives the example of someone who fails at a competitive examination.) To this it may be objected that the pains are *not* being *discounted* in such examples—they enter into the calculation and fall far short of the benefits involved. After all, Bentham said punishment was an *evil*, to be imposed only in order to avoid a greater evil. A balance has to be struck, and the factors entering into the calculation are clearly not being discounted in the literal sense. However, when a *utilitarian* says that some pains are not even to enter into the calculation at all, i.e. the distress felt by persons holding groundless antipathies, then he is abandoning pain as such as the criterion of a right action. What can be said in defence of this position?

It might be argued that the pain felt by a person holding a groundless antipathy ('mere prejudice') can be distinguished from the pain resulting from the action which distresses him. *A* witnesses a mugging and is terribly shocked, but the mugging is wrong independently of *A*'s distress at seeing it. *A* also thinks that mugging is wrong and its being a legal offence reflects the fact that *A* shares this belief with most other people. However, even a shared belief of this sort is not enough. It needs to be shown that mugging is productive of pain (or a balance of pain over pleasure) quite apart from the shared belief. And this cannot be done, so it is argued, in the case of eating pork or taking liquor on a Sunday. In short, the test is: is the action wrong independently of a belief that is wrong?

In presenting this line of argument—which is implicit in what Bentham, James Mill, and John Stuart say—I do not wish to commit myself to accepting it. More important is the way it connects up with the claim that 'harm' and 'injury' are 'objective', whereas likings and dislikings are 'subjective'.

For Bentham and James Mill at any rate, for an action, or type of action, to be regarded as harmful or injurious it was necessary (but not sufficient) that it had a tendency to be productive of a balance of pain. Following on from what was said earlier, the balance of pain is a consequence of (involved in) the action itself, not our personal feelings about the action. Whether or not a type of action causes pain was certainly taken to be an *objective* question, to be settled by empirical observation in the same sort of way that, say, we settle the question of smoking and lung cancer or whisky and liver disease. At least, that is how many passages in Bentham strike me. Of course, if that is how they saw it then they could be just plain wrong. On the other hand it makes sense of their claim that judgements about right and wrong were 'objective'.

It will be objected that 'harm' is not synonymous with or reducible to 'pain'. I would agree. But they wished to make it so. Again, they could be wrong.

Someone concerned with elucidating the notion of 'harm' quite apart from the Benthamite interpretation might point out that the question whether X is harmful is not equivalent to the question, 'does X cause a balance of pain over pleasure?' Pornography, abortion, etc. are matters which bring this our clearly. Pornographic films rate an X certificate and persons under 18 (in the UK) are not allowed into the cinema. Obviously this is not a decision based on an inquiry into the balance of pain over pleasure. A Benthamite would complain that decisions as to what is harmful taken in this way, without a felicific calculus, are indeed arbitrary because people will have different ideas of what is harmful. The suffering of pain is an event, it *happens*, just as rainfall happens—whereas the judgement as to harm depends on evaluative considerations; i.e. if one is going to use 'harm' in the loose sense typical of ordinary discourse.

Thus, although Bentham and James Mill seem to link harm (injury) to pain, John Stuart's use of harm—to 'interests' and 'rights'—points to our third alternative (harm = violation of the rules of justice) as the right answer. But I conclude this chapter by considering some of the main obstacles standing in the way of my interpretation, though it may be that there can be no single interpretation which captures the whole of Mill's argument in a precise and convincing manner.

Let me deal with one of the less formidable obstacles first. Mill says that only harmful conduct should be subjected to social control, be made subject to punishment. He stipulates a necessary but *not* a sufficient condition for restricting liberty. For instance, the costs of inflicting punishment may be too high. As a utilitarian and, in this respect, a follower of Bentham, he looked on punishment as an evil to be visited on a person only when the gains outweighed the losses. It is for this reason that the principle of liberty needs to be formulated to accommodate the fact that punishment does not necessarily have to be inflicted on persons whose conduct is harmful. A formulation of Mill's principle designed to take account of this fact would therefore read: 'The liberty of action of the individual ought *prima facie* to be interfered with if and only if his conduct is harmful to others.'[22]

Let me state quite baldly that I am happy to accept the amendment. It does not seem to me to go against the substance of what I have been arguing.

A more serious obstacle derives from what are called Mill's 'co-operation' and 'good samaritan' examples. Let me explain. Mill says that we may be subjected to coercion, legal or moral, to prevent harmful conduct—but he also says that we may be compelled to perform many positive acts for the *benefit* of others. Among the examples he gives are:

(*a*) To give evidence in a court of justice;

(*b*) To do military service

(*c*) To perform certain acts of individual beneficence, such as saving a man's life.

But it is important to notice that he utters a warning about cases of this kind. He remarks:

A person may cause evil to others not only by his actions but by his inaction, and in either case he is justly accountable to them for the injury. The latter case, it is true, requires a much more cautious exercise of compulsion than the former . . .[23]

I mentioned Mill's debt to his father and Bentham. It will be remembered that Bentham (*Principles of Morals and Legislation*, Ch. XVII) had said:

As to rules of beneficence, these, as far as concerns matters of detail must necessarily be abandoned to the jurisdiction of private ethics . . . [BUT] in cases where the person is in danger, why should it not be made the duty of every man to save another from mischief, when it can be done without prejudicing himself . . . ?

Among his examples are:

(*i*) A woman's head-dress catches fire: water is at hand: a man, instead of assisting to quench the fire, looks on, and laughs at it;

(*ii*) A drunken man, falling with his face downwards into a puddle, is in danger of suffocation: lifting his head a little on one side would save him: another man sees this and lets him lie.

He concludes: 'Who is there that in any of these cases would think punishment misapplied?[24]

As I have admitted, there are problems here which make this a *much* more serious obstacle than the first one. The danger must be obvious that if we allow examples of this kind to fall under the harmful conduct rubric then Mill's principle could also become one of 'conferring benefits' on others. Hence the distinct sense of unease on the part of some commentators who rather than attempt to bring such examples within the ambit of the harm principle are content to see Mill as being plainly inconsistent. Others, however, like David Lyons, are prepared to amend Mill's principle yet again in order to maintain consistency. He offers us this: 'The prevention of harm to others is a good reason, and the only good reason, for restricting behaviour',[25] calling it a 'harm—prevention principle' as opposed to a 'harmful conduct—prevention principle', which is what is usually taken to be Mill's principle. However, I do not find anything in what Mill says about the rules of justice that would support the extension of his principle to confer benefits on others in the form of saving or protecting them from injury or death. Certainly the notion of disappointed expectations, as Mill presents it, cannot be pushed as far as that, for it is manifested in such actions as breach of promise or returning good for good. Perhaps the idea of wrongfully withholding from someone something which is his due can be made to cover them? Whatever the stand each of us may be inclined to take on this problem, there is the farther question of how far our duties may be thought to extend. Would we want to take them so far as to favour the plaintiff in the following case reported in America?

An asbestos worker, Robert McFall (39), was suffering from a fatal form of anaemia and needed bone marrow to save his life. His cousin, David Shimp, was the only known compatible match for a marrow transplant, but was unwilling to undergo an operation to effect the transfer. McFall brought a court action against Shimp (32), his lawyers posing the question: 'In order to aid a dying man . . . may society compel an unwilling donor to undergo a medically safe, experientially proven, minor procedure . . . ?' In court, McFall's lawyer claimed that an English common law precedent dating back to the 13th century was applicable to the case:

That law says society has the right to force an individual to uphold a moral and legal obligation to secure the well-being of other members of society.

The judge, however, refused to allow the injunction, saying that, despite 'the moral implications involved in the case', to grant McFall's request 'would be to set a dangerous precedent . . . for a society to sink its teeth into the jugular vein or neck of one of its members is revolting to . . . concepts of jurisprudence . . . such a precedent could conceivably extend into the spectra of the swastika and the Inquisition, with experiments on humans'. His decision was, he said, based on US common law precedents which 'uphold the sanctity of the individual and recognize *no legal compulsion to give aid or take action to save another person's life.*' (My emphasis, J.C.R.) After delivering the judgement he is reported as having said: 'In essence, I have condemned someone to death to be carried out by fate.'[26]

I now come to the most serious obstacle of all. How to distinguish morality from justice in the matter of *punishment*? And why is this a problem for me? Well, in the extract I quoted from Mill's editorial comment on his father's *Analysis* it was argued that 'duty' and 'obligation', moral concepts, and the ideas of the 'immoral' and 'wrong' were conceptually tied to the notion of punishment. Whoever commits the wrong or violates the duty is a fit object of punishment—whether by the law or the 'displeasure and ill-offices of his fellow-creatures'. But, surely, it will be said, punishment in either mode is reserved for actions that are harmful to others. This would therefore make the category of 'harm' coextensive with that of immoral actions. And immorality is not the same as injustice. Actions that are wrong, whether in ordinary ethical discourse or in Mill's account, are not necessarily also injust. So what has happened? Did not Mill say, very clearly, that the moral rules which forbid mankind to *hurt* one another are more vital to human well-being than any other rules, because it is their observance which alone preserves peace among men? And did he not also go on to say that it is these moralities, primarily, which compose the obligations of justice? When, then, in other passages he links harm (or hurt) with punishment, and punishment with the immoral, how can he reconcile that with his description of justice?

To put the question in a slightly different way. If liberty of action must remain within the limits consistent with the essential interests of others, and if these essential interests coincide with the vital interests which are protected by the rules of justice, is not the requirement that wrongful but not unjust conduct be subject to punishment an additional and severe restriction on liberty?

I have indeed argued that the rules of justice (in which the notion of a *right* is essential) mark off the 'other-regarding sphere' from the province of liberty. And the rules of justice are part of morality. Yet Mill does also say that actions may be 'hurtful' to others 'without going to the length of violating any of their constituted rights'. In such cases the offender may be justly punished by opinion, though not by law. This would make a threefold division:

(*a*) Actions that do not harm others;
(*b*) Actions that harm others but do not violate their 'constituted rights';
(*c*) Actions that violate 'constituted rights'.

Would it be right to regard (*c*) as the area of 'justice', and (*b*) and (*c*) together as the area of morality? And that *legal* punishment is appropriate only for (*c*) and 'moral punishment' for (*b*)? Of course, moral punishment may be added to legal punishment when rights are violated, e.g. when the public reacts strongly to particularly vicious crimes.

Well, this suggestion looks neat and tidy and seems to correspond to much that Mill says. But there are passages that do not quite fit and it seems to me that Mill did not work it out at all carefully. He makes it clear beyond doubt that, when he talks of the 'compulsion and control' which society is entitled to exercise to 'prevent harm to others' he means both 'legal penalties' and 'the moral coercion of public opinion'. He also makes it clear that 'moral coercion' is different (in his mind at least) from merely showing distaste or contempt for a person's conduct. The former involves 'visiting him with evil', the latter does not.

But what of the respective areas of legal and moral coercion? One suggestion, made above, is that they correspond to justice and the rest of morality. Yet he says, of actions 'which concern the interest of other people', that 'if any one does an act hurtful to others, there is a *prima facie* case for punishing him, by law, or, where legal penalties are not safely applicable, by general disapprobation'.[27] So the distinction here is not between legal punishment for breach of the rules of justice and moral punishment for moral wrongs other than injustice but rather one based on the criterion of whether the legal penalties are 'safely applicable'. For example, many cases of breaking promises are not open to legal remedy: we think it wrong, for various reasons, to bring in the heavy hand of the law in such cases. This is what Mill seems to have in mind. It certainly does not seem to be based on the distinction between injustice (or breach of the rules of justice) and moral wrongs other than injustice.

Mill says: 'Acts, of whatever kind, which, without justifiable cause, do harm to others, may be, and in the more important cases absolutely require to be, controlled by the unfavourable sentiments, and, when needful, by the active interference of mankind'.[28] What force has 'unfavourable sentiments' here? They *seem* to be the same as the 'dislike' and 'contempt', falling short of *punishment*, that we must show toward self-regarding deficiencies. Maybe it is just unintentional, loose use of language. Unfortunately there are too many cases of that sort to make a clear-cut interpretation of Mill fit all passages.

There is a passage early on in Chapter IV of *On Liberty* where Mill appears to be choosing his words with special care. He is referring to the line of conduct we should be made to observe towards others. He says: 'This conduct consists . . . in not injuring the interests of one another; or rather certain interests, which, either by express legal provision or by tacit understanding, ought to be considered as rights . . .'.[29]

The use of 'rights' here seems to identify the conduct he has in mind as linked to the rules of justice. But shortly after he makes it clear that violation of *interests*, short of the violation of 'constituted rights', can be met with 'moral punishment'. This seems to confirm the division suggested above.

An explanation of the apparent untidiness in Mill's theory of liberty which must be allowed as a possibility is that the hard-core meaning or primary test of the harmful is set by the rules of justice. Mill, however, came to see that some actions deserving of punishment did not fall into that category; moreover, they were cases approvingly cited by Bentham. Rather than let lie around as *ad hoc* and inconsistent additions to the requirements of justice they were brought in under the standard of morality. There is an air of unkindness or desperation about this explanation, and as yet I cannot bring myself to accept it.

Finally, although, as I have tried to show, the account of *interests* in *On Liberty*, as outlined in the previous chapter, needs further elaboration in terms of Chapter V of *Utilitarianism* I would still attach importance to this notion. I do not think that Mill was being careless when in Chapter III of *On Liberty* he linked 'rights and interests', 'the injury of others', and 'rigid rules of justice' together, all in the same paragraph. What these rules of justice are gets attention in Chapter V of *Utilitarianism* where Mill talks of vital interests and the essentials of human well-being, and the need to uphold the moral rules which protect those interests. To repeat, he is talking here of those 'paramount interests' referred to in his note in his father's *Analysis*. And the 'permanent interests' which enter into his conception of utility 'in the largest sense' seem to me to be identifiable in these terms. Thus not everything that could be called an interest would figure among the interests which Mill wants protected. So a process of selection is involved; and that also implies that not all cases of being painfully affected are also cases of interests being harmed. Whether someone is painfully affected is an empirical question requiring no appeal to standards of evaluation. Picking out certain interests and assigning priority to their protection is not a simple empirical procedure and *does* require appeal to criterion of importance, criteria such as are summed up in the phrases 'permanent interests', 'essential interests', 'paramount interests'—all of which feature in key passages in Mill.

APPENDIX

On Social Freedom

AN essay attributed to Mill and entitled *On Social Freedom* was published for the first time in the *Oxford and Cambridge Review* of June 1907. The editor of the journal explained that the manuscript was found among Mill's papers at Avignon and that Mary Taylor, described as Mill's living representative,[1] had approved the publication of the essay. It is a remarkable fact that historians of political ideas and students of Mill have largely ignored the essay, even since 1941 when, in order to make it better known, it was brought out in the United States as a separate volume.[2] However, from a comparison of certain of its ideas with what we know to be genuinely Mill's and an examination of the original manuscript, part of which, as I shall explain, has never been published, I have come to think that Mill did not write this essay, although I very much doubt whether suspicions as to its authenticity are the main reason for its having been so much neglected in the past. Before going into the reasons which have led me to hold this view I propose to give a brief outline of the essay. This would seem necessary both because many readers are likely to be unfamiliar with it and because some of the arguments I put forward will, I hope, be better understood in the context of the essay as a whole. And if it should be thought that I have not established my case there would still remain to be explained a number of puzzling aspects of the essay to which I shall shortly be referring. Furthermore, if this is genuinely Mill's a widely accepted version of his political philosophy would have to be modified and the explanation of the change in his thinking sought in the criticisms summarized in the preceding pages. For Mill is generally regarded, we have already indicated, as a leading exponent of the negative idea of liberty—'liberty is just absence of restraint'—which prevailed in England until the Idealists reconstructed the philosophy of liberalism. But if the essay *On Social Freedom* was written by him we should have to admit that his role as the harbinger of the new

This appendix first appeared as pp. 38–54 of *Mill and his Early Critics* (University of Leicester Press, 1956).

liberalism is much greater than is usually allowed. So far, at any rate, there are few signs that political theorists are aware of the essay's possible significance in this respect.

The essay begins with a brief discussion of the problem of free-will. By a purely rational process, the author says, the determinist argument can easily be established, 'that every act of every human creature is absolutely determined by unalterable laws'. Although this conclusion is not capable of being refuted we cannot act as if it were true. We believe we are free, we sense it immediately, and that is enough. It can be assumed, therefore, that not only are men free, but also that they desire to be free, and that this desire is widespread. Hence it is important to know the extent to which freedom is necessarily limited by living in society with other men ('the limitations which arise inevitably out of the conditions under which we live'), because we may destroy valuable features of social life through a failure to distinguish 'those restraints which must be borne for the sake of our moral and social culture, from those which arise from abuses in our social system . . .'. Now freedom is freedom to *act*, and to act as we want to act. Since there are all sorts of men there must be many kinds of freedom. Thus freedom is not one uniform thing. Some wish to be free to get drunk, others to be insolent to passers-by, others to maltreat their wives, and so forth.

The author then moves on to consider what he calls the Individualist Theory of Freedom. To quote:

I believe that some persons have been disposed to regard each human individual as occupying, or as having a right to occupy, a certain 'sphere of activity', in sole and exclusive possession. Within this sphere he is to exercise perfect freedom, unimpeded by the free action of any other human creature. . . . According to this theory, a state of perfect and universal freedom may be attained by merely assigning to each individual his own sphere of activity, by securing to him free and unimpeded action within this sphere and by strictly and absolutely limiting his activity to this sphere.

Something like this theory, the author submits, is at the basis of all endeavours to extend human liberty. But it is an ideal quite impossible to realize. Moreover, if we were able to discover the degree of self-sufficiency such a condition would necessitate, it is probable that we should not even desire freedom of this sort.

I have not the slightest doubt that the life of each human individual, thus penned up in his own 'sphere', would be a life of continual misery. His freedom would be practically limited, in most cases, to the freedom to *starve* . . . the far greater number of human desires are such as can only be satisfied through some kind of *social relation*, or relation between fellow-beings.

The final section of the essay is concerned with 'the essential nature of freedom'. Freedom, it is stated, implies choice. But the choice may be good or bad, and depending on the nature of the motives which lead us to choose this rather than that course of action, so we are more or less free. How do we decide which are the better motives? Feeling, rather than intellect, is the test, for we have

> a strong and unmistakable *feeling* that some motives are higher, and others lower. . . . That man seems to me to act with freedom who yields to the impulse of the *highest motive* which demands his obedience or which presents itself to his consciousness, at the moment of determination . . . [but] it is not merely because an action is impelled by a low or base motive that it seems wanting in freedom, but because there is, *at the same time*, a higher and nobler motive which claims the obedience of the agent.

The idea is commonly held that human freedom is most severely checked by the laws of civil governments. This is very far from being true. Civil and judicial coercion limit human freedom to a very small extent, since persons of ordinary decency will rarely find themselves constrained by the law. The force that prevents us from behaving in unusual ways is not so much the law as public opinion. What keeps the majority of us in the old track of use and wont is the opinion of that class or section of the public whose opinion we most regard.

> There is a vast, vague, mysterious authority which casts its shadow over all human affairs, and which governs men's actions with a far more stringent rule than that exercised by the civil governor—the authority of Conventionalism or Conventional Propriety. There is a strange and vague dread of doing what no one else ever does, of being altogether singular, which far more frequently restrains men—excepting the lowest or poorest classes in society, and perhaps *not* excepting these—from the indulgence of their personal fancies and caprices, than the prohibitions of civil law.[3]

In her introduction to the reprint of the essay (1941) Dorothy Fosdick says that there is no mention of the work in any history of political theory or in any study of Mill, and that it is not listed in any bibliography of Mill's writings. Since 1941 the situation has remained substantially the same. Of the books published in England during the period from 1941 to 1954 in which it would be reasonable to expect some reference to the essay the only one to mention it, so far as I know, is the recent biography of Mill by Michael Packe, where it is listed in the bibliography, but Mr Packe does not discuss it in the text.[4] More surprising is its omission from the *Bibliography of the Published Writings of John Stuart Mill* (edited by MacMinn and others, Northwestern University, 1954). It is true that this bibliography, based on a notebook containing what seems to be a complete record of Mill's publications from 1822 to 1873, purports only to cover the

writings which were actually made public in Mill's own lifetime, but
the editor also gives a list of posthumous publications (p. xii) in which
the essay does not appear.[5]

Miss Fosdick thinks it strange that the essay's significance has been
overlooked because, she maintains, it represents 'a marked advance
in Mill's thinking'. The central argument of *On Liberty* is modified
and new light is thrown on 'the shift in his position from individualism toward socialism and idealism during the latter years of his life'.
More clearly than any other of his works this essay shows that Mill
'was . . . a potential idealist'.[6] Now, at first sight, there do seem to be
a number of considerations favouring Miss Fosdick's view, that this
essay was written by Mill in his last years when he was throwing off
the last shackles of the individualism he inherited from his father and
Bentham and so clearly manifested in the essay *On Liberty*. The following are the most important.

(*a*) Mill read the reviews of his own works very closely. Later
editions of the *Examination of Sir William Hamilton's Philosophy*, for
example, contain replies to the criticisms made of some of his arguments in the earlier editions. In particular, we know that he was
aware of some of the things said against the essay *On Liberty*.[7] As the
previous section shows, between the time of its first appearance in
1859 and Mill's death in 1873 a substantial number of reviews were
published, many of them early enough for him to have given careful
consideration to their criticisms. Much of this review literature, it will
have been noticed, is taken up with the individualistic foundations of
Mill's theory of freedom which, it was contended, underlay the whole
essay *On Liberty*. It is this individualism that seems to be the principal
target in the essay *On Social Freedom*. So it would not have been surprising if Mill had attempted to square these criticisms with what
he had written in 1859, even to the extent of abandoning some of the
positions he had formerly held. He was certainly flexible enough in
mind to give up doctrines he had previously accepted with confidence
(e.g. the Wage Fund Theory).

(*b*) Miss Fosdick observes that the idea of freedom which is based
on the distinction between various motives of human actions—'the
free action differs from the unfree, or the action which is more free
from the action which is less free, in the different orders of motives
which prompt them'—is strikingly similar to what Mill says in his
Utilitarianism about some pleasures being of a higher quality than
others. And had not Mill recognized in the *Logic* the truth of the saying that 'none but a person of confirmed virtue is completely free'?[8]

(*c*) There is an important element common to both the essay *On
Liberty* and this essay *On Social Freedom*, namely, the same fear of

the effects of public opinion, and the conviction that the informal pressures of convention and custom can work greater mischief than the explicit sanctions of the law.

(*d*) If Mill had wanted to acknowledge publicly that he had given up or modified some of the ideas expressed in the *Liberty* it would not have been through a revised edition of that work, as had been the case with the *Logic* and the *Political Economy*. In the *Autobiography* he says that the *Liberty* is consecrated to Harriet's memory and that no alteration or addition will ever be made to it.[9] This suggests that Mill would have written a separate work on the problem of human freedom if he had wished to revise his earlier opinions. But there is, in fact, no evidence that he did wish to retract or modify anything he had written in the *Liberty*; and this brings me to the first of the reasons for doubting whether the essay *On Social Freedom* is the work of a Mill having second thoughts about liberty.

(1) Miss Fosdick says that Mill probably wrote the essay shortly before his death in 1873. This seems very unlikely. As we have seen, most of the important criticisms that can be made of Mill's various arguments in the *Liberty* had been made in the early reviews, thus giving him ample opportunity to record any change of opinion in the later 1860s and the 1870s. In those passages of the *Autobiography* dealing with the *Liberty* there is no hint of dissatisfaction with any of the doctrines he had once professed.[10] In September 1871 (i.e. less than two years before his death) he wrote from Avignon to Émile Acollas and refers to the essay *On Liberty* in terms which hardly suggest second thoughts. Mill is commenting on a pamphlet written by Acollas, with much of which he agrees. He deals first with the historical section of the pamphlet and then moves on to consider the philosophical part in these words:

Quant à la partie philosophique, vous savez probablement par mon 'Essai sur la Liberté', dans quel sens et avec quelles limites j'entends notre principe commun, celui de l'autonomie de l'individu. Je reconnais cette autonomie comme une règle rigoureuse dans les choses qui ne regardent que l'individu lui-même ou, si elles intéressent les autres, ne les intéressent que par l'influence de l'exemple ou par l'intérêt indirect que d'autres peuvent avoir au bonheur et à la prospérité de chacun. Par cette doctrine j'affranchis de tout contrôle, hors celui de la critique, le cercle de la vie individuelle proprement dite. Mais dans ceux de nos actes qui touchent directement aux intérêts d'autrui, il faut à mon sens une autre règle, celle de l'intérêt général.'[11]

And just a few months before his death Mill read what was up to that time the most comprehensive assault on the *Liberty*, Fitzjames Stephen's *Liberty, Equality, Fraternity*. Stephen, as I have said, repeats many of the criticisms of the earlier reviews and brings together most of the objections to the Essay that have since been generally accepted as valid. Mill, however, saw no ground for repudiating any of his principles, and remarked to Bain that Stephen 'does not know what he is arguing against; and is more likely to repel than to attract people.'[12]

(2) Anyone familiar with Mill's other works must find it difficult to believe that he wrote the introductory section of the essay *On Social Freedom* which deals with the problem of the freedom of the will. The author of this section is obviously worried by the problem. He fears that it is possible to demonstrate that 'human freedom is altogether an illusion . . . that every act of every human creature is absolutely determined by unalterable laws'. He says that he cannot refute this theory but claims that no sane person 'can adopt and consistently carry out this doctrine . . . [because] every reasonable act of every sane man is a practical assertion of the existence of individual freedom'. He contends that the ability, within certain limits, to do as we please (the faculty of voluntary action) undoubtedly exists. It cannot be proved by any process of logical argumentation but rests on 'some immediate or spontaneous sense, on some movement of consciousness. Men believe that they are free . . . in perhaps the same way as they believe that they are *men*, and not mere locomotive vegetables or two-legged beasts—mainly because they cannot help believing it'. Clearly the writer thinks the free-will problem is an insoluble one— logic and immediate awareness tell different stories. But this is not Mill's position—at least, not from the 1830s until his death. From the time when he claimed to have solved the problem on the lines set out in the *Logic*[13] until the fourth, revised, edition of the *Examination of Sir William Hamilton's Philosophy* in 1872, Mill's views on the subject did not change. They can be summed up by an entry in his diary written in 1854: 'The doctrines of free-will and necessity rightly understood are both true. It is necessary, that is, it was inevitable from the beginning of things, that I should freely will whatever things I do will.'[14] In the *Autobiography* Mill tells us how he was at one period disturbed by the implications of the doctrine of necessity. 'I felt as if I was scientifically proved to be the helpless slave of antecedent circumstances.' Gradually he came to see the way out: 'though our character is formed by circumstances, our own desires can do much to shape those circumstances'. The doctrine of free-will—the conviction that we have real power over the formation of our own characters—was entirely consistent with the doctrine of circumstances. 'I no longer suffered the burden of thinking one doctrine true and the contrary doctrine morally beneficial'.[15]

It is not possible to date with accuracy the time when Mill worked out this theory. He refers to it in the part of the *Autobiography* dealing with his mental crisis (autumn 1826 onwards) and states that it was 'during the later returns of my dejection' that the doctrine of Necessity 'weighed on my existence like an incubus'. In the preceding paragraphs he recounts his connections with the Saint-Simonians in 1829 and 1830, so it seems probable that he had solved his problem some years before the first draft of the *Logic* was completed in November 1840. This point is important because it might be supposed that though Mill did not write the essay in his last years he may have done so in early life. Against this view is the fact that there is in it a reference to the Queen ('One man would be free to wear his hat while "God save the Queen" is being played or sung'),[16] making it certain that the essay could not have been written before 1837; and by this date Mill had probably arrived at the theory of the will expounded in the *Logic*. Since this theory is reasserted in 1854 (in his diary), in 1867 (in a letter),[17] in 1870 (when the *Autobiography* was finally revised), and in 1872 (the fourth edition of the *Examination of Sir William Hamilton's Philosophy*)—as well as in the later editions of the *Logic* itself, i.e. third edition 1851, eighth edition 1872—there is no way of accounting for this first section of the essay *On Social Freedom* save on the assumption that it is not Mill's.[18]

(3) No conclusions about the free-will problem entail any particular theory of civil or political liberty. Questions about human actions being determined by unalterable laws are not questions about legal or social restraints. The eighteenth-century philosophers Price and Priestley, for example, stood in definite opposition to each other on the issue of free-will versus determinism, yet agreed, as radical democrats, on a common political programme to extend the area of political liberty. But the distinction between the two kinds of problem involved is blurred, if not downright confused, by the author of *On Social Freedom*. He says: 'I assume not only that men have the power of exercising freedom [i.e. that all our actions are *not* absolutely determined by unalterable laws—J. C. R.], but that this power is generally regarded by men as an object of desire.' He then goes on to say that though we desire freedom, the fact of living in society inevitably involves restrictions upon it, and that some of these restrictions are not only unavoidable but desirable, because 'men may sometimes rebel against those restraints which are necessarily associated with the most valuable forms . . . of our social life'. Miss Fosdick sees that these problems are on different levels. 'The issue of liberty', she says, 'does not depend on whether or not our acts are absolutely determined by unalterable psychical and physical laws'.[19] And there is every sign that Mill, too, was fully aware of the distinction. Guilty of many logical blunders, he can escape the charge of failing to differ-

entiate civil liberty from freedom of the will. The opening lines of the essay *On Liberty* run: 'The subject of this Essay is not the so-called Liberty of the Will, so unfortunately opposed to the misnamed doctrine of Philosophical Necessity; but Civil, or Social Liberty: the nature and limits of the power which can be legitimately exercised by society over the individual.'

(4) The similarity between the idea of freedom presented in the essay *On Social Freedom* and the distinction between higher and lower pleasures in *Utilitarianism*, which led Miss Fosdick to say that the former 'bears the unmistakable marks of Mill's utilitarian ethics', is not so complete as it might seem. For there is a significant difference between the procedures by which the conclusions are reached. In *Social Freedom* the author appeals to 'feelings' as having 'a more distinct and unquestionable reality than . . . intellectual conceptions'. He admits that he cannot demonstrate 'to the critical reader' that some motives are higher than others: 'the fact to which I appeal is that we—meaning those persons to whom this work is mainly addressed [i.e. those who rely on feelings rather than intellect— J. C. R.]—have a strong and unmistakable *feeling* that some motives are higher, and others lower'. Now in the *Utilitarianism* Mill's thesis is that one pleasure is more valuable than another if those who have experienced both prefer the former, and he is sure that, as a matter of fact, those who are equally familiar with the various kinds of pleasure have a marked preference for those of the intellect. 'On a question', says Mill, 'which is the best worth having of two pleasures . . . the judgment of those who are qualified by knowledge of both, or, if they differ, that of the majority among them, must be admitted as final.'[20] Thus Mill has a definite and objective criterion for deciding which pleasures are higher in the scale than others—the majority—whereas the author of *Social Freedom* rests his case on the feelings of a restricted class of people, namely those who agree with him in acknowledging the importance of feelings as decisive in questions of this kind. *Utilitarianism* first appeared in *Fraser's Magazine* in 1861: it seems scarcely credible that Mill should later have become so utterly vague about the criteria for discriminating good from bad motives.[21]

Moreover, all this is admitting that motives and pleasures are the same thing, which of course they are not. It is not a tautology to say that one's motive for doing so and so was mere pleasure. So to argue from an account of motives to a theory of pleasures is to move from one type of mental phenomenon to another. If, however, one chooses to say that they are so closely related that statements about motives are good evidence for a person's likely opinions about pleasures no serious objection could be made. It so happens in this case that appreciable differences in the rest of the argument weaken what could otherwise have been accepted as strong evidence.

(5) Miss Fosdick gives as one reason for thinking that the essay *On Social Freedom* was written after the publication of *On Liberty* in 1859 the fact that 'it contains a pointed criticism of the individualist argument for liberty presented there'. But would it not have been extraordinary for Mill to have been referring to the essay *On Liberty*, and its principle of self-protection, in these words:

I believe that some persons have been disposed to regard each human individual as occupying, or as having a right to occupy, a certain 'sphere of activity', in sole and exclusive possession. Within this sphere he is to exercise perfect freedom, unimpeded by the free action of any other human creature?

There is no doubt that the principle of self-protection (and its associated idea of a realm of self-regarding actions) can, and has been, interpreted in this way. If we take this to be Mill's account of his own theory, how are we to explain his failure to criticize it on those occasions (up to 1871) when we know for certain that it is Mill who is writing?

These reasons seemed to me to be sufficient to establish a strong prima facie case against Mill's being the author of the essay and so I was led to search for the original manuscript. The manuscript was located and its owner, Sir David Kelly, has been kind enough to let me see it. A few facts about it can be stated briefly. It consists of 109 pages, the last twelve of which (pp. 98 to 109 inclusive) were not published in the *Oxford and Cambridge Review*. This concluding section is a set of outline notes of what the author hoped to add to the first ninety-seven pages and is headed, 'Partial analysis of succeeding portion of the work'. There is no indication of authorship in the MS itself, but a small label inside the case in which the MS is contained reads: 'De la Bibliothèque de JOHN STUART MILL. Vendue à Avignon les 21 . . . 28 Mai 1905.' The handwriting of the MS, I would say, is quite different from Mill's, at any time of his life. Nor does it appear to be Helen Taylor's, who frequently wrote for him during the last years at Avignon.

A number of remarks in the unpublished part of the MS are so unlike anything Mill would be likely to say that they can be taken to strengthen the case I have been making. Since this section has not been published I will describe some of its features.[22] The first topic noted for discussion is the 'practical realization' of freedom. The solution of this problem, it is said, is impossible so long as we regard freedom in its merely negative aspect, as limited by the restraints imposed by other human wills. Freedom can be limited by mere external circumstances, though these limitations are not felt to be so oppressive as restraints imposed by a hostile or arbitrary human will. Social inequalities cause a feeling of deprivation, and so a sense of limitation of freedom, on the part of the many. 'Does this limitation of Individual freedom arise from human injustice or from the mere force of circumstances?' This is a difficult question: it involves the great problem of Property and Socialism. Man's power over nature is infinitely increased by *organization*, thus organization is a means of extending human freedom. But freedom may be sacrificed to organization. The grand problem of society is, 'the *greatest* possible increase of power, with the *least* possible sacrifice of individuality'.

The writer then considers special forms of freedom. In regard to freedom of speech he says that freedom to dissociate from those whose opinions we disapprove could isolate the outstanding thinkers and result in the most complete bondage in the expression of opinions. It would help if *honest* thinkers were to organize themselves. Freedom in dress may seem trivial, but it is really an important matter. Dress has an evil moral influence—the desire to dress 'the lady' or 'the gentleman'. It would be better if a costume were strictly prescribed to each social class, which would adopt its own costume 'designed according to *taste* and *reason*, *not* to suit the interests of trade. Each man should be *proud* of his order, rather than ashamed of it'. The costumes now in use—army, clergy, law, Quakers, 'Sisters of Mercy'—could aid in the reformation of dress. Co-operative societies might adopt a dress, perhaps also trades-unions.

As in the essay itself so in these notes the writer is eager to state his opposition to 'regarding freedom in its merely negative aspects'. Freedom, he says, can actually be promoted by the restraints that go with efficient organization. A great increase in the extent of social control should therefore be welcomed so long as individuality is not sacrificed in the process. Mill would not have objected to this. In the *Liberty* he had spoken in a similar vein: 'All that makes existence valuable to any one, depends on the enforcement of restraints upon the actions of other people. Some rules of conduct, therefore, must be imposed, by law in the first place, and by opinion on many things which are not fit subjects for the operation of law.' Further, in his belief that individual character is too little valued by mass opinion, in the importance he attaches to the role of gifted men in all walks of life, and in his fear lest the right to dissociate from persons whose views we disapprove should lead to the isolation of outstanding men, the writer of these notes certainly resembles Mill. But the case is different when he proposes uniformity of dress for social classes or occupational groups. It is surely unthinkable that Mill, who until 1871 was still pleading for 'liberty of tastes and pursuits', freedom to frame 'the plan of our life to suit our own character', and who gave no sign of ever wishing to abandon his conception of liberty as 'pursuing our own good in our own way, so long as we do not attempt to deprive others of theirs', should have contemplated such a proposal. He had drawn heavy fire from his critics for the remark that 'in this age, the mere example of non-conformity, the mere refusal to bend the knee to custom, is itself a service', but he did not yield an inch of his ground. No one upbraided him more mercilessly on this score than did Fitzjames Stephen, yet Mill does not appear to have seen in Stephen's criticisms any cause for second thoughts.

The last paragraph of the notes (enclosed in square brackets) reads: 'I feel some temptation to attempt a somewhat elaborate essay on "The Province of Civil Government", having particular reference to the views of the "Voluntaryist", "laissez-faire", and Manchester schools of politicians, but I have strong doubts as to my capacity for the task.' Is it likely that Mill, who had already dealt so comprehensively with 'the province of government' in the fifth book of Political Economy, would have written this passage, even in the declining years of his life?[23]

NOTES

Chapter I

1. Note the remark by John Robson, *The Improvement of Mankind* (Toronto, 1968), p. viii. 'A man must grow and a man must change . . .' One is reminded of attempts to relate the 'young' with the 'mature' Marx—to show that the whole corpus of Marx's writings 'hang together'.
2. For a discussion of the 'periods' of Mill's intellectual development, see ibid., pp. vii–x, 32–5, 117; R. P. Anschutz, *The Philosophy of J. S. Mill* (Oxford, 1953) pp. 30–2; R. J. Halliday, *John Stuart Mill* (London, 1976) pp. 15–16; K. Britton, *John Stuart Mill* (Penguin, 1953) p. 23; C. L. Ten, 'Mill and Liberty', *Journal of the History of Ideas* Vol. XXX, 1969.
3. For details of the origins and activities of the Debating Society, see J. S. Mill's *Autobiography*, ed. H. J. Laski (World's Classics Edition, 1952) pp. 106–9.
4. Ibid., pp. 132–3.
5. Ibid., p. 194.
6. Ibid., p. 161.
7. F. C. Montague, *The Limits of Individual Liberty* (London, 1885) p. 183.
8. G. H. Sabine, *A History of Political Theory*, 1st edition (New York, 1937) pp. 666–7.
9. L. Stephen, *The English Utilitarians*, Vol. III (London, 1900) p. 244.
10. L. W. Lancaster, *Masters of Political Thought*, Vol. III (London, 1959) pp. 136–7.
11. W. E. Houghton, *The Victorian Frame of Mind* (New Haven, 1964) pp. 287, 290. See also G. Hirsch, 'Organic Imagery and the Psychology of Mill's *On Liberty*' in *The Mill News Letter* (Toronto) Vol. X, No.2, 1975.
12. Anschutz, p. 5.
13. Ibid., pp. 172–3.
14. G. Himmelfarb, *On Liberty and Liberalism* (New York, 1974).
15. Ibid., p. 262.
16. Ibid., p. 272.
17. P. Feyerabend, *Against Method* (London, 1975).
18. *Autobiography*, p. 54.

19. Ibid., p. 56. Mill adds 'My previous education had been, in a certain sense, already a course of Benthamism . . .'
20. Ibid., p. 86.
21. J. Hamburger, *Intellectuals in Politics* (New Haven, 1965) p. 37.
22. J. Mill, 'Essay on Government', in J. Lively and J. Rees, *Utilitarian Logic and Politics* (Oxford, 1978) p. 56.
23. Ibid., p. 69.
24. Ibid., p. 57.
25. Ibid., p. 62.
26. Ibid., p. 63.
27. Ibid., p. 68.
28. Ibid., p. 87.
29. *Autobiography*, p. 89.
30. Ibid., p. 90.
31. J. S. Mill, 'Formations of Opinions', *Westminster Review*, July 1826, pp. 13–14.
32. Ibid., p. 14.
33. Ibid., p. 13.
34. J. S. Mill, article on the *Edinburgh Review* in the *Westminster Review*, Jan. 1824, pp. 208–9.
35. Ibid.
36. J. S. Mill, article on 'The Ballot' in the *Westminster Review*, July 1830, p. 2, clearly reflecting his father's views.
37. J. S. Mill, *On Liberty*, in *Utilitarianism, On Liberty, and Representative Government* (Everyman edition) p. 114.
38. J. Mill, 'Liberty of the Press' in *Essays* . . . (London, n.d.) p. 4.
39. Ibid., pp. 18–19.
40. Ibid., p. 22.
41. Ibid., p. 22.
42. Ibid., p. 14.
43. Ibid., p. 15.
44. Ibid., p. 30.
45. Ibid., p. 4.
46. J. Mill 'Essay on Jurisprudence' in *Essays*, p. 5.
47. Ibid., p. 10.
48. Ibid., p. 14.
49. Ibid., p. 15.
50. 'Liberty of the Press', p. 4.
51. Ibid., p. 6.
52. Ibid., p. 9.
53. Ibid., p. 10.
54. Ibid., p. 11.
55. Ibid., p. 11; my emphasis [JCR].

56. Ibid., p. 11.
57. Ibid., p. 12.
58. Ibid., pp. 12–13.
59. *Autobiography*, p. 87.
60. 'Jurisprudence', p. 15.
61. J. Bentham, *Principles of Morals and Legislation*, Ch. XVI, section 1.
62. Ibid., Ch. I, sections 3 and 4.
63. Ibid., Ch. IV, section 7.
64. 'Jurisprudence', p. 21.
65. *On Liberty*, p. 74.
66. Ibid., p. 74.
67. *Autobiography*, p. 215.
68. *On Liberty*, p. 70.
69. Ibid., p. 68.
70. *Collected Works*, Vol. X, pp. 106–8.
71. *Autobiography*, p. 171.
72. 'Jurisprudence', p. 21.
73. *Principles*, Ch. XVIII, section 11. We may assume once more that Mill shared Bentham's opinion—see 'Jurisprudence', p. 20.
74. *Principles*, Chaps. XIII and XVII. See also 'Jurisprudence', p. 15 for example.
75. D. Lyons, *In the Interest of the Governed* (Oxford, 1973) p. 62.
76. *Principles*, Ch. XIII, sections 1 and 2.
77. Ibid., Ch. XIII, section 5.
78. Ibid., Ch. XIII, section 13.
79. Ibid., Ch. XVII, section 12.
80. All quotations in the summary that follows are taken from *Principles*, Ch. XVII, section 1.
81. Ibid., Ch. XVII, section 8.
82. Ibid., Ch. XVII, section 14.
83. Ibid., Ch. XVII, section 15.
84. Ibid., Ch. XVII, section 18.
85. Ibid., Ch. XVII, section 19.
86. 'Liberty of the Press', p. 12.
87. Ibid., pp. 10–11.
88. *Utilitarianism* (Everyman edition) p. 19.
89. *Autobiography* p. 54; see also *On Liberty*, p. 140 and the article on Whewell in *Collected Works*, Vol. X, pp. 176–9.
90. *Principles*, Ch. II, section 11.
91. Ibid., Ch. II, section 13.
92. Ibid., Ch. II, section 19.
93. *On Liberty*, pp. 69–70, p. 140.
94. *Collected Works*, Vol. X, p. 179.

95. *Principles*, Ch. XVI, sections 1–10.
96. Ibid., Ch. XVI, section 64.
97. Ibid., see notes to Ch. XVI, sections 33, 34, 35, 52; Ch. XVI, section 15; Ch. XVII, sections 15 to 18.
98. *On Liberty*, p. 135.
99. Ibid., pp. 137–8.
100. *Principles*, Ch. XVII, section 15.
101. *On Liberty*, p. 138.
102. Ibid., p. 142.

Chapter II

1. *Autobiography*, ed. J. Stillinger (Oxford, 1971) pp. 144.
2. *Collected Works*, Vol. XIV, p. 294; see G. Himmelfarb, pp. 247 ff.
3. Speech (never spoken) on the British Constitution (unpublished). This and other unpublished speeches referred to below are located in the Mill Collection at the LSE.
4. The British Constitution in Laski's ed. of *Autobiography*, p. 278.
5. Speech against Sterling in ibid., p. 308.
6. Speech (never spoken) on the British Constitution (unpublished).
7. *Autobiography*, p. 131.
8. Speech on the Influence of the Aristocracy, 1825 (unpublished).
9. Ibid.
10. See *System of Logic*, Bk. VI, Ch. VIII.
11. Speech against Sterling in Laski, p. 305.
12. *Essay on Government*, pp. 68–72.
13. Speech on Parliamentary Reform (unpublished).
14. Ibid.
15. Influence of the Aristocracy.
16. Speech on Parliamentary Reform.
17. Ibid.
18. Ibid. It is interesting to note that Mill uses the same argument when arguing against the co-operative system and in favour of free competition, in another unpublished speech—Against the Co-operative Society, 1825.
19. Influence of the Aristocracy.
20. Speech (never spoken) on the British Constitution.
21. *Autobiography*, pp. 275–87.
22. Ibid., pp. 285–6.
23. Ibid., p. 291.
24. Ibid., p. 293.
25. See J. Mill's article on 'Education', in *Essays*.
26. *Autobiography*, p. 294.

27. Ibid., pp. 297-9.
28. B. Wishy (ed.), *Prefaces to Liberty* (Boston, 1959) p. 52.
29. 'On the Present State of Literature' (unpublished speech).
30. Ibid.
31. *Collected Works*, Vol. I, p. 330.
32. Article on the *Edinburgh Review, Westminster Review*, Vol. I (1824), p. 510.
33. Letters to d'Eichtal (1829), *Collected Works*, Vol. XII, pp. 36 and 42.
34. Speech on Perfectibility, Laski, p. 294.
35. *Westminster Review*, Vol. II (1824), pp. 9-10.
36. Speech on the Church, Laski, p. 323.
37. Letters to d'Eichtal (1830), *Collected Works*, Vol. XVII, pp. 45-6.
38. 'The Law of Libel and Liberty of the Press', *Westminster Review*, Vol. III (1825), reprinted in G. L. Williams (ed.), *J. S. Mill on Politics and Society* (London, 1976) p. 149.
39. *Autobiography*, pp. 161-2.
40. M. St. John Packe, *The Life of John Stuart Mill* (London 1954) pp. 133-4 and 203-4.
41. *Collected Works*, Vol. XII, p. 84.
42. Packe, p. 134.
43. *Collected Works*, Vol. XII, p. 77.
44. Ibid., p. 40.
45. *Spirit of the Age*, in G. Himmelfarb, *Essays on Politics and Culture by J. S. Mill* (New York, 1963) pp. 12 and 15.
46. Ibid., p. 7.
47. See R. K. P. Pankhurst, *The Saint-Simonians, Mill and Carlyle* (London, 1957) pp. 20 and 22.
48. *Edinburgh Review*, Vol. XLIX (1829), pp. 443 and 457.
49. Pankhurst, p. 22. William Ellery Channing (1780–1842) was an American Unitarian preacher and writer who came to dislike the narrow Calvinistic view of human nature (cf. Mill's attack on the Calvinist conception of good conduct) and claimed that man was capable of a natural development into goodness. The possibility that Channing's opinions may have had some influence on Mill was first suggested to me by a remark on the similarity of the emphasis on individuality in Channing's works to that in Mill's *Liberty*, by J. T. Mackenzie in the *Contemporary Review*, Vol. XXXVII (1880), p. 562.
50. The preceding quotations are all taken from W. E. Channing, *Remarks on the disposition which now prevails to form associations and to accomplish all objects by organised masses* (London, 1830).
51. *On Liberty*, p. 74.
52. Ibid., p. 74.

53. Ibid., p. 73.
54. Ibid., p. 137.
55. Ibid., p. 121.

Chapter III

1. Crane Brinton, *English Political Thought in the Nineteenth Century* (London, 1933) p. 98; and *Ideas and Men* (London, 1951) pp. 432 and 445.
2. John Morley, *Recollections* (2 Vols., London, 1917), I, p. 60.
3. Frederic Harrison, *Tennyson, Ruskin, Mill* (London, 1899) pp. 292–3. It must not be supposed that Harrison and Morley were uncritical of the essay. Both of them had important reservations to make. See, e.g. Morley, *On Compromise*, Ch. VI, and Harrison, op. cit., pp. 296–300.
4. Michael St. John Packe, *The Life of John Stuart Mill* (London, 1954) pp. 402–4.
5. Morley, I, p. 55.
6. *The Saturday Review*, 12 Feb. 1859, p. 187. The review was unsigned, but according to Leslie Stephen it was written by Fitzjames (*Life of Sir James Fitzjames Stephen*, London, 1895, p. 314).
7. *Fraser's Magazine*, NS, VI (Aug. 1872), p. 150.
8. *Dublin Review*, XIII (1869), p. 65.
9. H. T. Buckle, 'Mill on Liberty', *Fraser's Magazine*, LIX (May, 1859) pp. 530 and 525. It might be said that the published comment is not fully representative of educated opinion of the time nor of the attitudes of those who participated in public life and shaped public policy. This may well be so: I grant that it is important to distinguish the reaction of a relatively small group of philosophically-minded readers from that of the large public Mill succeeded in reaching. But even if we could track down that elusive entity we call 'public opinion' we should still be entitled to regard the reviews I have summarized as having an interest and significance of their own and as the sort of opinion by which Mill himself would be likely to be influenced.
10. *Bentley's Quarterly Review*, II (January, 1860) pp. 435 and 471–3.
11. Tocqueville, *Democracy in America* (Trans. Henry Reeve, 3rd edn., London, 1838) II, p. 90.
12. *Edinburgh Review*, Oct. 1840. The review was reprinted in *Dissertations and Discussions* (4 Vols., London, 1859–75), II.
13. *On Liberty*, pp. 115, 119, 123, and 127. I do not wish to imply that Mill's ideas on this matter were derived solely from his reading of de Tocqueville. There is evidence that both Harriet

Taylor and Mill were becoming alarmed by the increasing power of public opinion before de Tocqueville's book was published. In an essay written in (or soon after) 1832 Harriet complains of the pervading spirit of conformity: 'Whether it would be religious conformity, Political conformity, moral conformity, or Social conformity, no matter which the species, the spirit is the same: all kinds agree in this one point, of hostility to individual character, and individual character if it exists at all, can rarely declare itself openly while there is, on all topics of importance, a standard of conformity raised by the indolent-minded many . . . which, though composed individually of the weakest twigs, yet makes up collectively a mass which is not to be resisted with impunity.' The essay is included in F. A. Hayek, *John Stuart Mill and Harriet Taylor* (London, 1951) pp. 275–9. Professor Hayek rightly observes that some of the views expressed in it anticipate what Mill says in *On Liberty* (p. 26), but he also makes it clear that Harriet's influence made itself felt from the times of their first meetings in the 1830s (see also Packe, pp. 133–4). What must be the first expression of this attitude to come from Mill himself is the letter he wrote to the *Monthly Repository* in 1832 (reprinted in *Four Dialogues of Plato*, ed. Ruth Borchardt, London, 1946), in which he counts among the characteristics of the age a loss in intellectual intensity, and suggests that the deficiency is being made up 'by the united efforts of a constantly increasing multitude of dwarfs' (p. 29). 'Is there anything', he asks, 'a man can do, short of swindling or forgery . . . which will so surely gain him the reputation of a dangerous, or, at least, an unaccountable person, as daring, without either rank or reputation as a warrant for the eccentricity, to make a practice of forming his opinions for himself?' (p. 38).

14. *On Liberty*, pp. 130–1.
15. Ibid., pp. 65 and 73.
16. Writing nearly ten years before the publication of *On Liberty*, Herbert Spencer refers to his own day as one in which there had been an 'abatement of intolerance' and a 'growth in free institutions'. 'A new Areopagitica . . . would surely be needless in our age of the world and in this country', he says (*Social Statics*, Ch. XIV, sec. 2).
17. *A Review of Mr. J. S. Mill's Essay "On Liberty"*, by A Liberal (London, 1867) p. 17.
18. *Bentley's Quarterly Review*, Vol. II (Jan. 1860), pp. 439 and 442.
19. *Review*, by A Liberal, pp. 23 and 31–2.
20. *London Review*, Vol. XIII (Oct. 1859), p. 273.
21. Buckle, pp. 532–3.

22. *Dublin Review*, Vol. XIII (July–Oct. 1869), p. 75.
23. *British Quarterly Review*, Vol. XXIX (1859), pp. 547–8.
24. *National Review*, Vol. III (1859), pp. 393–4.
25. *Saturday Review*, 19 Feb. 1859, p. 213.
26. Ibid.
27. *National Review*, 1859, p. 407.
28. *London Review*, 1859, pp. 274–5.
29. Vol. IV (1868), p. 148. *The Southern Review* was an American journal published in Baltimore and edited by A. T. Bledsoe, who represented the unrepentant pro-slavery element in the decade after the Civil War. Bledsoe wrote most of the articles himself. Mill read some North American periodicals and this particular journal propounds a theory of liberty closely similar to that put forward in the essay *On Social Freedom*.
30. Ibid., Vol. V (1869), pp. 250 and 258–60.
31. Ibid., pp. 260–2. The passages in Mill which the writer has in mind are: *On Liberty*, p. 73 and *Representative Government*, pp. 178–9 and 197–9.
32. Ibid., Vol. II (1867), pp. 61–6.
33. *On Liberty*, pp. 72–3.
34. *Fraser's Magazine*, Vol. VI, NS (1872), p. 150.
35. *Meliora*, Vol. II (1860), pp. 83–4.
36. Joseph Parker, *John Stuart Mill on Liberty. A Critique* (London, 1865) pp. 4–6 and 17. Joseph Parker (1830–1902) was a prominent Congregationalist minister and a staunch prohibitionist.
37. *Bentley's*, p. 463.
38. Index, *Individual Liberty, Legal, Moral, and Licentious; in which The Political Fallacies of J. S. Mill's Essay "On Liberty" are pointed out*, pp. 108–12. (The second edition, 1877, gives the author's name as George Vasey.)
39. *London Review*, p. 274.
40. *Bentley's*, pp. 463 and 473. In a review of Mill's *Autobiography* published just after the close of our period the *Edinburgh Review* commented on the principle of self-protection thus: 'We hold this to be a false and detestable principle in morals, for it amounts to this, that no action is bad or immoral in itself, but only in so far as it tends to injure other men; and that the penalties with which society visits the actions it regards as immoral in themselves are unjust.' (Jan. 1874, pp. 122–3).
41. *On Liberty*, p. 136.
42. Ibid., pp. 137–9.
43. Parker, pp. 18–19. The passages he has in mind are probably those on pp. 97, 119, and 123–7 of *On Liberty*.

44. Vasey, pp. 115–17.
45. *National Review*, VIII, 1859, pp. 415–17.
46. *Dublin*, pp. 74–5,
47. *Review*, by A Liberal, p. 22.
48. Vasey, pp. 94–5.
49. *Bentley's Quarterly Review*, II (Jan. 1860), pp. 465–7. The secretary of a temperance association had declared: 'If anything invades my social rights, certainly the traffic in strong drink does. It destroys my primary right of security, by constantly creating and stimulating social disorder. . . . It impedes my right to free moral and intellectual development . . . by weakening and demoralizing society, from which I have a right to claim mutual aid and intercourse.' This, asserted Mill, amounted to an 'absolute social right of every individual, that every other individual shall act in every respect exactly as he ought . . . it ascribes to all mankind a vested interest in each other's moral, intellectual, and even physical perfection, to be defined by each claimant according to his own standard.' (*On Liberty*, pp. 145–6.)
50. *Meliora*, pp. 87–93. The passage quoted from Mill occurs on p. 132 of *On Liberty*.
51. *On Liberty*, pp. 151–2.
52. *Review*, by A Liberal, pp. 38–9. Better known writers were later to fasten on this example of the man crossing the unsafe bridge and interpret it as the embryo of a theory of liberty altogether at odds with Mill's main thesis. D. G. Ritchie in *The Principles of State Interference* (London, 1891) takes the statement, 'liberty consists in doing what one desires', to be a sign of a more positive idea of liberty and argues that the development of this view would justify the most insidious incursions into individual freedom. For example, the inquisitor could have said to the heretic he was torturing: 'This man desires salvation, and I am seeking to prevent him being damned.' Mill's defence of liberty, paradoxically enough, contains what could be turned into an apology for despotism, observes Ritchie (pp. 86–7). Of course, Ritchie is not accusing Mill of being a totalitarian in disguise. He is concerned, mainly, to demonstrate the ambiguity of the word 'desire' in the statement quoted and to point out what he considers are the inevitable confusions in, and inconsistent implications of, an abstract theory like Mill's. Bosanquet thinks that Mill's weakness lies in the treatment of 'the central life of the individual as something to be carefully fenced round against the impact of social forces' and contends that in Mill there is to be found another principle, quite incompatible with the essential

NOTES TO CHAPTER III   195

theme of the essay. He cites two examples to support this claim, the one we have already referred to and the case of the man who sells himself as a slave. (Mill argues that a contract to restrict one's own freedom is morally invalid because it is inconsistent with liberty to be free to make oneself unfree—'it is not freedom to be allowed to alienate one's freedom' (*On Liberty*, pp. 157–8). Bosanquet comments: '. . . he [Mill] is aware that it might be right, according to the principle of liberty, to restrain a man, for reasons affecting himself alone, from doing what at the moment he proposes to do. For we are entitled to argue from the essential nature of freedom to what freedom really demands, as opposed to what the man momentarily seems to wish. . . . Here we have in germ the doctrine of the "real will", and a conception analogous to that of Rousseau when he speaks of a man "being forced to be free".' (*Philosophical Theory of the State*, Ch. III.))

53. *Bentley's*, p. 472.
54. Vol. II (1867), pp. 57–60.
55. *National Review*, pp. 398–401.
56. *Fraser's Magazine*, VI (Aug. 1872), pp. 155–7.
57. Ibid., pp. 154-5.
58. *Liberty, Equality, Fraternity* (London, 1873) pp. 13–14. Stephen had read the article by 'L.S.' (see. p. 42).
59. *London Review*, XIII (1859), p. 275.
60. *Dublin University Magazine*, LIV (1859), p. 389.
61. Parker, pp. 14–15.
62. 'L.S.', pp. 162–4,
63. *Dublin*, p. 397.
64. *On Liberty*, p. 97.
65. *London*, p. 271.
66. *Bentley's*, pp. 445–8.
67. 'L.S.', pp. 163–4. From here to the end of the paragraph I am summarizing pp. 450–61 of *Bentley's Quarterly Review*.
68. The writer in *Bentley's Quarterly Review* is referring here to Mill's essay on Coleridge (*London and Westminster Review*, 1840: reprinted in *Dissertations and Discussions*, Vol. 1) in which he says that one condition of a permanent political society is 'the existence, in some form or other, of the feeling of allegiance, or loyalty . . . that there be in the constitution of the State something which is settled, something permanent, and not to be called in question . . .' This feeling may attach itself to a common God, to laws, or to the principles of individual freedom and political and social equality. And another essential condition, Mill argues, is 'a strong and active principle of cohesion among the members of the same community or state . . . a feeling of common interest

among those who live under the same government, and are contained within the same natural or historical boundaries.'
69. *Dublin University*, p. 396.
70. *On Liberty*, pp. 101, 108–9, and 119–20.
71. Parker, pp. 24–9; *Bentley's Quarterly Review*, pp. 469–70; *Saturday Review*, 19 Feb. 1859, p. 214.
72. *Dublin*, pp. 65–7. Several other reviewers make similar points about what they claim is an inconsistency in Mill, i.e. on the one hand stating that we can never be sure that an opinion is false and, on the other, asserting that some things are no longer doubtful. See W. W. English, *An Essay on Moral Philosophy* (1869) pp. 24–5; and Parker, pp. 13–15.
73. Ernest Barker, *Political Thought in England* (London, 1915) p. 10.
74. Thus Miss Dorothy Fosdick in her introduction to the essay *On Social Freedom* (NY, 1941) says that the conception of man as 'inevitably bound into society' is familiar enough to twentieth-century readers but in Mill's day 'it was popular only among socialist writers'.
75. Opposition to what they consider a false individualism and an excessive regard for individual freedom on Mill's part was especially vehement among temperance reformers. One of them, Mr George Vasey, is convinced that 'every healthy man is in process of deterioration from the moment he becomes a regular drinker of any intoxicating fluid, even in a moderate degree' and thinks that if Mill's theory of liberty were applied to English society it would not only encourage intemperance, and produce 'a more licentious state of manners than that under which we are at present suffering', but would even make ignorant people critical of law as such. Mill, he claims, by a false individualistic conception of society is led to under-value those restraints without which civilized communities cannot exist (pp. 149 *et seq.* and 171).
76. *National*, pp. 407–11 and 424–5.
77. *London Review*, pp. 272–3; *National Review*, pp. 411–12; *Bentley's Quarterly Review*, pp. 463–4. 'L.S.' questions Mill's assumption that variety of character is good in itself. Would not a nation, he asks, in which everyone was sober be better than one divided equally into the drunk and the sober? If and when the millennium comes we shall all be agreed upon a vast range of matters over which there is at the moment much controversy. Variety is, of course, a desirable thing, but always within limits.

Chapter IV

1. *Autobiography*, p. 132.
2. G. Himmelfarb, *On Liberty and Liberalism* (New York, 1974);

B. Mazlish, *James and John Stuart Mill* (London, 1975); P. Feyerabend, *Against Method* (London, 1975).

3. C. Douglas, *John Stuart Mill* (London, 1895).
4. Douglas, p. 5.
5. Douglas, p. 7.
6. R. P. Anschutz, *The Philosophy of J. S. Mill* (London, 1953).
7. Anschutz, p. 5.
8. Anschutz, p. 172.
9. J. S. Mill, *Essays on Politics and Culture* (New York, 1962) edited by G. Himmelfarb, p. vii.
10. Himmelfarb, *On Liberty and Liberalism*, pp. xxi–xxii.
11. *Autobiography*, p. 215.
12. Himmelfarb, *On Liberty and Liberalism*, p. 272.
13. Ibid., p. 178.
14. Ibid., p. 15.
15. For example, on p. 181 of *On Liberty and Liberalism*.
16. Ibid., p. 107.
17. Ibid., pp. 106–7.
18. P. Feyerabend, 'Imre Lakatos', *British Journal for the Philosophy of Science*, 26 (1975), p. 10.
19. 'An individual fact is said to be explained by pointing out its cause, that is, by stating the law or laws of causation of which its production is an instance', and 'a law of uniformity in nature is said to be explained when another law or laws are pointed out, of which that law itself is but a case, and from which it could be deduced'.
20. P. Feyerabend, 'Against Method', *Minnesota Studies in the Philosophy of Science*, 4 (1970).
21. Ibid., p. 29.
22. Ibid., p. 112.
23. J. S. Mill, *Utilitarianism, On Liberty and Considerations on Representative Government* (London, Dent, 1972), introduction by Acton, p. xxi.
24. M. Cowling, *Mill and Liberalism* (Cambridge, 1963).
25. The inclusion of 'rights' here is deliberate. See the following two chapters.

Chapter V

1. *Autobiography*, p. 215.
2. *On Liberty*, p. 119.
3. Ibid., p. 123.
4. *Autobiography*, p. 212.
5. *Collected Works*, Vol. XIV, p. 294.

6. As well as the essay on 'Civilization', *Collected Works*, Vol. XVIII, see the essay on 'Genius' (1832), *Collected Works*, Vol. I, and Chapter II above.

7. *On Liberty*, p. 68.

8. Ibid., pp. 71–2.

9. Before the publication of the first part of Tocqueville's work in 1835 the American Unitarian preacher and writer, William Ellery Channing, had uttered warnings similar to Tocqueville's at a number of points. Channing's writings were known in England and there were reviews of some of them in the *Edinburgh Review* and the *Westminster Review* in 1829 and 1830. I argued in Chapter II that Mill was influenced by Channing's views. Apart from the 'Remarks on the Formation of Associations', which Mill certainly knew, there is the election sermon of 1880. The latter was reprinted in a two-volume edition of Channing's works published in Britain in 1835 (see Vol. II, pp. 255ff.). One or two passages are worth quoting.

> 'The advantages of civilization have their peril. In such a state of society, opinion and law impose salutary restraint, and produce general order and security. But the power of opinion grows into a despotism, which, more than all things, represses original and free thought, subverts individuality of character, reduces the community to a spiritless monotony, and chills the love of perfection' [p. 268]. 'An espionage of bigotry may as effectually close our lips and chill our hearts, as an armed and hundred-eyed police' [p. 271]. 'Our great error as a people, is, that we put an idolatrous trust in free institutions; as if these, by some magic power, must secure our rights, however we enslave ourselves to evil passions. We need to learn that forms of liberty are not its essence; that whilst the letter of a free constitution is preserved, its spirit may be lost; that even its wisest provisions and most guarded powers may be made weapons of tyranny. In a country called free, a majority may become a faction, and a proscribed minority may be insulted, robbed, and oppressed. Under elective governments, a dominant party may become as truly a usurper, and as treasonably conspire against the state, as an individual who forces his way by arms to the throne' [p. 278].

10. *On Liberty*, pp. 72–3.

11. Ibid., pp. 149–50.

12. Leading article in the *Times Literary Supplement*, 10 July 1948. Reprinted as part of a pamphlet, *Western Values*, published by *The Times*.

13. 'Including some important ones' is necessary here in order to prevent the issue from being trivialized. When Mill's critics say that no action is free from social consequences they must be assumed to be ignoring many petty acts which are obviously free

from social effects, or else they are mistaken in refusing to admit their existence. For example, if I shave in a well-lit room before a mirror that reflects the face with uniform clarity and I can, in these conditions, shave equally well no matter which side I begin to shave, then starting with the left or the right is a matter which cannot be considered to have any effects on other persons. Hence it is of no concern to society how I, or anyone else, begins to shave each morning. The debate between Mill and his critics clearly does not hinge on trivial acts of this kind.

14. *London Review*, Vol. XIII, p. 274.
15. J. F. Stephen, p. x, preface to the 2nd edn., 1874.
16. Ibid., p. 128 (1st edn., 1873). Mill's remarks appear in *On Liberty*, pp. 145–6.
17. D. G. Ritchie, pp. 96–8.
18. B. Bosanquet, *Philosophical Theory of the State* (London, 1899) p. 60. Writing about the same time Frederic Harrison (*Tennyson, Ruskin, Mill*) states: 'The attempt to distinguish between conduct which concerns oneself, and conduct that may remotely concern others, is quite fallacious. No distinction can be drawn, for human acts are organically inseparable' (p. 300). See also F. C. Montague's *The Limits of Individual Liberty*, pp. 185–8: Mill's distinction, says Montague, is an offshoot of the doctrine of the social contract and 'is impossible to those who look upon man as receiving from society his whole character and his whole endowment, and as reacting upon society at every moment of his life'.
19. MacIver, *Modern State* (Oxford, 1926) pp. 457 and 459.
20. E. Barker, *Principles of Social and Political Theory* (Oxford, 1951) p. 217.
21. R. P. Anschutz, p. 48.
22. My italics.
23. See note 13 above.
24. The quotations in this paragraph are from *On Liberty*, pp. 136–8.
25. Ibid., p. 75.
26. Ibid., pp. 134–6.
27. Ibid., pp. 120 and 135 (my italics).
28. These last quotations are from ibid., p. 132.
29. I have found the word on the following pages: 74 (twice), 75, 120, 132 (four times), 135, 138, 142, 149 (twice), and 150 (twice).
30. Ibid., p. 75 (my italics).
31. Ibid., pp. 115 and 132. It should be noted, however, that 'primarily' and 'chiefly' are not equivalent to 'directly' or 'in the first instance'.
32. In my draft of this the words 'to say' did not appear. I have inserted them in response to a remark made by Mr J. M. Brown

in some very valuable comments he kindly sent me on the draft. Mr Brown pointed out that to allow 'conduct which affects only himself' to mean 'conduct which only affects his own interests' would undermine the distinction I have sought to make between these two types of statement.

33. I am leaving out the complications connected with 'primarily', 'chiefly', and 'directly'.
34. *Political Studies*, Vol. II, 1954.
35. R. M. MacIver, *Community* (London, 1917) 3rd edn., pp. 98–101.
36. R. M. MacIver, *Society* (London, 1937) pp. 20–1.
37. See A. Ross, *On Law and Justice* (London, 1958), pp. 358–9.
38. *On Liberty*, pp. 145–6.
39. And even if it came to be accepted that a man's interests were affected by the noisy interruption of his privacy there is still the question of whether these interests should be protected against other claims, such as, for example, freedom to converse outside public houses, the demand for air travel, or the desire to listen to music.
40. *On Liberty*, p. 150.
41. Ibid., p. 132.
42. Ibid., p. 150.
43. Ibid., p. 132.
44. Ibid., p. 153.
45. This is one of Mill's examples (pp. 141–2). 'There are few acts which Christians and Europeans regard with more unaffected disgust than Mussulmans regard this particular mode of satisfying hunger', says Mill. He goes on to argue that the only good reason for condemning an attempt to ban the eating of pork in a country where the Mussulmans were a majority would be 'that with the personal tastes and self-regarding concerns of individuals the public has no business to interfere'.
46. *On Liberty*, pp. 153–5.

Chapter VI

1. D. D. Raphael, *Justice and Liberty* (London, 1980), p. v.
2. F. A. Hayek, *The Road to Serfdom* (London, 1944).
3. F. A. Hayek, *Law, Legislation and Liberty*, Vol. II (London, 1976) p. 32.
4. Ibid., p. 63.
5. Ibid., pp. 63–4.
6. *Utilitarianism*, p. 38.
7. *On Liberty*, p. 120.

8. Ibid., p. 121.
9. Ibid.
10. *Auguste Comte and Positivism* in Everyman edition of *Utilitarianism*, p. 406.
11. *On Liberty*, p. 72.
12. J. Mill, *Analysis of the Phenomena of the Human Mind* (London, 1869) Vol. II, p. 325.
13. See Chapter V above.
14. *Utilitarianism*, pp. 50-1.
15. Ibid., pp. 55-6.
16. Ibid.
17. Ibid., pp. 56-7.
18. Ibid., pp. 57-8.
19. Ibid., p. 59.
20. Ibid., pp. 46-7.
21. H. L. A. Hart, 'Are there any natural rights?' in A. Quinton, *Political Philosophy* (Oxford, 1967).
22. See D. G. Brown, 'Mill on Liberty and Morality' in *Philosophical Review*, Vol. LXXXI (1972); and 'Mill on Harm to Others' Interests', *Political Studies*, Vol. XXVI (1978).
23. *On Liberty*, p. 74.
24. *Principles*, Ch. XVII, section 19.
25. D. Lyons, 'Mill's Theory of Morality', *Nous*, X (1976), and *Forms and Limits of Utilitarianism* (Oxford, 1965).
26. The facts on the McFall case cited above are derived from the *Montreal Gazette*, 26 and 27 July 1978 and the *Toronto Globe and Mail*, 11 August 1978. I am grateful to Mr Roger Bennett for providing me with this information.
27. *On Liberty*, p. 74.
28. Ibid., p. 114.
29. Ibid., p. 132.

Appendix

1. Mary Taylor was the daughter of Harriet Taylor's son, Algernon, and therefore Helen Taylor's niece. Mill's papers passed from Helen to Mary.
2. *On Social Freedom*, by John Stuart Mill. With an introduction by Dorothy Fosdick (Columbia University Press, NY, 1941).
3. All the words in italics in the original.
4. There is no reference to the essay in any of the following: R. P. Anschutz, *The Philosophy of J. S. Mill*, 1953; Crane Brinton, *English Political Thought in the Nineteenth Century*, 2nd edn., 1952;

K. Britton, *John Stuart Mill*, 1953; R. B. McCallum (ed.), *Mill's Liberty and Representative Government*, 1946; J. Plamenatz, *The English Utilitarians*, 1949; G. H. Sabine, *History of Political Theory*, 2nd edn., 1951; Basil Willey, *Nineteenth-Century Studies*, 1949.

5. The only place where I have seen the essay discussed before Miss Fosdick's reprint appeared is in a short article in *Mind* by Carveth Read (NS, No. 65, Jan. 1908, pp. 74–8).

6. D. Fosdick, pp. 3, 25, and 28.

7. See the two letters to Alexander Bain in *Collected Works*, Vol. XV, pp. 631 and 640.

8. Book VI, Ch. II, section 3.

9. *Autobiography*, p. 213.

10. This part of the *Autobiography* was probably written in 1869 or 1870. See A. W. Levi, 'The Writing of Mill's Autobiography', *Ethics*, LXI (1950/51), pp. 284–96.

11. *Collected Works*, Vol. XVII, pp. 1831–2.

12. Alexander Bain, *John Stuart Mill* (London, 1882) p. 111.

13. Book VI, Ch. II. Mill said of this chapter: 'It is short and in my judgement the best in the two volumes'. (W. L. Courtney, *Life and Writings of J. S. Mill* (1889) pp. 76–7.)

14. In H. S. R. Elliot (ed.), *The Letters of John Stuart Mill* (2 vols., 1910) Vol. II, p. 375.

15. *Autobiography*, pp. 143–4.

16. Fosdick, p. 39.

17. *Collected Works*, Vol. XVI, p. 1240–2.

18. The author of *On Social Freedom* justifies his belief in freedom of the will by appealing to 'immediate or spontaneous sense'. This is the position attributed to Sir William Hamilton by Mill ('for the *fact* of Liberty we have immediately or mediately, the evidence of Consciousness', *Examination*, 1872 edn., p. 573), which Mill goes on to reject (pp. 578 *et seq.*) on the ground that if our internal consciousness tells us we are possessed of freedom of the will it tells us something quite inconsistent with our whole experience of outward behaviour. To be conscious of free-will, Mill argues, 'is to be conscious, before I have decided, that I am able to decide either way. . . . Consciousness tells me what I do or feel. But what I am *able* to do, is not a subject of consciousness.' Mill denies any inconsistency between what he was then saying and a passage in the *Logic* in which he had written of 'a feeling of Moral Freedom which we are conscious of'. He explains that this conviction of free-will is just the fact that we feel we could, and even should, have chosen different courses of action had we preferred them. What we cannot do, he insists, is to act 'in opposition to the strongest present desire or aversion'. Whether right or

wrong, these are not the views to be found in the essay *On Social Freedom*.

19. D. Fosdick, p. 23.
20. *Utilitarianism*, p. 10.
21. In an article published in 1908 (see note 5) Carveth Read observes the difference in the criteria suggested in *Utilitarianism* and *On Social Freedom* and describes the appeal to the feelings of a special class in *On Social Freedom* as 'strangely unlike the persuasive public utterance that we are accustomed to from Mill'. He is also struck by the absence of any reference in it to the other works of Mill where the free-will question is discussed: he wonders 'whether this paper *On Social Freedom* is really Mill's own', but decides that 'Miss Taylor, who has sanctioned its publication, is the best possible judge'.
22. The form of the text makes it unsuitable for direct quotation to any great extent, but I have kept to the original as closely as possible. I am indebted to Sir David Kelly for permission to quote from this unpublished section.
23. I do not think there is much in the suggestion that Mill's faculties deteriorated in the last few years, or even months, before his death and that it was in such a condition that he wrote the essay *On Social Freedom* (see Fosdick, pp. 4–5). The doctor who attended him at the end wrote: 'His expressed desire that he might not outlive his mental faculties . . . was gratified, for his great intellect remained clear to the last moment' (quoted by Packe, p. 507). An example of what Mill was capable of doing during the closing weeks of his life is in the *Tract on Right of Property in Land* written in April 1973 for the Land Tenure Reform Association (*Letters*, ed. Elliot, II, pp. 387–95).

If Mill did not write *On Social Freedom*, who did and how did it come to be among his papers? Perhaps the answer lies in the letter Mill wrote to a certain E. R. Edger in September 1862, acknowledging the receipt of a manuscript entitled *On Social Freedom* (*Collected Works*, Vol. XV, pp. 792–3). Apparently Edger had not asked Mill for detailed observations on the essay: he wanted advice on his capacity for a career as a writer in the field of social philosophy. Mill's reply therefore does not help very much so far as the contents of the manuscript are concerned.

BIBLIOGRAPHY

Works by Mill

The Collected Works of John Stuart Mill (Toronto and London, 1963–)
is being produced by the University of Toronto, under the General
Editorship first of F. E. L. Priestley and then of J. M. Robson.
Volumes that have so far appeared are:

<table>
<tr><td>I</td><td>Autobiography and Literary Essays</td></tr>
<tr><td>II–III</td><td>Principles of Political Economy</td></tr>
<tr><td>IV–V</td><td>Essays on Economics and Society</td></tr>
<tr><td>VI</td><td>Essays on England, Ireland, and the Empire</td></tr>
<tr><td>VII–VIII</td><td>A System of Logic</td></tr>
<tr><td>IX</td><td>An Examination of Sir William Hamilton's Philosophy</td></tr>
<tr><td>X</td><td>Essays on Ethics, Religion, and Society</td></tr>
<tr><td>XI</td><td>Essays on Philosophy and the Classics</td></tr>
<tr><td>XII–XIII</td><td>The Earlier Letters, 1812–1848</td></tr>
<tr><td>XIV–XVII</td><td>The Later Letters, 1849–1873</td></tr>
<tr><td>XVIII–XIX</td><td>Essays on Politics and Society</td></tr>
<tr><td>XX</td><td>Essays on French History and Historians</td></tr>
<tr><td>XXI</td><td>Essays on Equality, Law, and Education</td></tr>
</table>

On Liberty appears in Vol. XVIII and *Utilitarianism* appears in Vol. X.
The following selections of Mill's essays are useful:

Acton, H. B. (ed.), *Utilitarianism, Liberty and Representative Government*,
  Everyman (London, 1910), much reprinted, new edition 1972.
  References to *On Liberty* and *Utilitarianism* in the text are to this
  edition.
Warnock, M. (ed.), *Utilitarianism*, Fontana (London, 1962), much
  reprinted, contains *On Liberty*.
Wishy, B. (ed.), *Prefaces to Liberty* (Boston, 1959).
Himmelfarb, G. (ed.), *Essays on Politics and Culture* (New York, 1963).
Schneewind, J. B. (ed.), *Mill's Ethical Writings* (New York and
  London, 1965).
Schneewind, J. B. (ed.), *Mill's Essays on Literature and Society* (New
  York and London, 1965).
Williams, G. L. (ed.), *John Stuart Mill on Politics and Society*, Fontana
  (London, 1976).
Laski, H. J. (ed.), *Autobiography* (World's Classics edition, 1924),
  much reprinted, contains an Appendix of Unpublished Speeches.
  References in the text are to this edition, unless otherwise stated.

Works cited in the text

Anschutz, R. P., *The Philosophy of J. S. Mill* (Oxford, 1953).
Barker, E. (ed.), *Mill's Essay on Government* (Cambridge, 1937).
Barker, E., *Principles of Social and Political Theory* (Oxford, 1951).
Bentham, J., *Introduction to the Principles of Morals and Legislation* (London, 1970).
Bosanquet, B., *The Philosophical Theory of the State* (London, 1899).
Brown, D. G., 'Mill on Liberty and Morality', *Philosophical Review*, Vol. LXXXI, 1972.
—— 'Mill on Harm to Others' Interests', *Political Studies*, Vol. XXVI, 1978.
Brinton, C., *English Political Thought in the Nineteenth Century* (London, 1933).
—— *Ideas and Men* (London, 1951).
Britton, K., *John Stuart Mill* (Penguin, 1953).
Carlyle, T., 'Signs of the Times', *Edinburgh Review*, Vol. XLIX, 1829, reprinted in Vol. XXVII of the Century Edition of *The Works, Critical and Miscellaneous Essays* (London, 1899) Vol. II; also in Tennyson, G. B. (ed.), *A Carlyle Reader* (Cambridge, 1984).
Cowling, M., *Mill and Liberalism* (Cambridge, 1963).
Douglas, C., *John Stuart Mill* (London, 1895).
English, W. W., *An Essay on Moral Philosophy* (London, 1869).
Feyerabend, P., *Against Method* (London, 1975).
—— 'Imre Lakatos', *British Journal for the Philosophy of Science*, Vol. XXVI, 1975.
—— 'Against Method', *Minnesota Studies in the Philosophy of Science*, Vol. IV, 1970.
Fosdick, D., *On Social Freedom*, by John Stuart Mill (New York, 1941).
Halliday, R. J., *John Stuart Mill* (London, 1976).
Hamburger, J., *Intellectuals in Politics* (New Haven, 1965).
Harrison, F., *Tennyson, Ruskin, Mill* (London, 1899).
Hayek, F. A., *John Stuart Mill and Harriet Taylor* (London, 1951).
—— *The Road to Serfdom* (London, 1944).
—— *Law, Legislation and Liberty*, 2 Vols. (London, 1976).
Himmelfarb, G., *On Liberty and Liberalism* (New York, 1974).
—— *J. S. Mill, Essays on Politics and Culture* (New York, 1962).
Hirsch, G., 'Organic Imagery and the Psychology of Mill's *On Liberty*' in *The Mill News Letter* (Toronto) Vol. X, No. 2, 1975.
Houghton, W. E., *The Victorian Frame of Mind* (New Haven, 1964).
Lancaster, L. W., *Masters of Political Thought*, Vol. III (London, 1959).
Lyons, D., *In the Interest of the Governed* (Oxford, 1973).
—— *Forms and Limits of Utilitarianism* (Oxford, 1965).
—— 'Mill's Theory of Morality', *Nous*, Vol. X, 1976.

Lively, J. and Rees, J., *Utilitarian Logic and Politics* (Oxford, 1978).
MacIver, R. M., *Modern State* (Oxford, 1926).
—— *Society* (London, 1937).
—— *Community* (London, 1917).
Mazlish, B., *James and John Stuart Mill* (London, 1975).
Mill, J., *Essays on Government, Liberty of the Press, Jurisprudence* (London, no date).
—— *Analysis of the Phenomena of the Human Mind* (London, 1869).
Montague, F. C., *The Limits of Individual Liberty* (London, 1885).
Morley, J., *Recollections*, 2 Vols. (London, 1917).
—— *On Compromise* (London, 1921).
Packe, M. St. John, *The Life of John Stuart Mill* (London, 1954).
Pankhurst, R. K.P., *The Saint Simonians, Mill and Carlyle* (London, 1957).
Parker, J., *John Stuart Mill on Liberty: A Critique* (London, 1865).
Raphael, D. D., *Justice and Liberty* (London, 1980).
Ritchie, D. G., *The Principles of State Interference* (London, 1891).
Robson, J., *The Improvement of Mankind* (Toronto, 1968).
Ross, A., *On Law and Justice* (London, 1958).
Sabine, G. H., *A History of Political Theory* (New York, 1937).
Spencer, H., *Social Statics* (London, 1851).
Stephen, J. F., *Liberty, Equality, Fraternity* (London, 1873).
Stephen, L., *Life of Sir James Fitzjames Stephen* (London, 1895).
—— *The English Utilitarians*, Vol. III (London, 1900).
Ten, C. L., 'Mill and Liberty', *Journal of the History of Ideas* Vol. 30, 1969.
Tocqueville, A. de, *Democracy in America*, 3rd Edition (London, 1838).

Additional works on J. S. Mill's On Liberty

Berlin, I., *Four Essays on Liberty* (London, 1969).
Gray, J., *Mill on Liberty: A Defence* (London, 1983).
Letwin, S. R., *The Pursuit of Certainty* (Cambridge, 1965).
McCloskey, H. J., *John Stuart Mill: A Critical Study* (London, 1971).
Radcliff, P. (ed.), *Limits of Liberty* (Belmont, California, 1966).
Robson, J. M. *et al.* (eds.), *The Mill News Letter* (Toronto).
Ryan, A., *The Philosophy of John Stuart Mill* (London, 1970).
—— *J. S. Mill* (London, 1974).
Spitz, D. (ed.), *John Stuart Mill: On Liberty* (New York, 1975).
Ten, C. L., *Mill on Liberty* (Oxford, 1980).

Works on Mill by John Rees

Mill and his early Critics (Leicester, 1956).

'A Note on Macaulay and the Utilitarians', *Politics Studies*, Vol. IV, 1956.
'A Phase in the Development of Mill's Ideas on Liberty', *Political Studies*, Vol. VI, 1958.
'A Re-reading of Mill on Liberty', *Political Studies*, Vol. VIII, 1960.
'Individualism and Individual Liberty', *Il Politico*, Vol. XXVI, 1961.
'H. O. Pappe on Mill', *Political Studies*, Vol. X, 1962.
'Hayek on Liberty', *Philosophy*, Vol. XXXVIII, 1963.
'Was Mill for Liberty?', *Political Studies*, Vol. XIV, 1966.
'The Reaction to Cowling on Mill', *The Mill News Letter*, Vol. I, No.2, 1966.
'The Thesis of the Two Mills', *Political Studies*, Vol. XXV, 1977.
with J. Lively (eds.), *Utilitarian Logic and Politics* (Oxford, 1978).

INDEX OF NAMES